barbri

HOW TO USE THE STEP 1: MBE EARLY BAR PREP

What is the Step 1: MBE Early Bar Prep?

The Step 1: MBE Early Bar Prep is the first MBE Workshop in BARBRI's Multistate Advantage™ program—an unparalleled collection of outlines, questions, and lectures that give you ***everything you need*** to succeed on the Multistate Bar Exam ("MBE").

What do I get with the Step 1: MBE Early Bar Prep?

The Step 1: MBE Early Bar Prep consists of excerpts from the Conviser Mini Review outline covering key topics in each of the Multistate subjects, an online video lecture in each subject that corresponds to the outline, and a set of practice questions and analytical answers covering those topics.

How do I use the Step 1: MBE Early Bar Prep book?

The Step 1: MBE Early Bar Prep Workshop is designed to start building your foundation of MBE knowledge. You can do this workshop before your regular BARBRI bar review course starts.

- ***Step One:*** Select a subject and start by reading the mini review excerpt for that subject. Pay particular attention to the Exam Tips that alert you to commonly tested issues.

- ***Step Two:*** Log in to the Enrolled Student Center on the BARBRI website (barbri.com) and watch the two-hour lecture for that subject—offered in on-demand streaming video. Some of the subjects have handouts in the book on which you can take notes during the lecture.

- ***Step Three:*** Finally, work through the practice questions on that subject in your book to reinforce your learning. Try to do the set of questions in about a half hour, and then review the explanatory answers to see how you did.

If you do that for each of the six Multistate subjects, you will have an invaluable head start in your MBE preparation before your BARBRI course even begins!

barbri®

Step 1: MBE Early Bar Prep

MULTISTATE ADVANTAGE™

FOR EACH SUBJECT:

- **READ** THE MINI REVIEW EXCERPT
- **WATCH** THE LECTURE AT BARBRI.COM
- **DO** THE QUESTIONS IN THIS BOOK

YOU CAN DO THIS WORKSHOP BEFORE YOUR COURSE STARTS

To be used in conjunction with the Summer 2011 and Winter 2012 BARBRI Bar Review Courses

EBP

Step 1: MBE Early Bar Prep

Table of Contents

Constitutional Law

Equal Protection
Fundamental Rights
First Amendment

CONSTITUTIONAL LAW

I. EQUAL PROTECTION

A. CONSTITUTIONAL SOURCE

The Equal Protection Clause of the Fourteenth Amendment is limited to state action. However, grossly unreasonable discrimination by the federal government violates the Due Process Clause of the Fifth Amendment. The Court applies the same tests under either constitutional provision.

B. APPLICABLE STANDARDS

If a ***fundamental right*** or ***suspect classification*** is involved, the ***strict scrutiny*** standard is used to evaluate the regulation. If a ***quasi-suspect classification*** is involved, ***intermediate scrutiny*** is the applicable standard. If the classification does not affect a fundamental right or involve a suspect or quasi-suspect classification, the ***rational basis*** standard applies.

C. PROVING DISCRIMINATORY CLASSIFICATION

For strict or intermediate scrutiny to be applied, there must be ***intent*** on the part of the government to discriminate. Intent may be shown by:

(i) A law that is ***discriminatory on its face***;

(ii) A ***discriminatory application*** of a facially neutral law; or

(iii) A ***discriminatory motive*** behind the law.

Note: The third way to show intentional discrimination is the most difficult to prove. A discriminatory effect alone is ***not*** enough. The legislature's discriminatory motive must be shown (*e.g.*, by evidence of a history of discrimination).

D. SUSPECT CLASSIFICATIONS

Classifications are suspect if they are based on race, national origin, or alienage.

1. Race and National Origin

Classifications based on race or national origin are judged by a strict scrutiny standard.

a. School Integration

Only intentional segregation violates the Constitution. If school systems and attendance zones are established in a racially neutral manner, there is no violation. Thus, there is no violation if housing patterns result in racial imbalance in schools.

b. "Benign" Government Discrimination—Affirmative Action

Government action—whether by federal, state, or local governmental bodies—that ***favors*** racial or ethnic minorities is subject to the same strict scrutiny standard as is government action discriminating ***against*** racial or ethnic minorities.

1) Remedying Past Discrimination

The government has a compelling interest in remedying past discrimination against a racial or ethnic minority. The past discrimination must have been persistent and readily identifiable. A race-based plan ***cannot*** be used to remedy ***general*** past "societal discrimination."

2) **Where There Was No Past Discrimination**

Even where the government has not engaged in past discrimination, it may have a compelling interest in affirmative action. However, the governmental action must be ***narrowly tailored*** to that interest.

a) **Diversity in Public Education**

The Supreme Court has not found diversity itself to be a sufficiently compelling reason to justify placing students in a particular elementary or secondary school on the basis of race. However, the law is different for colleges and universities. Public colleges and universities have claimed that they have a compelling interest in having a diverse student body, and the Supreme Court has deferred to that claim. But the Court has also held that each applicant to such schools must be considered as an individual. Admissions officers may consider an applicant's race in making admissions decisions, but only as a ***plus among a range of factors***. If race or ethnicity is the defining criterion for admission, the admission policy will not be narrowly tailored to achieving the compelling interest of ensuring a diverse student body.

c. **Discriminatory Legislative Apportionment**

Race can be considered in drawing up new voting districts, but it ***cannot be the predominant factor***. If a plaintiff can show that a redistricting plan was drawn up predominately on the basis of racial considerations, the plan will violate the Equal Protection Clause unless the government can show that the plan is narrowly tailored to serve a compelling state interest.

2. **Alienage Classifications**

a. **Federal Classifications**

Because of Congress's plenary power over aliens, federal alienage classifications are ***not*** subject to strict scrutiny. Such classifications are valid if they are not arbitrary and unreasonable.

b. **State and Local Classifications**

Generally, state/local laws on alienage are suspect classifications subject to strict scrutiny. *Examples:* It is unconstitutional for United States citizenship to be required for welfare, civil service jobs, or to become a lawyer.

1) **Exception—Participation in Self-Government Process**

If a law discriminates against alien participation in state government (*e.g.,* voting, jury service, elective office), the ***rational basis*** standard is applied. Also, the rational basis standard is used for state and local laws limiting certain nonelective offices involving important public policy (*e.g.,* police officers, probation officers, and primary and secondary school teachers).

c. **Undocumented Aliens**

Undocumented ("illegal") aliens are ***not*** a suspect classification. Thus, state laws regarding them are subject to a "rational basis" standard. (However, denial of free public education to undocumented alien children is invalid, and more than a simple rational basis standard was used by the Court.)

E. QUASI-SUSPECT CLASSIFICATIONS

Classifications based on legitimacy and gender are "quasi-suspect."

1. Gender Classifications

Gender classifications are reviewed under the intermediate scrutiny standard: They must be ***substantially related*** to an ***important*** government purpose. The government bears the burden of showing an "exceedingly persuasive justification" for the discrimination.

a. Women

Intentional discrimination ***against*** women generally is invalid. Classifications ***benefiting*** women that are designed to ***remedy past discrimination*** generally are valid.

b. Intentional Discrimination Against Men

Intentional discrimination against men is generally invalid. However, certain laws have been found to be substantially related to an important government interest (*e.g.,* statutory rape laws, all-male draft).

2. Legitimacy Classifications

Legitimacy classifications are also reviewed under the intermediate scrutiny standard: They must be ***substantially related*** to an ***important*** government interest. Discriminatory regulations intended to punish illegitimate children (*e.g.,* law providing a benefit to legitimate children but not to illegitimate children) are invalid. *Example:* A law allowing only legitimate children to recover from their father's estate is invalid. *But note:* A law allowing illegitimate children to recover from their father's estate only if parenthood is established before the father's death is ***valid***.

F. OTHER CLASSIFICATIONS

All other classifications are evaluated under the ***rational basis*** standard. These include age, disability, and wealth classifications. For example, mandatory retirement ages may be established; and because education is not a fundamental right, there is no denial of equal protection when wealthier children can afford to pay for access to the best state-operated schools.

CMR Exam Tip For the MBE, you must memorize the suspect classifications (race, national origin, and sometimes alienage), quasi-suspect classifications (gender and legitimacy), and the fundamental rights (right to interstate travel, privacy, voting, and First Amendment rights). Any other classification or any other right is ***not*** entitled to more than the rational basis test, and thus the government regulation will usually be valid. Do not let your personal feelings lead you to apply the wrong standard (and pick the wrong answer) because you think the right is important or the group is worthy.

II. FUNDAMENTAL RIGHTS

A. INTRODUCTION

Certain fundamental rights are protected under the Constitution. If they are denied to everyone, it is a substantive due process problem. If they are denied to some individuals but not others, it is an equal protection problem. The applicable standard in either case is strict scrutiny. Thus, government action must be ***necessary*** to protect a ***compelling*** governmental interest. (Remember that there must be no less restrictive means to achieve this goal.)

B. RIGHT OF PRIVACY

Various privacy rights including marriage, sexual relations, abortion, and childrearing are fundamental rights. Regulations affecting these rights are reviewed under the ***strict scrutiny*** standard.

1. Marriage

The right of a male and female to enter into (and, probably, to dissolve) the marriage relationship is a fundamental right. However, a statute restricting the rights of prison inmates to marry will be upheld if reasonably related to legitimate penological interests.

2. Use of Contraceptives

A state cannot prohibit distribution of nonmedical contraceptives to adults.

3. Abortion

The right of privacy includes the right of a woman to have an abortion without interference from the state under certain circumstances. However, normal strict scrutiny analysis cannot be applied because the state has two compelling interests here that often compete: protecting the woman's health and protecting the fetus that may become a child. In its latest abortion rights approach, the Supreme Court has adopted two basic rules: a pre-viability rule and a post-viability rule.

a. Pre-Viability Rule—No Undue Burdens

Before viability (a realistic possibility that the fetus could survive outside the womb), a state may adopt a regulation protecting the mother's health and the life of the fetus if the regulation does not place an "undue burden" on or substantial obstacle to the woman's right to obtain an abortion.

b. Post-Viability Rule—May Prohibit Abortion Unless Woman's Health Threatened

Once the fetus is viable, the state's interest in the fetus's life can override the woman's right to obtain an abortion, but the state cannot prohibit the woman from obtaining an abortion if it is necessary to protect the woman's health or safety.

c. Remedy

When a court is faced with a statute restricting access to abortions that may be applied in an unconstitutional manner so as to harm the mother's health, it should ***not*** invalidate the statute in its entirety if the statute has valid applications. Instead, the court should attempt to fashion narrower declaratory and injunctive relief against the unconstitutional application.

d. Financing Abortions

The government has no obligation to pay for abortions.

4. Obscene Reading Material

The right to privacy includes freedom to read obscene material in one's home (except for child pornography), but not the right to sell, purchase, or transport such material.

5. Keeping Extended Family Together

Zoning regulations that prevent family members—even extended ones—from living together are invalid. However, this right does ***not*** extend to unrelated people.

6. **Rights of Parents**
Parents have a fundamental right to make decisions concerning the care, custody, and control of their children (*e.g.,* a parent has a fundamental right to send a child to private school or to forbid visitation with grandparents).

7. **Intimate Sexual Conduct**
The state has no legitimate interest in making it a crime for fully consenting adults to engage in private intimate sexual conduct (*e.g.,* sodomy) that is not commercial in nature.

8. **Collection and Distribution of Personal Data—No Privacy Right**
The state may reasonably gather and distribute information about its citizens. Thus, there is no privacy right to prohibit the accumulation of names and addresses of patients for whom dangerous drugs are prescribed.

C. **RIGHT TO VOTE**
The right to vote is a fundamental right. Thus, restrictions on that right, other than on the basis of residence, age, and citizenship, are ***invalid*** unless they can pass ***strict scrutiny***.

1. **Restrictions on Right to Vote**

a. **Residency Requirements**
Reasonable time periods for residency (*e.g.,* 30 days) are valid. Note that Congress may override state residency requirements in ***presidential*** elections and substitute its own.

b. **Property Ownership**
Conditioning the right to vote or hold office on ownership of property is usually invalid. *Exception:* Special purpose elections (*e.g.,* water storage districts); *see infra.*

c. **Poll Taxes**
Poll taxes are unconstitutional.

d. **Primary Elections**
States may require early registration to vote in primaries. However, states cannot prohibit political parties from opening their primary elections to anyone, whether or not registered with the party.

2. **Dilution of Right to Vote**

a. **One Person, One Vote Principle**
The "one person, one vote" principle applies whenever any level of government, state or local, decides to select representatives to a governmental body by popular election from ***individual districts***.

1) **Congressional Elections**
States must use ***almost exact mathematical equality*** when creating congressional districts within the state. This is not true of Congress, however, when it apportions representatives among the states; Congress's good faith method for apportioning representatives commands more deference and is ***not*** subject to a precise mathematical formula, as are state plans.

2) State and Local Elections
For state and local elections, the variance in the number of persons included within districts must not be more than a few percentage points.

3) Exception—Appointed Officials and Officials Elected "At Large"
The apportionment requirement is inapplicable to officials who are appointed or elected at large.

4) Exception—Special Purpose Election
The one person, one vote principle does not apply to elections of officials who do not exercise "normal governmental authority" but rather deal with matters of special interest in the community (*e.g.,* water storage districts).

b. Gerrymandering
Race (and presumably other suspect classifications) cannot be the predominant factor in drawing the boundaries of voting districts unless the district plan can pass muster under strict scrutiny.

3. Candidates and Campaigns

a. Candidate Qualifications

1) Fee Must Not Preclude Indigents
States may not charge candidates a fee that results in making it impossible for indigents to run for office.

2) Restrictions on Ability to Be a Candidate
A ballot access regulation must be a reasonable, nondiscriminatory means of promoting important state interests. A state may require candidates to show reasonable support to have their names placed on the ballot.

b. Campaign Funding
The government may allocate more public funds to the two "major" parties than to "minor" parties for political campaigns.

D. RIGHT TO TRAVEL

1. Interstate Travel
An individual has a fundamental right to migrate from state to state and to be treated equally after moving into a new state. However, not every restriction on the right to cross state lines is an impairment of the right to travel (*e.g.,* increased penalties for a father abandoning his children and leaving the state are valid). A problem arises when a state imposes a minimum durational residency requirement for receiving its benefits or otherwise dispenses state benefits based on the length of time a person has resided in the state. It is not clear whether the Court always reviews these regulations under the strict scrutiny standard.

2. Right to International Travel
International travel is ***not a fundamental right***. It is, however, protected from arbitrary federal interference by the Fifth Amendment Due Process Clause; the rational basis standard applies.

FIRST AMENDMENT FREEDOMS

The First Amendment prohibits Congress from establishing a religion or interfering with the free exercise of religion, abridging the freedoms of speech and press, or interfering with the right of assembly. These prohibitions are applicable to the states through the Fourteenth Amendment.

III. FREEDOM OF SPEECH AND ASSEMBLY

A. GENERAL PRINCIPLES

Whenever the government seeks to regulate the freedoms of speech or assembly, the Court will weigh the great importance of speech and assembly rights against the interests or policies sought to be served by the regulation. Keep the following guidelines in mind:

1. Government Speech

The Free Speech Clause restricts government ***regulation of private speech***; it does not require the government to aid private speech nor restrict the government from expressing its views. The government generally is free to voice its opinions and to fund private speech that furthers its views while refusing to fund other private speech, absent some other constitutional limitation, such as the Establishment Clause or Equal Protection Clause. Because government speech does not implicate the First Amendment, it is not subject to the various levels of scrutiny that apply to government regulation of private speech (*see infra*). Generally, government speech and government funding of speech will be upheld if ***rationally related to a legitimate state interest***.

a. Public Monuments

A city's placement of a ***permanent*** monument in a public park is government speech and thus is not subject to Free Speech Clause scrutiny, even if the monument is privately donated.

b. Compare—Government Funding of Private Speech

When the government chooses to fund private messages (*e.g.*, college group newsletters), it generally must do so on a viewpoint neutral basis.

1) Exception—Funding of the Arts

From a financial standpoint, the government cannot fund all artists, and choosing among those it will fund and those it will not inevitably must be based on the content of the art.

2. Content vs. Conduct

Speech and assembly regulations can generally be categorized as either ***content*** regulations (regulations forbidding communication of specific ideas) or ***conduct*** regulations (regulations of the conduct associated with speaking, such as the time of the speech, sound level, etc.). Different standards are used to assess the validity of a regulation within each category.

a. Content

It is presumptively unconstitutional to place burdens on speech because of its content except for certain categories of speech (obscenity, defamation, etc.). Content-neutral speech regulations generally are subject to ***intermediate scrutiny***; *i.e.*, they must advance ***important*** interests unrelated to the suppression of speech and ***must not burden substantially more speech than necessary*** to further those interests.

b. Conduct

Conduct related to speech can be regulated by content-neutral time, place, and manner restrictions. (These rules will be discussed at B., *infra.*) Additionally, all regulations of speech are subject to the following restrictions.

3. Reasonableness of Regulation

a. Overbroad Regulation Invalid

If a regulation of speech or speech-related conduct punishes a ***substantial amount of protected speech*** in relation to its plainly legitimate sweep (*e.g.,* a regulation outlawing ***all*** First Amendment activity in an airport terminal; a regulation prohibiting all canvassers from going onto private residential property to promote ***any*** cause without first obtaining a permit), the regulation is ***facially invalid*** (*i.e.,* it may not be enforced against anyone—not even a person engaging in activity that is not constitutionally protected) unless a court has limited construction of the regulation so as to remove the threat to constitutionally protected expression. If the regulation is ***not substantially overbroad***, it can be enforced against persons engaging in activities that are not constitutionally protected.

b. Void for Vagueness Doctrine

If a criminal law or regulation fails to give persons reasonable notice of what is prohibited (*e.g.,* a prohibition of "lewd" speech), it may violate the Due Process Clause. This principle is applied somewhat strictly when First Amendment activity is involved.

c. Cannot Give Officials Unfettered Discretion

A regulation cannot give officials broad discretion over speech issues; there must be ***defined standards*** for applying the law. If a statute gives licensing officials ***unbridled discretion***, it is ***void on its face*** and speakers need not even apply for a permit. If the licensing statute includes standards, a speaker may not ignore the statute; he must seek a permit and if it is denied, he can challenge the denial on First Amendment grounds.

4. Scope of Speech

The freedom to speak includes the freedom ***not to speak***. Thus, the government generally cannot require people to salute the flag or display other messages with which they disagree (*e.g.,* a person need not display the state motto "live free or die" on a license plate). The freedom can extend to ***symbolic acts*** undertaken to communicate an idea (*e.g.,* wearing a black armband to protest the war), although the government may regulate such conduct if it has an ***important*** interest in the regulation ***independent*** of the speech aspects of the conduct and the incidental burden on speech is no greater than necessary (*e.g.,* to facilitate a smooth draft, the government can prohibit the burning of draft cards).

a. Mandatory Financial Support

Although the government may not compel a person to express a message, it may tax people and use the revenue to express a message with which they disagree (*e.g.,* a beef producer can be required to pay an assessment to support government-sponsored generic advertising of beef even if the producer thinks generic advertising is a waste of

money). However, it appears that people ***cannot*** be compelled to subsidize private messages with which they disagree (*e.g.,* while lawyers may be compelled to pay bar dues and government teachers can be compelled to pay union dues, they cannot be compelled to pay sums to such private associations that will be used to support political views that, or candidates whom, they do not endorse).

1) **Exception—University Activity Fees**
The government can require public university students to pay a student activity fee even if the fee is used to support political and ideological speech by student groups whose beliefs are offensive to the student, as long as the program is viewpoint neutral.

B. TIME, PLACE, AND MANNER RESTRICTIONS—REGULATION OF CONDUCT

The government has power to regulate the ***conduct*** associated with speech and assembly, although the breadth of this power depends on whether the forum involved is a public forum, a designated public forum, a limited public forum, or a nonpublic forum.

1. Public Forums and Designated Public Forums

Public property that has historically been open to speech-related activities (*e.g.,* ***streets, sidewalks, and public parks***) is called a public forum. Public property that has not historically been open to speech-related activities, but which the government has thrown open for such activities on a permanent or limited basis, by practice or policy (*e.g.,* schoolrooms that are open for after-school use by social, civic, or recreation groups), is called a designated public forum. The government may regulate speech in public forums and designated public forums with reasonable time, place, and manner regulations that:

(i) Are ***content neutral***;

(ii) Are ***narrowly tailored*** to serve an ***important*** government interest; and

(iii) Leave open ***alternative channels*** of communication.

Note: Almost every legitimate governmental interest satisfies the significant/important standard.

CMR **Exam Tip** Remember that even if a regulation meets the time, place, and manner requirements above, it could still be invalid if it is overbroad, vague, or gives unfettered discretion.

a. Injunctions

Injunctions against speech in public forums are treated differently from generally applicable laws. If the injunction is content based, it must be necessary to achieve a compelling interest. If the injunction is content neutral, it must burden no more speech than is necessary to achieve an important government interest.

2. Limited Public Forums and Nonpublic Forums

Speech and assembly can be more broadly regulated in limited public forums (*i.e.,* government-owned property opened for use by certain groups or dedicated solely to the discussion of certain subjects, such as a school hosting a public debate on a particular issue in its gym) and nonpublic forums (*i.e.,* government-owned property not historically linked with speech and assembly and not held open for speech activities, such as military bases, schools while classes are in session, government workplaces, etc.). The government can regulate speech in such a forum to ***reserve the forum for its intended use***. In such locations, regulations are valid if they are:

a. ***Viewpoint neutral***; and

b. ***Reasonably related to a legitimate*** government purpose.

C. UNPROTECTED SPEECH—REGULATION BASED ON CONTENT

To be valid, restrictions on the content of speech must be ***necessary*** to achieve a ***compelling*** government interest. The government has a compelling interest in the following categories of speech, which are deemed "unprotected" speech under the First Amendment:

1. Inciting Imminent Lawless Action

Speech can be burdened if it creates a clear and present danger of imminent lawless action. It must be shown that imminent illegal conduct is ***likely*** and that the speaker intended to cause it.

2. Fighting Words

True threats (*e.g.,* cross-burning carried out with an intent to intimidate) are not protected by the First Amendment. Speech also can be burdened if it constitutes fighting words (personally abusive words that are likely to incite immediate physical retaliation in an average person). Words that are merely annoying are not sufficient. Note also that the Supreme Court will not tolerate fighting words statutes that are designed to punish only certain viewpoints (*e.g.,* proscribing only fighting words that insult on the basis of race, religion, or gender).

Exam Tip While this classification of punishable speech exists in theory, as a practical matter, statutes that attempt to punish fighting words are usually vague or overbroad. Thus, on the examination, they generally should be regarded as ***invalid***.

3. Obscenity

Obscene speech is not protected.

a. Elements

Speech is obscene if it describes or depicts sexual conduct that, taken as a whole, by the average person:

1) ***Appeals to the prurient interest*** in sex, using a ***community standard***;

2) Is ***patently offensive*** and an affront to contemporary ***community standards***; and

3) ***Lacks serious value*** (literary, artistic, political, or scientific), using a ***national reasonable person standard***.

Exam Tip Note the two different standards used in the obscenity test: appeal to the prurient interest and offensiveness are judged by contemporary ***community*** standards (local or statewide, not necessarily national standards), while value is judged on a ***national reasonable person*** basis.

b. Standard May Be Different for Minors

The state can adopt a specific definition of obscenity applying to materials sold to minors, even though the material might not be obscene in terms of an adult audience. However, government may not prohibit the sale or distribution of material to adults merely because it is inappropriate for children.

1) **Pictures of Minors**
To protect minors from exploitation, the government may prohibit the sale or distribution of ***visual*** depictions of sexual conduct involving minors, even if the material would not be found obscene if it did not involve children.

2) **Compare—Simulated Pictures of Minors**
The government may not bar visual material that only appears to depict minors engaged in sexually explicit conduct, but that in fact uses young-looking adults or computer generated images.

c. **Land Use Regulations**
A land use (or zoning) regulation may limit the location or size of adult entertainment establishments if the regulation is designed to reduce the secondary effects of such businesses (*e.g.*, rise in crime rates, drop in property values, etc.). However, regulations may not ban such establishments altogether.

d. **Liquor Regulation**
Under the Twenty-First Amendment, states have broad power to regulate intoxicating beverages. Laws relating to this power that affect free speech rights generally will not be set aside unless they are irrational.

e. **Private Possession of Obscene Material**
Private possession of obscene material ***in the home*** cannot be punished (except for possession of child pornography). However, the protection does not extend outside the home.

4. **Defamatory Speech**
Defamatory statements can be burdened. If the defamatory statement is about a ***public official*** or ***public figure*** or involves a ***public concern***, the First Amendment requires the plaintiff to prove all the elements of defamation ***plus falsity*** and some degree of ***fault***. (*See* Torts outline for detailed discussion.)

CMR **Exam Tip** The First Amendment may also play a role in certain privacy actions. (*See* Torts outline.)

5. **Some Commercial Speech**
As a general rule, commercial speech is afforded First Amendment protection if it is truthful. However, commercial speech that proposes ***unlawful activity*** or that is ***misleading or fraudulent*** may be burdened. Any other regulation of commercial speech will be upheld only if it:

(i) Serves a ***substantial government interest***;

(ii) ***Directly advances*** that interest; and

(iii) Is ***narrowly tailored*** to serve that interest.

Exam Tip "Narrowly tailored" does ***not*** require the least restrictive means of accomplishing the legislative goal; there just must be a ***reasonable fit*** between the goal and the means chosen.

a. Complete Bans

Complete bans on truthful advertisement of lawful products are very unlikely to be upheld due to a lack of tailoring.

b. Required Disclosures

The government may require commercial advertisers to make disclosures if the disclosures are not unduly burdensome and they are reasonably related to the state's interest in preventing deception.

D. PRIOR RESTRAINTS

Prior restraints prevent speech before it occurs, rather than punish it afterwards. They are rarely allowed. The government has a heavy burden in justifying a prior restraint; it must show that some ***special societal harm*** will otherwise result.

1. Procedural Safeguards

To be valid, a system for prior restraint must provide the following safeguards:

(i) The standards must be ***narrowly drawn, reasonable, and definite***;

(ii) Injunction must ***promptly*** be sought; and

(iii) There must be ***prompt and final determination*** of the validity of the restraint.

A number of other cases, especially in the area of movie censorship, require that the ***government bear the burden*** of proving that the speech involved is unprotected.

2. Obscenity Cases

a. Seizures of Books and Films

Seizures of a single book or film may be made with a ***warrant*** based on probable cause, although if the item is available for sale to the public, a police officer may purchase a book or film to use as evidence without a warrant. Large-scale seizures must be ***preceded by a full scale adversary hearing*** and a judicial determination of obscenity.

b. Movie Censorship

The Court has found that time delays incident to censorship are less burdensome on movies than on other forms of expression. Thus, the Court allows the government to establish censorship boards to screen movies before they are released, as long as the procedural safeguards discussed above are followed.

c. Burden of Government

When the government adopts a content-based, prior restraint of speech, the government has the burden of proving that the restriction is ***narrowly tailored*** to accomplish its goal.

E. FREEDOM OF THE PRESS

Generally, the press has ***no greater First Amendment freedom*** than does a private citizen. Thus, the concepts discussed above apply.

1. Publication of Truthful Information

Generally the press has a right to publish truthful information regarding a matter of public concern, and this right can be restricted only by a sanction that is narrowly tailored to further an interest of the highest order.

2. **Access to Trials**
The First Amendment guarantees the public and press a right to attend criminal (and probably civil) trials. However, the right may be ***outweighed*** by an overriding interest stated in the trial judge's findings (*e.g.*, to protect children who are victims of sex offenses). The right includes the right to be present at voir dire and at other pretrial proceedings, unless the judge makes specific findings that closure was narrowly tailored to preserve a higher value.

3. **Requiring Press to Testify Before Grand Jury**
Members of the press may be required to testify before grand juries.

4. **Interviewing Prisoners**
The First Amendment does not give journalists a right to interview specified prisoners of their choice or to inspect prison grounds.

5. **Business Regulation or Tax**
The press and broadcasting companies can be subjected to ***general*** business regulations or taxes but cannot be targeted for special regulation or taxes. A tax or regulation impacting on the press or a subpart of the press cannot be based on the content of a publication (*e.g.*, a tax exemption cannot be given to "medical journals") absent a compelling justification.

6. **Broadcasting Regulations**
Radio and television broadcasting may be more closely regulated than the press. The paramount right is the right of ***viewers and listeners*** to receive information of public concern rather than the right of broadcasters to broadcast what they please. This paramount right allows government to forbid newspaper ownership of radio stations and to prohibit indecent speech over the airwaves.

   a. **Fairness Doctrine**
   The First Amendment does not require broadcasters to accept political advertisements. However, a radio station may constitutionally be required to offer free broadcasting time to certain individuals (*e.g.*, opponents of political candidates or views endorsed by the station, or persons who have been personally attacked in a broadcast).

7. **Cable Television Regulation**
While generally regulations of newspapers are subject to strict scrutiny, and regulations of the broadcast media are subject to less critical review, regulations of cable television transmissions generally are subject to review by a standard somewhere between these two (*e.g.*, a law requiring cable operators to carry local stations is subject to "intermediate scrutiny"—because it is content-neutral (*see* A.2.a., *supra*)—and is constitutional because it serves the important interest of preserving economic viability of local broadcasters). However, content-based restrictions (*e.g.*, a law forbidding sexually oriented cable programs before 10 p.m.) are subject to strict scrutiny.

8. **Internet Regulation**
The strict standard of First Amendment scrutiny, rather than the more relaxed standard applicable to broadcast regulation, applies to regulation of the Internet.

IV. FREEDOM OF RELIGION

A. CONSTITUTIONAL PROVISION

The First Amendment prohibition on establishment of religion and its protection of the free exercise of religion is applicable to the states through the Fourteenth Amendment.

B. FREE EXERCISE CLAUSE

1. No Punishment of Beliefs

The Free Exercise Clause prohibits government from punishing someone on the basis of her religious beliefs. For example, the Clause forbids:

(i) State governments from requiring office holders or employees to take a ***religious oath*** (the federal government is similarly restricted by Article VI);

(ii) States from ***excluding clerics*** from holding public office; and

(iii) Courts from ***declaring a religious belief to be false***.

The Supreme Court has not defined what constitutes religious belief, but it is clear that religious belief need not come from an organized religion or involve a supreme being. The Court has never held an asserted religious belief to be not religious for First Amendment purposes.

CMR **Exam Tip** Technically, the government may deny benefits to or impose a burden on someone based on her religious beliefs ***if there is a compelling interest***. However, the Supreme Court has ***never*** found an interest so compelling that it justifies such action.

2. General Conduct Regulation—No Religious Exemptions Required

The Free Exercise Clause cannot be used to challenge government regulation unless the regulation was ***specifically designed*** to interfere with religion (*e.g.*, a law that prohibits the precise type of animal slaughter used in a ritual by a particular religious sect is unconstitutional). Moreover, the Free Exercise Clause does ***not require religious exemptions*** from generally applicable governmental regulations that happen to burden religious conduct; *i.e.*, a law that regulates the conduct of ***all*** people can be applied to prohibit the conduct of a person despite the fact that his religious beliefs prevent him from complying with the law.

a. Exception—Unemployment Compensation Cases

A state cannot refuse to grant unemployment benefits to persons who quit their jobs for religious reasons (*i.e.*, the work or conditions of work conflict with tenets of the worker's religion). The worker need not even belong to a formal religious organization in such a situation, as long as the belief is sincere.

b. Exception—Right of Amish Not to Educate Children

The Supreme Court has granted the Amish an exemption from a law requiring compulsory school attendance until age 16, based on the Free Exercise Clause ***and*** the fundamental right to educate one's children.

CMR **Exam Tip** To summarize, the Free Exercise Clause prohibits government interference with religious ***beliefs***, but it generally does ***not*** prohibit regulation of ***conduct***. If the governmental action regulates ***general conduct***—including religious conduct—it is ***valid*** (*e.g.,* banning any use of peyote is valid even though a group's religious beliefs require its use during its ceremonies). The only exceptions to this rule are those pertaining to unemployment compensation and the education of Amish children.

C. ESTABLISHMENT CLAUSE

The Establishment Clause prohibits laws respecting the establishment of religion.

1. Sect Preference

If government action includes a preference for one religious sect over another, it is invalid unless it is ***narrowly tailored*** to promote a ***compelling*** interest.

CMR **Exam Tip** Although you should know the standard (narrowly tailored to promote a compelling interest) for government preference of a religious sect (or sects), it is unlikely that the government could ever have a compelling interest in preferring one religious group.

2. No Sect Preference—*Lemon* Test

If government action does not involve sect preference, it is ***valid*** under the Establishment Clause ***if*** it:

(i) Has a ***secular purpose***;

(ii) Has a ***primary effect that neither advances nor inhibits religion***; and

(iii) Does not produce ***excessive government entanglement*** with religion.

This is known as the *Lemon* test. (Note that some recent cases have simply focused on whether the action is neutral between the religious and nonreligious when there is no endorsement of a particular religion.)

a. Cases Unconnected to Financial Aid or Education

A good rule of thumb here is that a law favoring or burdening religion or a specific religious group will be invalid (*e.g.,* exempting certain religious groups—traditional religions—from state registration requirements), but a law favoring or burdening a large segment of society that happens to include religious groups will be upheld (*e.g.,* a Sunday closing law).

b. Cases Involving Financial Benefits to Religious Institutions

The Supreme Court applies the three-part test above with greater strictness when government financial aid is going to a religiously affiliated ***grade or high school*** than it does when the aid is going to another type of religious institution.

1) Recipient-Based Aid

The government may give aid in the form of financial assistance to a defined class of persons as long as the class is defined without reference to religion or religious criteria. Such a program is valid even if most of the people receiving the aid use it to attend a religiously affiliated school.

2) **Aid to Colleges and Hospitals**
Aid to colleges or hospitals will be upheld as long as the government program requires the aid to be used ***for nonreligious purposes*** and the recipient so agrees.

3) **Aid to Grade Schools and High Schools**
Aid to religious grade schools and high schools is usually found to have a secular purpose, but may fail the other parts of the test. For example, if the program has detailed administrative regulations to prevent the effect of advancement of religion, the law will be stricken for excessive government entanglement.

c. **Religious Activities in Public Schools**
School ***sponsored*** religious activity is ***invalid***, but school ***accommodation*** of religion is ***valid***. Moreover, if a public school allows members of the public and private organizations to use school property when classes are not in session, it cannot deny a religious organization permission to use the property for meetings merely because religious topics will be discussed.

barbri®

Constitutional Law

1. Ⓐ Ⓑ Ⓒ Ⓓ
2. Ⓐ Ⓑ Ⓒ Ⓓ
3. Ⓐ Ⓑ Ⓒ Ⓓ
4. Ⓐ Ⓑ Ⓒ Ⓓ
5. Ⓐ Ⓑ Ⓒ Ⓓ

6. Ⓐ Ⓑ Ⓒ Ⓓ
7. Ⓐ Ⓑ Ⓒ Ⓓ
8. Ⓐ Ⓑ Ⓒ Ⓓ
9. Ⓐ Ⓑ Ⓒ Ⓓ
10. Ⓐ Ⓑ Ⓒ Ⓓ

11. Ⓐ Ⓑ Ⓒ Ⓓ
12. Ⓐ Ⓑ Ⓒ Ⓓ
13. Ⓐ Ⓑ Ⓒ Ⓓ
14. Ⓐ Ⓑ Ⓒ Ⓓ
15. Ⓐ Ⓑ Ⓒ Ⓓ

16. Ⓐ Ⓑ Ⓒ Ⓓ
17. Ⓐ Ⓑ Ⓒ Ⓓ

CONSTITUTIONAL LAW QUESTIONS

Question 1

A state law permitted young men and women to apply for a license to operate a motorcycle when they reach the age of 18. Recently, however, because of a marked increase in motorcycle accidents involving teenage girls, the state legislature raised the age for women who apply for such a license to age 21, while leaving the age for men who apply unchanged.

A 19-year-old woman applied for a motorcycle license in the state but was denied because of her age. She subsequently sues in federal court, alleging that the statute unconstitutionally discriminates against women.

Which of the following statements best reflects the burden of persuasion that the court will apply in the woman's suit?

(A) The state must show that the law is substantially related to a legitimate government interest.

(B) The state must show that the law is necessary to achieve a compelling or overriding government purpose.

(C) The woman must show that the law is rationally related to a legitimate government interest.

(D) The state must show that the law is substantially related to an important government purpose.

Question 2

To reduce incidents of violence among male gang members at a youth center, a city passed an ordinance forbidding any male between the ages of 13 and 19 to enter the center unless accompanied by a female.

An 18-year-old male who was refused admission at the center because he was not escorted by a female filed suit in federal court to strike down the ordinance as unconstitutional.

The court should find the ordinance:

(A) Constitutional, because in these situations the government is performing a parens patriae function.

(B) Constitutional, if the city can show a rational relationship between the ordinance and maintaining order at the center.

(C) Unconstitutional, if the plaintiff can show that the ordinance was not necessary to promote a compelling government interest.

(D) Unconstitutional, unless the city can show that the ordinance is substantially related to important government objectives.

Question 3

A state public employee retirement act provided that, while legitimate children under 18 qualify for survivor benefits, an employee's children born out of wedlock may recover only if they lived with the employee in a regular parent-child relationship. A state employee lived with a woman in the state for ten years, after which they separated. They had two children, both of whom were the employee's natural children born out of wedlock. The employee supported the children under a state child support decree until he died a year ago. At the time of his death, he was covered by the retirement act. The state retirement commission determined that the children did not qualify because they were living with their mother and not living with the employee at the time of his death.

The mother sued in federal court alleging that, if the children were born in wedlock, they would have been entitled to benefits, and that it was discriminatory to treat illegitimate children differently.

The court should hold that the statutory provision is:

(A) Constitutional, because a state may allocate survivor benefits to its employees without restriction.

(B) Constitutional, if there was a rational basis for the classification of illegitimate versus legitimate children.

(C) Unconstitutional, unless the classification of legitimate and illegitimate children is substantially related to an important state purpose.

(D) Unconstitutional, unless the different treatment of legitimate and illegitimate children is necessary to promote a compelling state interest.

Question 4

To better reflect the age range of its citizens, a city council passed an ordinance providing that no city employee could be hired or promoted unless that employee had reached the age of 55. A 25-year-old city mechanic in the lower pay classification had recently finished first on a promotional exam for the senior mechanic position, which would entitle him to a substantial increase in pay. His supervisor told him that, under instructions from the head of the city administrative office, a 56-year-old city mechanic who scored lower on the exam would be promoted to the position instead.

If the mechanic brings an appropriate action in federal court to challenge the ordinance, the burden of proof would be on:

(A) The mechanic, to prove that there is no compelling state interest furthered by the challenged ordinance.

(B) The mechanic, to prove that the challenged ordinance is clearly arbitrary and irrational.

(C) The city, to prove that its ordinance is necessary to further a compelling state interest.

(D) The city, to prove that there was a rational basis for enacting the challenged ordinance.

Question 5

A state enacted health care legislation to provide comprehensive insurance coverage on prescription drugs for all of its citizens. The legislation provided state reimbursement for the cost of all prescription drugs with one exception—a drug commonly known as the "abortion pill," which was prescribed to induce early term abortions without surgery. All other prescription drugs for pregnant women were covered. A pregnant woman who had received a prescription for the drug and was subsequently denied reimbursement filed suit in federal district court challenging the constitutionality of the legislation.

Which of the following best describes the appropriate standard by which the court should review the constitutionality of the state legislation?

(A) Because the state legislation does not improperly discriminate against a suspect class or burden a fundamental right, the woman will have to show that the legislation is not rationally related to any legitimate state interest.

(B) Because the state legislation discriminates against women by not providing coverage for all of their prescription medications as it does for men, the state will have to demonstrate that the legislation is substantially related to an important government interest.

(C) Because the state legislation impinges on a woman's constitutional right to choose whether to terminate her pregnancy, the state will have to show that the legislation does not constitute an undue burden on that right.

(D) Because the state legislation discriminates against women seeking to exercise their fundamental right to terminate their pregnancy in favor of women incurring the regular expenses of pregnancy, the state will have to demonstrate that the legislation is necessary to vindicate a compelling state interest.

Question 6

A state prohibited speechmaking, noisy picketing, or other public gatherings within 100 feet of the state legislative building when the legislature was in session to vote or debate on any legislation. The statute did permit silent picketing or silent vigils at any time, as long as the pickets did not interfere with pedestrians or traffic. The nearest place to the building where speeches could be made during a session was a large public park directly opposite the building.

During a controversial debate on a proposed bill to reinstate the state's death penalty, supporters of the bill gathered for a rally and speeches. One of the leaders of the group was giving a speech when he was informed that the legislature had decided to send the bill back to committee and that there would be no vote on the bill until the next legislative session. He told the crowd that they should all go across the street and let the legislators hear the voices of the people. When he led the chanting crowd to the front of the building, the state police dispersed them and arrested the leader, charging him with violating the statute.

This statute likely would be held:

(A) Constitutional on its face and as applied to the leader.

(B) Constitutional on its face, but not as applied to the leader.

(C) Unconstitutional on its face, because a state's citizens have a right to take their complaints to their state legislature.

(D) Unconstitutional on its face, because it permits silent picketing while prohibiting other picketing.

Question 7

A state statute makes it a felony for anyone in the corridors or on the grounds of any building in which a court may be in session to make a speech or carry a sign intended to influence judicial proceedings. When the head of a street gang was on trial for murder, a gang member was arrested for carrying a sign on the steps of the courthouse warning that if the gang leader was not freed, "the judge will die."

In the criminal proceeding against the gang member, he:

(A) Cannot be convicted, because the statute could apply to others whose speech is constitutionally protected.

(B) Cannot be convicted, unless he personally intended to harm the judge.

(C) Can be convicted, if there was a clear and present danger that the judge would be influenced by the sign.

(D) Can be convicted, because the statute does not violate the freedom of expression guaranteed by the First Amendment.

Question 8

A private organization created to counter what its members view as environmental extremism organized an annual parade extolling the benefits of industry. Shortly after the organization obtained all of the necessary city permits to hold the parade, it was contacted by a local environmental group that wanted to march in the organization's parade armed with anti-pollution signs. The environmental group correctly informed the organization that the city's parade ordinance provided that all private parade organizers must allow into their parade any group wishing to participate in the parade. The organization's parade organizers immediately filed suit in federal court challenging the constitutionality of the ordinance.

Is the court likely to find the ordinance unconstitutional?

(A) Yes, because it violates the organizers' freedom of speech.

(B) Yes, because a state cannot interfere with the speech activities of a private organization.

(C) No, because it promotes the right to freedom of speech.

(D) No, because it falls within the reaches of the state's police power to protect public health, safety, welfare, and morals.

Question 9

Responding to complaints from city residents that a proliferation of adult-oriented businesses, such as bookstores and video arcades, lowered property values and increased crime, the city council passed an ordinance banning the operation of adult-oriented businesses in any area of the city zoned "residential" or "commercial." The ordinance provided that such businesses would be allowed to operate in areas zoned "industrial," providing that they complied with other laws, such as those against prostitution. There were a number of industrial zones in the city where adult-oriented businesses could operate, but they were in areas remote from the central business district. The owner of a marginally profitable bookstore located in a commercially zoned area of the downtown business district wanted to increase his profits by converting to an adult bookstore, but he did not want to move the business. He filed suit in federal court to prevent enforcement of the statute against him, claiming violation of his free speech rights.

The court is likely to rule for:

(A) The city, because speech-related activities may be regulated to prevent effects that are distasteful to neighboring businesses and residents.

(B) The city, because zoning may be used to regulate the time, place, and manner of speech-related activities if such zoning does not constitute an effective ban on such activities.

(C) The bookstore owner, because governmental entities may not regulate free speech merely because people dislike its content.

(D) The bookstore owner, because the city has no right to infringe upon the rights of businesspeople to operate speech-related businesses wherever they choose.

Question 10

In response to a state study concluding that the state had a substantial interest in combating the obesity epidemic and improving the general health of its citizens, the legislature passed legislation to advance those goals. One statute regulated the time, duration, frequency, and content of all television advertisements for food, food retailers, and restaurants. An association of food retailers brings an action in federal court challenging the statute's constitutionality.

Should the court find the statute constitutional?

(A) Yes, if it does not prohibit the dissemination of truthful information about price and the availability of products, and is narrowly tailored to serve the state's interest in combating obesity.

(B) Yes, because it serves a substantial government interest and restricts only commercial speech.

(C) No, because it infringes on the freedom of speech rights of food sellers in violation of the First Amendment.

(D) No, if it interferes with existing contracts between food sellers and television broadcasters.

Question 11

To protect the privacy rights of its citizens, a state statute required that all records be sealed when a person charged with a crime was later acquitted, or when the charges were dropped by the prosecutor. The public was denied access to arrest records and any other records relating to such cases, and the statute made it a misdemeanor to publish material from the sealed records. The same information was allowed to be published only if it came from a source other than the officially sealed records. A reporter for a local newspaper discovered through private sources that the mayor of the city had once been charged with molesting a child, but that the district attorney had ordered the charges dropped. The district attorney's office refused the newspaper's demand for the arrest records, citing the statute. The newspaper filed suit, demanding the unsealing of the records and attacking the constitutionality of the state statute.

The state's best argument in defense is:

(A) The privacy rights of state citizens outweigh the public's right to know.

(B) The mayor's records are not being specially withheld from the newspaper, because the statute treats all such cases equally.

(C) A newspaper has no greater claim to information than the public at large, and the First Amendment does not create a right to government documents.

(D) The statute is not a prior restraint on publications.

Question 12

A state legislature passed a statute making the possession of rattlesnakes illegal. The legislative debates made clear that the purpose of the statute was to reduce the number of venomous snakebites in the state.

A local church practiced the doctrine of rattlesnake worship, and members of the congregation handled rattlesnakes as an integral part of the church's services. The leader of the church brought suit to have the statute declared unconstitutional for violating the church members' right to practice their religion.

The court will most likely:

(A) Uphold the statute, because of the compelling state interest involved.

(B) Uphold the statute, because it is a neutral law of general application.

(C) Invalidate the statute, because it is not the least restrictive means of accomplishing the state's purpose.

(D) Invalidate the statute, because as applied to the church, it interferes with an integral part of the church's services.

Question 13

A church developed a sex education program for children of church members, ages 12 to 16. The program included lectures and slides, including some slides depicting explicit sexual activity between males and females. Parents would be required to give their consent before any child could participate. The program was conducted by the church board, consisting of the minister, a doctor, and a psychologist. The church board called the program "an integral part of involving the church in the real world of a teenager."

A state statute provides in relevant part, "It is unlawful to sell, give, or display to any person under the age of 17 any lewd or obscene article, picture, or depiction."

If the church board members are convicted of violating the above statute and they appeal:

(A) Their convictions will be reversed because the freedom to engage in conduct connected with one's religion is absolutely protected under the First and Fourteenth Amendments.

(B) Their convictions will be reversed if it can be shown that the statute is being applied only to interfere with religion.

(C) Their convictions will be upheld because the state's interest in regulating activities involving children necessarily outweighs any rights of the church board members under the Free Exercise Clause of the First Amendment.

(D) Their convictions will be upheld because the members of the church board lack standing to challenge the statute on "free exercise of religion" grounds.

Question 14

A state legislature enacted a statute requiring the parents of every child to have the child vaccinated for chicken pox before the child's second birthday. Failure to comply was a misdemeanor. A parent refused to have her child vaccinated, claiming that any injections or vaccinations violate the tenets and beliefs of her religion.

If the state commences a criminal prosecution against the parent for violation of the statute, the state court may constitutionally inquire as to whether:

(A) The tenets of the parent's religion are true.

(B) The parent's religion is a traditional, established one.

(C) The parent believes that the tenets of her religion are derived from a supreme being or are merely internally derived.

(D) The parent sincerely believes the tenets of her religion.

Question 15

A member of a religion that celebrated Saturday as the Sabbath and proscribed any form of servile work on that day worked at a plant that manufactured tractors and other tracked vehicles used in agriculture and construction work. After the plant landed a big government contract to produce armored personnel carriers for the military, the managers required all full-time assembly-line workers to work an overtime shift every other Saturday. Rather than compromise his religious beliefs, the worker voluntarily quit the plant. A co-worker who was also a member of that religion continued to work at the plant but failed to report for work on his first scheduled Saturday shift, citing religious objections. He was promptly fired by plant management. Both workers applied for state unemployment benefits. Benefits were granted to the worker who had been fired but not to the worker who had quit.

If the worker denied benefits wishes to sue to obtain them, his best constitutional argument is based on:

(A) The Establishment Clause, because the policies prefer a majority religion in violation of the First and Fourteenth Amendments.

(B) The Free Exercise Clause, because his attempts to practice the tenets of his religion have denied him benefits in violation of the First and Fourteenth Amendments.

(C) The Equal Protection Clause of the Fourteenth Amendment, because persons who elected to be involuntarily dismissed for the same reason as he voluntarily quit are being treated differently from him.

(D) The Due Process Clause of the Fourteenth Amendment, because unemployment benefits are a property right of which he has been deprived without due process of law.

Question 16

The council of a city with a rich and diverse heritage established a city-run ethnic sculpture garden. City residents and groups were encouraged to erect statues and other displays in the garden depicting ethnic, cultural, and religious heritages. Many of the displays included religious symbols. The city maintained the property and administered the affairs of the garden. While the garden was paid for primarily by a small admission fee, the city contributed about $1,000 each year for the garden's upkeep from general city funds.

If a local citizen brings an action in federal court challenging the city's funding of the garden, the court should find the city's acts:

(A) Constitutional, because the amount of city funds spent on the garden is de minimis.

(B) Constitutional, because the garden also includes secular displays depicting the city's ethnic and cultural heritage.

(C) Unconstitutional, because the city is helping to maintain religious symbols in violation of the First Amendment.

(D) Unconstitutional, because the city does not have a compelling interest in running the garden.

Question 17

A state legislature enacted a statute providing for loaning certain textbooks on secular subjects to students in all public and private schools. In accordance with the statute, the state board of education distributed textbooks to a private school that offered religious instruction and admitted only Caucasian students.

Which of the following is the strongest argument against the constitutionality of free distribution of textbooks to the students at the private school?

(A) A state may not constitutionally aid private schools through distribution of textbooks.

(B) Segregation is furthered by the distribution of textbooks to these students.

(C) The distribution of textbooks advances religion because it is impossible to separate their secular and religious uses.

(D) The distribution of textbooks fosters excessive government entanglement with religion.

CONSTITUTIONAL LAW ANSWERS

Answer to Question 1

(D) The state must show that the law is substantially related to an important government purpose. Cases of gender discrimination are tested under intermediate scrutiny—the state must prove that the government action in question is substantially related to an important government interest. (A) is incorrect. While it properly places the burden on the state, it provides a muddled statement of the correct standard by combining the language for the intermediate standard with that for the minimal, rational basis standard. (B) is incorrect because, while it properly places the burden on the state, it provides a statement of the strict scrutiny standard, which is too stringent a standard for gender discrimination. (C) is incorrect. It states the minimal scrutiny, or "rational basis," standard. This standard places the burden on the wrong party (the plaintiff) and is too lenient for gender discrimination cases.

Answer to Question 2

(D) The court should find the ordinance unconstitutional unless the city shows that the ordinance is substantially related to important government objectives. Classifications based on gender, such as the ordinance here, are quasi-suspect and violate equal protection unless they are substantially related to an important government objective. (A) is incorrect; even if the government were performing a parens patriae function, it would not be permitted to violate equal protection. (B) states the wrong equal protection test; because a quasi-suspect class is involved, the rational relationship test does not apply. (C) states the wrong test and places the burden of proof on the wrong party.

Answer to Question 3

(C) The statutory provision should be found unconstitutional unless the classification is substantially related to an important government purpose. Discrimination against illegitimate children is judged by a quasi-suspect standard similar to that used in gender discrimination cases. The standard requires that the classification be substantially related to an important state purpose. (A) is incorrect because state action is restricted by federal constitutional protections. (B) and (D) state the wrong tests for this type of discrimination.

Answer to Question 4

(B) The burden of proof will be on the mechanic to prove that the challenged ordinance is arbitrary and irrational. Because age is neither a suspect classification nor the type of discrimination entitled to an intermediate level of constitutional scrutiny, the rational basis test applies in an equal protection analysis. Under that test, the challenger must show that the law has no rational basis, and the statute will be presumed constitutional unless a clear showing of arbitrariness and irrationality is made. (A) is wrong because it applies the compelling state interest test, which is the wrong standard. (C) and (D) are incorrect because they place the burden of proof on the wrong party. The mechanic has the burden. Also, (C) requires a stricter test than would be applied.

Answer to Question 5

(A) The court should require the woman to show that the legislation is not rationally related to any legitimate state interest. The Supreme Court has held that the right of privacy includes the right of a woman to have an abortion under certain circumstances without undue interference from the government. However, neither federal nor state government is required to grant medical benefit payments for abortions, even if it grants benefits for childbirth services. The Court has held that a state's failure to provide funding for a woman's abortion decision does not constitute interference with her constitutional right to make that decision; hence, such legislation is valid unless the plaintiff can show that it is not rationally related to a legitimate state interest. [*See* Maher v. Roe (1977)] (B) is incorrect because the legislation does not create a gender-based classification that would require application of an intermediate scrutiny standard. The fact that the restriction applies to a drug prescribed only to women does not establish gender-based discrimination. [*See* Geduldig v. Aiello (1974)] (C) is wrong because, as discussed above, legislation excluding abortion-related expenses from government funding has been held not to constitute interference with a woman's constitutional right to choose to have an abortion. Therefore, the undue burden test does not apply. (D) is incorrect for the same reason as in (C), and also because it does not state the standard that the Court uses to evaluate abortion regulations. Regulations restricting pre-viability abortions will be invalidated if they constitute an "undue burden" on a woman's right to have an abortion. [Planned Parenthood of Southeastern Pennsylvania v. Casey (1992)]

Answer to Question 6

(A) The statute likely will be held constitutional on its face and as applied. The statute appears to be a time, place, and manner restraint on speech-related activities in a public forum rather than an unconstitutional burden on a fundamental right. This is so, despite its breadth of coverage, since it applies only to times when the legislature is in session and likely to be disturbed by noisy picketing. The application of the statute to the leader of the group does not make it unconstitutional as applied; there is no reason why he could not have remained in the park and spoken as noisily as he wanted to. Thus, (B) is incorrect. (C) is wrong because there are many methods to direct complaints to a legislature without speechmaking right in front of the building. (D) is incorrect because silent picketing can be considered to be reasonable at the same time that noisy picketing is prohibited.

Answer to Question 7

(D) The gang member can be convicted because the statute does not violate the First Amendment. Certain public property (*e.g.*, public streets or parks) is so historically associated with the exercise of First Amendment rights that speech thereon can be regulated only by content-neutral proscriptions. Other places controlled by the government, however, are not so historically linked to speech activities, and in such locations free speech might interfere with the intended use of such locations. Thus, the government can regulate access to these limited public forums and nonpublic forums based on the subject matter of the speech, as long as the regulation is reasonably related to the purpose served by the property and is not designed merely to suppress a particular point of view. A courthouse and its grounds are not a public forum. (The surrounding sidewalks are, but that is not in issue here.) The statute, although based on the subject matter of speech, is viewpoint neutral and reasonably related to the courthouse purpose of promoting a stable, orderly atmosphere in which judicial proceedings can take place, free of improper outside influence or coercion. Thus, the statute is valid and the gang member can be convicted for his actions. (A) is wrong because it is based on an over-breadth argument and the statute here is not overbroad. A regulation of speech that restricts substantially more speech than necessary is unenforceable, even if the speech in question could have been properly restricted by a narrower statute. This doctrine is inapplicable here because the statute is not overbroad: It reaches only speech ***in the courthouse or on its grounds*** and only that speech ***that might improperly influence the judicial proceedings***; it does not limit all speech at that location. (B) is wrong because the gang member's personal intent to harm the judge is irrelevant. The statute makes it a crime to make a speech or carry a sign intended to influence the judicial proceeding. The statute does not require that the violator intend to harm anyone. Since the state is entitled to regulate speech or conduct in the courthouse or on its grounds that might interfere with the judicial proceedings, it is entitled to convict the gang member for his actions here regardless of his intent to harm the judge. (C) is wrong because it improperly applies the "clear and present danger" test to these facts. Under the current version of the "clear and present danger" test, a state cannot forbid advocating the ***use of force or violation of law*** unless such advocacy is (i) directed to producing or inciting imminent lawless action, and (ii) likely to produce such action. The state statute here does not purport to punish advocacy of force or lawlessness, but rather seeks to further the purpose of maintaining the stability and integrity of the judicial proceedings by regulating access to certain nonpublic areas. Therefore, the restrictions are constitutionally valid and the "clear and present danger" test is inapplicable.

Answer to Question 8

(A) The court will likely find that the ordinance violates the organizers' freedom of speech rights. The First Amendment right to freedom of speech includes the right to refrain from speaking or endorsing beliefs with which one does not agree. In keeping with this principle, the Supreme Court has held that government may not require private parade organizers to include in their parade other groups that have messages with which the organizers disagree. Accordingly, (C) is incorrect. (B) is incorrect because it is an overbroad misstatement of the law. While private speech is broadly protected by the First Amendment, government may regulate the conduct (*e.g.*, activities) associated with speech (*e.g.*, through time, place, and manner regulations). (D) is incorrect. Under their police power, states and their subsidiaries can enact laws that protect the health, safety, welfare, and morals of their citizens. It is arguable whether the ordinance here relates to health, safety, welfare, or morals. In any case, the police power cannot usurp citizens' First Amendment rights, and as discussed above, the ordinance here violates the organizers' First Amendment rights.

Answer to Question 9

(B) The court is likely to find in favor of the city because the zoning ordinance is a reasonable regulation of these businesses. In two leading zoning cases, the Supreme Court has upheld the right of a city to regulate the location or size of adult bookstores and adult theaters, provided the ordinance was content-neutral and did not constitute a total ban. [*See* Young v. American Mini Theatres, 427 U.S. 50 (1976)—city may separate adult theatres from adult bookstores to reduce high crime rates and prevent lower property values; City of Renton v. Playtime Theatres, Inc., 475 U.S. 41 (1986)—city ordinance prohibiting adult theatres within 1,000 feet of any dwelling, church, park, or school upheld] (A) is wrong because the city may not regulate activities merely because they are "distasteful" to others. (C) is incorrect because the purpose of the ordinance is not to regulate unpopular speech. (D) is wrong because a city may regulate businesses even in speech-related areas provided the regulation is not aimed at its content and serves an important governmental interest.

Answer to Question 10

(A) The test stated in choice (A) most accurately reflects the balance between the scope of First Amendment protection for the dissemination of truthful commercial speech and the state's ability to enact narrowly drawn regulations to advance substantial governmental interests. Although commercial speech is protected by the First Amendment, it is subject to significant regulation. A state may outlaw commercial speech that proposes an unlawful transaction or that is misleading or fraudulent. If commercial speech concerns a lawful activity and is not misleading or fraudulent, the government regulation, to be valid, must directly advance a substantial government interest and must be no more extensive than necessary to serve that interest. In addition, the regulation must be narrowly drawn, and there must be a reasonable fit between the legislation's end and the means chosen. If, as (A) states, the legislation here does not prohibit the dissemination of truthful information about prices and product availability, and is otherwise narrowly tailored to serve the state's substantial interest, it probably will constitute a valid regulation of commercial speech. (B) is incorrect because it does not correctly state the standard for permissible restriction of commercial speech. This legislation may infringe the federal constitutional right of free speech (which extends to commercial speech) if it does not satisfy the test for reasonable regulations of commercial speech stated in choice (A). (C) could be a true statement, but the question lacks facts sufficient to reach the conclusion in (C). The legislation would not be constitutional if it prohibits the dissemination of truthful information about price or availability of products, or is not narrowly tailored. Because the facts do not indicate, *e.g.*, how the content of the television advertisements is regulated, (A) is the better choice. (D) is incorrect because it is too broad. Under the Contract Clause, states may not enact laws that retroactively and ***substantially*** impair contract rights unless the action (i) serves an important and legitimate government interest, and (ii) is a narrowly tailored means of promoting that interest. Here, we do not know if the impairment is substantial or, as indicated above, whether the law is narrowly tailored. Thus, (D) is not as good a choice as (A).

Answer to Question 11

(C) The state's best argument is that neither the press nor the public has a right under the First Amendment to these documents. Although freedom of the press is a fundamental right, the press is not entitled to special governmental assistance in obtaining information. For example, in *Pell v. Procunier,* 417 U.S. 817 (1974), the Supreme Court upheld state and federal regulations that prohibited press interviews with any specific inmate. The Court reasoned that the press is not entitled to any special treatment beyond that of other members of the public in obtaining information not shared by the general public. [*See also* Houchins v. KQED, 438 U.S. 1 (1978)—press has no right of access to jails over general public] Thus, choice (C) presents the strongest argument. (A) is incorrect because it is too broad. Although it is not established that the public has a right to know the details of charges in a case such as this, there is a First Amendment right to attend criminal trials, and perhaps pretrial proceedings as well. (B) is weak because it addresses an equal protection argument, whereas the challenge here will be based on the First Amendment. (D) is a true statement but it is not the best defense because it is too narrow. The First Amendment can be violated by statutes that do not amount to a prior restraint.

Answer to Question 12

(B) The court will most likely uphold the statute because it is a religiously neutral law of general application. The First Amendment provides that the free exercise of religion shall not be abridged; however, the prohibition is far from absolute. The Supreme Court has stated that the amendment prohibits the government from outlawing religious beliefs and probably from outlawing conduct merely because it is religious (*i.e.,* the state could not forbid the handling of snakes only in religious ceremonies), but states may validly proscribe general conduct; *i.e.,* a law of general application will not be held invalid under the First Amendment merely because it happens to proscribe conduct that is required by one's religious beliefs. Neither will the state be required to provide religious exemptions from the statute. [Employment Division v. Smith

(1990)] Thus, the statute here is probably valid. (A) is incorrect because the state need not show a compelling interest to have the statute upheld; it will be held valid as long as it is a religiously neutral law of general application. (C) is incorrect because the state need not show that a statute is the least restrictive means for achieving its legislative goal merely because the statute happens to burden religious conduct. (D) is incorrect because it is irrelevant whether the religious practice interfered with is an integral function of a religion or merely a minor belief—the Court will not assess the centrality of religious belief, but will only inquire into whether a person's belief is sincere.

Answer to Question 13

(B) The convictions will be reversed if it can be shown that the statute is being applied only to interfere with religion. The Free Exercise Clause prohibits government from punishing religious belief. The Clause prevents government from punishing conduct merely because it is religious and from regulating conduct for the purpose of interfering with religion. However, the Clause does not prohibit government from regulating general conduct, even if the regulation happens to interfere with a person's ability to conform conduct to sincerely held religious beliefs. Thus, if it can be shown here that the statute is not really a regulation of general conduct but rather is being applied only to interfere with religion, the convictions will be reversed. (A) is incorrect because, as stated above, a person's conduct can be regulated by a generally applicable conduct regulation; religiously motivated conduct has very narrow protection. (C) is incorrect because it implies that the court will balance the interests involved in determining the validity of the application of the statute here. Since *Employment Division v. Smith* (1990), the Court has abandoned the balancing approach in favor of the approach discussed above. (D) is incorrect because the church board would have standing. All that is required is a concrete stake in the outcome of the litigation; having been prosecuted for violating the statute, the board's stake is about as concrete as it can get.

Answer to Question 14

(D) The sincerity of the parent's religious beliefs is a factor that can be inquired into as a way of determining whether she can avail herself of the protection of the Free Exercise Clause. The Free Exercise Clause of the First Amendment, applicable to the states through the Fourteenth Amendment, prohibits punishing people for their religious beliefs. When a person claims that she is being punished for her religious beliefs, the court may consider whether the person challenging the law sincerely holds those beliefs. Thus, the court may consider whether the parent's beliefs are sincerely held. (A) is incorrect because the First Amendment forbids a court from determining whether a person's religious beliefs are true. A court must respect a sincerely held religious belief, even if it appears to be illogical or incapable of proof. (B) is incorrect because the Free Exercise Clause protects all sincerely held religious beliefs, regardless of whether a specific religion is deemed to be "established" or "traditional." (C) is incorrect because religious beliefs need not be theistic to qualify for constitutional protection. An asserted religious belief must occupy a place in the believer's life parallel to that occupied by orthodox religious beliefs. Even an internally derived belief is entitled to protection.

Answer to Question 15

(B) The worker's best constitutional argument is based on the Free Exercise Clause. In a handful of cases, the Supreme Court has struck down state practices that, in effect, punish an individual for exercising his religious beliefs. [*See, e.g.*, Sherbert v. Verner, 374 U.S. 398 (1963)—state may not deny unemployment benefits to claimant who refuses to work on Saturdays because of religious beliefs; Thomas v. Review Board of Indiana Employment Security Division, 450 U.S. 707 (1981)—state may not deny unemployment benefits to claimant who left job because of religious beliefs; Frazee v. Illinois Department of Employment Security, 489 U.S. 829 (1989)—state may not deny unemployment benefits to worker who believed it was "unchristian" to work on Sunday] In each case, the state failed to prove a compelling reason for the state policy. The facts in this question are similar to those of the *Thomas* case, *supra.* In *Employment Division v. Smith,* the Supreme Court narrowed the scope of the Free Exercise Clause, but expressly reaffirmed these earlier decisions involving unemployment benefits. (A) is incorrect because the Establishment Clause prohibits a state from directly aiding religion. Here, the facts do not support direct state aid to religion. (C) is not the best answer because the law does not unconstitutionally classify according to any impermissible criteria. Even under an equal protection argument, economic benefits are tested under a weak rational basis test. (D) is incorrect because the Supreme Court has never ruled that unemployment benefits are a "property right" under the Due Process Clause.

Answer to Question 16

(B) The city may continue to operate the garden because the display is not primarily religious in nature. In a case such as this, where state action does not involve a preference of one religious sect over another, the action is valid under the Establishment Clause if (i) it has a secular purpose, (ii) its primary effect neither advances nor inhibits religion, and (iii) it does not involve excessive government entanglement with religion. This is known as the *Lemon* test. This test is met here: The secular purpose is to promote pride in heritage and perhaps to encourage people to learn about the heritage of others. The primary effect does not promote or inhibit religion, but merely acknowledges the religious backgrounds of the city residents. Finally, the maintenance and administration of the garden by the city does not constitute excessive entanglement between government and religion. Therefore, (B) is correct and (C) is incorrect. [*See* Lynch v. Donnelly (1984)—permitting government-maintained Christmas display that includes religious as well as nonreligious symbols] (A) is incorrect because if the garden did fail one of the above tests, the fact that only a relatively small amount of municipal funds were used would not remedy the constitutional violation; de minimis is not a defense. (D) is incorrect because it states the wrong test. Establishment Clause cases not involving a sect preference are resolved under the above three-part test and not under the compelling interest test.

Answer to Question 17

(B) The strongest argument is that state provision of textbooks to the segregated private school violates the Equal Protection Clause by giving state support to a racially segregated educational process. (A) is wrong because it is too broad. A state may, under certain situations, aid a private school through distribution of textbooks, as discussed below. (C) and (D) are parts of the test for violation of the Establishment Clause. The Supreme Court has held that a state lending textbooks on secular subjects to all students, including those at religious schools, does not violate the Establishment Clause. Thus, (C) and (D) are incorrect.

Contracts

Offer and Acceptance

Remedies

CONTRACTS AND SALES

I. WHAT IS A CONTRACT?

A. GENERAL DEFINITION

A contract is a promise or set of promises for the breach of which the law gives a remedy or the performance of which the law, in some way, recognizes as a duty.

B. COMMON LAW VS. ARTICLE 2 SALE OF GOODS

Generally, the common law governs contracts. However, special rules have been developed for contracts involving the sale of ***goods***, and those rules are contained in Article 2 of the Uniform Commercial Code ("U.C.C."). Article 2 has adopted much of the common law of contracts, but when the common law and Article 2 differ, Article 2 prevails in a contract for the sale of goods.

1. "Goods" Defined

Article 2 defines "goods" as all ***things movable*** at the time they are identified as the goods to be sold under the contract. Thus, Article 2 applies to sales of most tangible things (*e.g.,* cars, horses, hamburgers), but does not apply to the sale of real estate, services (*e.g.,* a health club membership), or intangibles (*e.g.,* a patent), or to construction contracts.

2. Merchants vs. Nonmerchants

A number of the rules in Article 2 depend on whether the seller and/or buyer are merchants. Article 2 generally defines "merchant" as one who regularly deals in goods of the kind sold or who otherwise by his profession holds himself out as having special knowledge or skills as to the practices or goods involved.

CMR **Exam Tip** For Article 2 provisions dealing with ***general business practices*** (*e.g.*, Statute of Frauds, confirmatory memos, firm offers, modification), almost anyone in business can be deemed a merchant. But remember that some Article 2 provisions are narrower and require a person to be a merchant ***with respect to goods of the kind involved in the subject transaction*** (*e.g.,* the implied warranty of merchantability).

C. TYPES OF CONTRACTS

1. As to Formation

Contracts are frequently described as express, implied, or quasi. Only the first two are actually contracts, and they differ only in the manner in which they are formed.

a. Express Contract

Express contracts are formed ***by language***, oral or written.

b. Implied in Fact Contract

Implied contracts are formed by manifestations of assent other than oral or written language, *i.e.,* ***by conduct***.

c. Quasi-Contract or Implied in Law Contract

Quasi-contracts are ***not contracts*** at all. They are constructed by courts to ***avoid unjust enrichment*** by permitting the plaintiff to bring an action in restitution to recover the amount of the benefit conferred on the defendant.

2. As to Acceptance

a. **Bilateral Contracts—Exchange of Mutual Promises**
The traditional bilateral contract is one consisting of the exchange of mutual promises, *i.e.,* a promise for a promise, in which each party is both a promisor and a promisee.

b. **Unilateral Contracts—Acceptance by Performance**
The traditional unilateral contract is one in which the offeror requests performance rather than a promise. Here, the offeror-promisor promises to pay upon the ***completion of the requested act*** by the promisee. Once the act is completed, a contract is formed. In such contracts, there is one promisor and one promisee.

c. **Modern View—Most Contracts Are Bilateral**
Under Article 2 and Second Restatement, a traditional unilateral contract (*i.e.,* a contract that can be formed only by full performance) occurs in only two situations: (i) when the offeror clearly (unambiguously) indicates that ***completion of performance is the only manner of acceptance***; and (ii) where there is an ***offer to the public***, such as a reward offer.

3. **As to Validity**

a. **Void Contract**
A void contract is one that is totally ***without any legal effect*** from the beginning (*e.g.,* an agreement to commit a crime). ***It cannot be enforced by either party***.

b. **Voidable Contract**
A voidable contract is one that one or both parties may ***elect to avoid*** (*e.g.,* by raising a defense that makes it voidable, such as infancy or mental illness).

c. **Unenforceable Contract**
An unenforceable contract is an agreement that is otherwise valid but which may not be enforceable due to a defense extraneous to contract formation, such as the statute of limitations or Statute of Frauds.

CMR **Exam Tip** The distinction between void and voidable contracts is sometimes important to an exam question. The key thing to remember is that ***void*** contracts cannot be enforced, but an aggrieved party may ***elect*** to enforce a ***voidable*** contract.

D. CREATION OF A CONTRACT
When a suit is brought in which one party seeks to enforce a contract or to obtain damages for breach of contract, a court must first decide whether there was in fact a contract. In making this determination, a court will ask the following three basic questions:

1. Was there ***mutual assent***?

2. Was there ***consideration*** or some substitute for consideration?

3. Are there any ***defenses*** to creation of the contract?

Exam Tip Contract formation is a major topic on the exam. For any contract question, be sure that there really is an enforceable contract; *i.e.,* ***all three*** of the above elements must be present. Fact patterns sometimes greatly emphasize some elements (*e.g.,* offer and acceptance) to try to

fool you into thinking that a contract has been formed, but on closer examination, you might find that another element (*e.g.,* consideration) is missing. Remember to check carefully for all three elements. (Of course, if the ***facts state*** that one or more of the elements is present—or that a valid contract has been formed—don't waste your time analyzing elements already given to you.)

II. MUTUAL ASSENT—OFFER AND ACCEPTANCE

A. IN GENERAL

For an agreement to be enforced as a contract, there must be mutual assent. In other words, one party must accept the other's offer. Whether mutual assent is present will be determined by an objective standard; *i.e.,* did words or conduct manifest a present intention to enter into a contract?

B. THE OFFER

An offer creates a power of acceptance in the offeree and a corresponding liability on the part of the offeror. For a communication to be an offer, it must create a ***reasonable expectation*** in the offeree that the offeror is willing to enter into a contract on the basis of the offered terms. In deciding whether a communication creates this reasonable expectation, you should ask the following three questions:

(i) Was there an expression of a ***promise***, ***undertaking***, ***or commitment*** to enter into a contract?

(ii) Were there ***certainty and definiteness*** in the essential terms?

(iii) Was there ***communication*** of the above to the offeree?

1. Promise, Undertaking, or Commitment

For a communication to be an offer, it must contain a promise, undertaking, or commitment to enter into a contract, rather than a mere invitation to begin preliminary negotiations; *i.e.,* there must be an ***intent*** to enter into a contract.

a. Language

The language used may show that an offer was or was not intended. Technical language such as "I offer" or "I promise" is useful, but it is not necessary. Phrases such as "I quote," "I am asking $30 for," and "I would consider selling for" tend to be construed merely as invitations to deal rather than offers.

b. Surrounding Circumstances

The circumstances surrounding the language will be considered by courts in determining whether an offer exists. For example, if a statement is made in jest, anger, or by way of bragging, and it is reasonably understood in this context, it will have no legal effect.

c. Prior Practice and Relationship of the Parties

In determining whether certain remarks constitute an offer rather than preliminary negotiations, a court will look to the prior relationship and practice of the parties involved.

d. **Method of Communication**

1) **Use of Broad Communications Media**
The broader the communicating media (*e.g.*, publications), the more likely it is that the courts will view the communication as merely the ***solicitation of an offer***.

2) **Advertisements, Etc.**
Advertisements, catalogs, circular letters, and the like containing price quotations are ***usually*** construed as mere ***invitations for offers***.

CMR **Exam Tip** Most offers are fairly easy to spot, but watch out for language that sounds like an offer but really is an invitation to deal. For example, advertisements often sound like offers but usually are just invitations for people to come in and deal. The more definite the language (*e.g.*, "I'll sell for . . ." or "I'll pay you $10 for . . ."), the more likely the statement is an offer. However, you need to examine the other factors (surrounding circumstances, prior relationship of parties, etc.). Don't be too hasty in your determination.

CMR **Exam Tip** If there has been a series of communications between the parties, pay attention to the legal significance, if any, of each statement. For example, if you determine that A's first statement to B is not an offer but rather is merely an invitation to deal, then B's response cannot be an acceptance (because there was nothing to accept). You must then consider whether B's response is another invitation to deal or a counteroffer. Keep checking until you find an offer and an acceptance.

2. **Definite and Certain Terms**
An offer must be definite and certain in its terms. The basic inquiry is whether enough of the essential terms have been provided so that a contract including them would be ***capable of being enforced***.

a. **Identification of the Offeree**
To be considered an offer, a statement must sufficiently identify the offeree or a class to which she belongs to justify the inference that the offeror intended to create a power of acceptance.

b. **Definiteness of Subject Matter**
The subject matter of the deal must be certain, because a court can enforce a promise only if it can tell with reasonable accuracy what the promise is.

1) **Requirements for Specific Types of Contracts**

a) **Real Estate Transactions—Land and Price Terms**
An offer involving realty must identify the ***land*** and the ***price*** terms. The land must be identified with some particularity but a deed description is not required (*e.g.*, "my house in Erewhon" is sufficient if the seller has only one house in Erewhon). Most courts will ***not*** supply a missing price term for realty.

b) **Sale of Goods—Quantity Term**
In a contract for the sale of goods, the ***quantity*** being offered must be certain or capable of being made certain.

(1) "Requirements" and "Output" Contracts
In a requirements contract, a buyer promises to buy from a certain seller all of the goods the buyer requires, and the seller agrees to sell that amount to the buyer. In an output contract, a seller promises to sell to a certain buyer all of the goods that the seller produces, and the buyer agrees to buy that amount from the seller. It is assumed that the parties will act in good faith; hence, there may not be a tender of or a demand for a quantity ***unreasonably disproportionate*** to (i) any stated estimate, or (ii) (in the absence of a stated estimate) any normal or otherwise comparable prior output or requirements.

c) Services—Nature of Work
The nature of the work to be performed is required in an offer for services.

2) Missing Terms
The fact that one or more terms are left open does ***not prevent the formation*** of a contract if it appears that the parties ***intended to make a contract*** and there is a ***reasonably certain basis*** for giving a remedy. In such a case, the majority of jurisdictions and Article 2 hold that the ***court can supply reasonable terms*** for those that are missing.

a) Price
Except in contracts for real property, the failure to state the price does not prevent the formation of a contract if the parties intended to form a contract without the price being settled. Note that if a contract for the sale of goods is missing a price term, Article 2 provides that the price will be a ***reasonable price at the time of delivery***.

3) Vague Terms
The presumption that the parties' intent was to include a reasonable term goes to supplying ***missing*** terms. The presumption ***cannot*** be made if the parties have ***included*** a term that makes the contract too vague to be enforced (*e.g.*, an agreement to split profits on a "liberal basis"). However, uncertainty can be cured by part performance that clarifies the vague term or by acceptance of full performance.

4) Terms to Be Agreed on Later
Often, an offer will state that some term is to be agreed on at a future date. If the term is a ***material*** term, the offer is ***too uncertain***.

3. Communication to Offeree
To have the power to accept, the offeree must have ***knowledge*** of the offer. Therefore, the proposal must be communicated to her.

C. TERMINATION OF OFFER
An offer cannot be accepted after it has been terminated. An offer may be terminated by an act of either party or by operation of law.

1. Termination by Acts of Parties

a. Termination by Offeror—Revocation

A revocation is the retraction of an offer by the offeror. An offeror may revoke by directly communicating the revocation to the offeree (*e.g.,* "I revoke my offer of May 25"). An offer made by publication can be directly revoked only by publication through comparable means (*e.g.,* an offer placed in the *Wall Street Journal* cannot be revoked by publishing in *Better Homes and Gardens*). An offer may also be revoked ***indirectly*** if the offeree receives: (i) correct information, (ii) from a reliable source, (iii) of acts of the offeror that would indicate to a reasonable person that the offeror no longer wishes to make the offer (*e.g.,* after offeror offers to sell his car to offeree, offeree is told by a reliable third party that offeror just sold his car to someone else).

1) Effective When Received

A revocation is generally effective when ***received*** by the offeree. Where revocation is by publication, it is effective when ***published.***

2) Limitations on Offeror's Power to Revoke

Offers can be revoked at will by the offeror, even if he has promised not to revoke for a certain period, except in the following circumstances:

a) Options

An option is a distinct contract in which the ***offeree gives consideration*** for a promise by the offeror not to revoke an outstanding offer (*e.g.,* an offeror offers to sell her farm to an offeree for $1 million and promises to keep the offer open for 90 days if the offeree pays the offeror $1,000 to keep the offer open).

b) Merchant's Firm Offer Under Article 2

Under Article 2: (i) if a ***merchant***; (ii) offers to sell goods in a ***signed writing***; and (iii) the writing ***gives assurances that it will be held open*** (*e.g.,* "this offer will be held open for 10 days," "this offer is firm for 10 days," "I shall not revoke this offer for 10 days"); the offer ***is not revocable*** for lack of consideration during the time stated, or if no time is stated, for a reasonable time (but in no event may such period exceed ***three months***).

c) Detrimental Reliance

When the offeror could reasonably expect that the offeree would rely to her detriment on the offer, and the offeree does so rely, the offer will be held ***irrevocable as an option contract for a reasonable length of time***. At the very least, the offeree would be entitled to relief measured by the extent of any detrimental reliance.

d) Part Performance—True Unilateral Contract Offers

(1) Implied Contract for Reasonable Time

Under the First and Second Restatements, as well as Article 2, an offer for a true unilateral contract becomes ***irrevocable once performance has begun***. The offeror must give the offeree a ***reasonable time to complete performance***. Note that the offeree is ***not bound*** to complete

performance—she may withdraw at any time prior to completion of performance and there is no acceptance until performance is complete.

(2) **Distinguish—Preparations to Perform**
Substantial preparations to perform (as opposed to the beginning of performance) do not make the offer irrevocable but ***may constitute detrimental reliance*** sufficient to make the offeror's promise binding to the extent of the detrimental reliance.

e) **Part Performance—Offer Indifferent as to Manner of Acceptance**
As noted above, most offers are indifferent as to the manner of acceptance, and thus, a bilateral contract may be formed ***upon the start of performance*** by the offeree. Therefore, once the offeree ***begins performance,*** the contract is complete and ***revocation*** becomes ***impossible.*** *But note:* Notification of the start of performance may be necessary. (*See* D.3.b., *infra.*)

b. **Termination by Offeree**

1) **Rejection**

a) **Express Rejection**
An express rejection is a statement by the offeree that she does not intend to accept the offer. Such a rejection will terminate the offer.

b) **Counteroffer as Rejection**
A counteroffer is an offer made by the ***offeree*** to the offeror that contains the same subject matter as the original offer, but differs in its terms (*e.g.,* "I'll take the house at that price, but only if you paint it first").

Exam Tip Remember that a counteroffer is ***both*** a rejection and a new offer. It terminates the original offer and reverses the roles of the parties: The offeree giving a counteroffer becomes the offeror of a new offer, which the other party may accept or reject. Thus, if A offers to sell his property, Blackacre, to B for $100,000, and B says, "I'll buy it for $90,000," what has happened? A's offer has been rejected and B has made an offer for $90,000, which A may accept or reject. B cannot later say to A, "All right, I'll take Blackacre for $100,000," and accept A's offer. It no longer exists because it was rejected. (Of course, A could accept B's new offer to buy it for $100,000.)

(1) **Distinguish—Mere Inquiry**
Distinguish between a counteroffer (which constitutes a rejection) and a mere inquiry. An inquiry will not terminate the offer when it is consistent with the idea that the offeree is still keeping the original proposal under consideration (*e.g.,* "Would you consider lowering your price by $5,000?"). The test is whether a ***reasonable person*** would believe that the original offer had been rejected.

c) **Effective When Received**
A rejection is effective when ***received*** by the offeror.

d) Rejection of Option
Because an option is a contract to keep an offer open, a rejection of or a counteroffer to an option does ***not*** constitute a termination of the offer. The offeree is still free to accept the original offer within the option period unless the offeror has ***detrimentally relied*** on the offeree's rejection.

2) Lapse of Time
An offer may be terminated by the offeree's failure to accept within the time specified by the offer or, if no deadline was specified, within a reasonable period.

2. Termination by Operation of Law
The following events will terminate an offer by operation of law:

a. ***Death or insanity of either party*** (unless the offer is of a kind the offeror could not terminate, *e.g.*, an option supported by consideration). Death or insanity need ***not*** be communicated to the other party;

b. ***Destruction*** of the proposed contract's ***subject matter***; or

c. ***Supervening illegality***.

D. THE ACCEPTANCE
An acceptance is a manifestation of assent to the terms of an offer.

1. Who May Accept
Generally, only the person to whom an offer is addressed has the power of acceptance. One may also have the power of acceptance if she is a member of a class to which an offer has been directed. Generally, an offeree's power of acceptance ***cannot be assigned***. However, if the offeree has paid consideration to keep the offer open (*i.e.,* an option contract was created), the right to accept ***is*** transferable.

2. Offeree Must Know of Offer
The offeree must know of the offer in order to accept it, and this is true whether the offer is for a bilateral or unilateral contract. Thus, if A sends B an offer and B sends A an offer unaware of A's offer (*i.e.,* a crossing offer situation), no contract is formed, even if the offers contain the same terms.

3. Acceptance of Offer for Unilateral Contract
If an offer provides that it may be accepted only by performance (*i.e.*, an offer for a unilateral contract), note the following particular rules.

a. Completion of Performance
Most courts hold that an offer to form a unilateral contract is not accepted until performance is completed. The beginning of performance may create an option so that the offer is irrevocable. (*See* C.1.a.2)d), *supra*.) However, the offeree is not obligated to complete performance merely because he has begun performance, as only complete performance constitutes an acceptance of the offer.

CMR **Exam Tip** Keep in mind that like all offerees, the offeree of a unilateral contract ***must know of the offer*** to accept it. If the "offeree" acts without knowledge and learns of the offer later, his acts were not an acceptance. Thus, if A finds O's watch and returns it to O without knowledge of O's reward offer, A has no contractual right to the reward.

b. **Notice**
Generally, the offeree is ***not*** required to give the offeror notice that he has begun the requested performance, but is required to notify the offeror within a reasonable time after performance has been completed. However, no notice is required if: (i) the offeror ***waived notice***; or (ii) the offeree's ***performance would normally come to the offeror's attention*** within a reasonable time.

4. **Acceptance of Offer for Bilateral Contract**
Recall that unless an offer specifically provides that it may be accepted only through performance, it will be construed as an offer to enter into a bilateral contract and may be accepted either by a promise to perform or by the ***beginning of performance*** (compare offers for true unilateral contracts, which may be accepted only by full performance).

a. **Generally, Acceptance Must Be Communicated**
Generally, acceptance of an offer to enter into a bilateral contract must be communicated to the offeror, unless the offer provides that acceptance need not be communicated.

b. **Method of Acceptance**
Unless otherwise provided, an offer is construed as inviting acceptance in ***any reasonable manner*** and by any medium reasonable under the circumstances. Any objective manifestation of the offeree's counterpromise is usually sufficient.

1) **Offers to Buy Goods for Current or Prompt Shipment**
Under Article 2, an offer to buy goods for current or prompt shipment is construed as inviting acceptance either by a ***promise to ship*** or by ***current or prompt shipment*** of conforming or nonconforming goods.

a) **Shipment of Nonconforming Goods**
The shipment of nonconforming goods is an ***acceptance*** creating a bilateral contract ***as well as a breach*** of the contract unless the seller seasonably notifies the buyer that a shipment of nonconforming goods is offered only as an ***accommodation***. The buyer is not required to accept accommodation goods and may reject them. If he does, the shipper is not in breach and may reclaim the accommodation goods, because her tender does not constitute an acceptance of the buyer's original offer.

CMR **Exam Tip** Remember that the accommodation shipment rule applies ***only*** when shipment is used as a form of acceptance. Watch out for a fact pattern in which a party accepts an order by promising to ship. He then discovers he lacks the specified goods and ships nonconforming goods as an "accommodation." This is a breach, not an accommodation. There was a contract at the promise to ship. The shipment was not the acceptance; thus, ***accommodation is not possible***.

c. **Acceptance Must Be Unequivocal**
Traditional contract law insists on an absolute and unequivocal acceptance of each and every term of the offer (the "mirror image rule").

1) **Common Law Rule**
At common law, any different or additional terms in the acceptance make the response a ***rejection and counteroffer***.

2) **Article 2 Rule—Battle of the Forms Provision**
Article 2 has abandoned the mirror image rule, providing instead that the proposal of additional or different terms by the offeree in a definite and timely acceptance does ***not*** constitute a rejection and counteroffer, but rather is ***effective as an acceptance***, unless the acceptance is ***expressly*** made conditional on assent to the additional or different terms. Whether the additional or different terms become part of the contract depends on whether or not both parties are merchants.

Exam Tip Recall that Article 2 changes the common law rule. Thus, for an offer for the purchase or sale of ***goods***, an acceptance with additional terms is still an acceptance and a contract is formed (with or without the new terms). If the offer is for something ***other than the sale of goods*** (*e.g.*, land), an acceptance proposing additional or different terms is a rejection and a counteroffer; no contract is formed.

3) **Bilateral Contracts Formed by Performance**
If a contract is not formed by the parties' communications, but they begin to perform as if they formed a contract, a contract is formed.

d. **When Effective—The Mailbox Rule**
Acceptance by mail or similar means creates a contract at the ***moment of dispatch***, provided that the mail is properly addressed and stamped, ***unless:***

1) The ***offer stipulates*** that acceptance is not effective until received; or

2) An ***option contract*** is involved (an acceptance under an option contract is effective only upon ***receipt***).

3) If the offeree sends a ***rejection and then sends an acceptance***, whichever arrives first is effective.

4) If the offeree sends an acceptance and then a rejection, the acceptance is effective (*i.e.*, the mailbox rule applies) ***unless the rejection arrives first and*** the offeror ***detrimentally relies*** on it.

Exam Tip Remember that the mailbox rule ("effective upon dispatch") applies ***only to acceptance***. It does not apply to other events in the contract setting, such as rejection or revocation.

1) **Acceptance by Unauthorized Means**
An acceptance transmitted by unauthorized means or improperly transmitted by authorized means may still be ***effective if it is actually received*** by the offeror while the offer is still in existence.

E. AUCTION CONTRACTS

The U.C.C. contains some special rules regulating auction sales. A sale by auction is complete

when the auctioneer so announces by the ***fall of the hammer*** or in another customary manner. An auction sale is with reserve unless the goods are explicitly put up without reserve. "***With reserve***" means the ***auctioneer may withdraw the goods*** at any time until he announces completion of the sale.

III. BREACH

A. WHEN DOES A BREACH OCCUR?

If it is found that (i) the promisor is under an absolute duty to perform, and (ii) this absolute duty of performance has not been discharged, then this failure to perform in accordance with contractual terms will amount to a breach of the contract. The nonbreaching party who sues for breach of contract must show that she is ***willing and able*** to perform but for the breaching party's failure to perform.

B. MATERIAL OR MINOR BREACH—COMMON LAW CONTRACTS

Once you have determined that there is a breach of contract, the next determination to be made in a common law contract situation is whether that breach is material or minor.

1. Effect of Breaches

a. Minor Breach

A breach of contract is minor if the obligee gains the ***substantial benefit of her bargain*** despite the obligor's defective performance. A minor breach does ***not relieve*** the aggrieved party of her duty of performance under the contract; it merely gives her a right to damages (setoff) for the minor breach.

b. Material Breach

If the obligee does not receive the ***substantial benefit of her bargain***, the breach is considered material. If the breach is material, the nonbreaching party (i) may treat the contract as at an end, *i.e.,* any duty of counterperformance owed by her will be discharged, and (ii) will have an ***immediate right*** to all remedies for breach of the entire contract, including total damages.

c. Minor Breach Coupled with Anticipatory Repudiation

If a minor breach is coupled with an anticipatory repudiation, the nonbreaching party may treat it as a material breach; *i.e.,* she may sue immediately for total damages and is permanently discharged from any duty of further performance. Indeed, the courts hold that the aggrieved party must not continue on, because to do so would be a failure to mitigate damages. The U.C.C. modifies this to permit a party to complete the manufacture of goods to avoid having to sell unfinished goods at the lower salvage value. (*See infra.*)

d. Material Breach of Divisible Contract

In a divisible contract, recovery is available for substantial performance of a divisible part even though there has been a material breach of the entire contract.

CMR **Exam Tip** The distinction between a material and a minor breach is important. A minor breach may allow the aggrieved party to recover damages, ***but she still must perform*** under the contract. If the breach is a material one, the aggrieved party need not perform.

2. Determining Materiality of Breach

In determining whether a breach is material or minor, courts look at:

(i) ***The amount of benefit received*** by the nonbreaching party;

(ii) ***The adequacy of compensation*** for damages to the injured party;

(iii) ***The extent of part performance*** by the breaching party;

(iv) ***Hardship*** to the breaching party;

(v) ***Negligent or willful behavior*** of the breaching party; and

(vi) ***The likelihood that the breaching party will perform*** the remainder of the contract.

The nonbreaching party must show that he was both willing and able to perform.

CMR **Exam Tip** On the ***MBE***, you will not be asked to make a fact determination about whether a breach is material. If you find yourself going down that road, reconsider what the question is asking. Note that it is still worthwhile to know the factors above should you need to discuss them in an ***essay answer***.

3. Timeliness of Performance

Failure to perform by the time stated in the contract is generally not a material breach if performance is rendered within a reasonable time. However, if the nature of the contract makes timely performance essential, or if the contract expressly provides that time is of the essence, then failure to perform on time is a material breach.

C. PERFECT TENDER RULE—SALE OF GOODS

Article 2 generally does not follow the common law substantial performance doctrine. Instead, it follows the perfect tender rule—if ***goods or their delivery fail to conform to the contract in any way***, the buyer generally may reject all, accept all, or accept any commercial units and reject the rest.

1. Right to Reject Cut Off by Acceptance

A buyer's right to reject under the perfect tender doctrine generally is cut off by acceptance. Under Article 2, a buyer accepts when:

a. After a reasonable opportunity to inspect the goods, she ***indicates to the seller that they conform*** to requirements or that she will keep them even though they fail to conform;

b. She ***fails to reject*** within a reasonable time after tender or delivery of the goods or fails to seasonably notify the seller of her rejection; or

c. She does any ***act inconsistent with the seller's ownership***.

2. Buyer's Responsibility for Goods After Rejection
After rejecting goods in her physical possession, the buyer has an obligation to hold them with reasonable care at the seller's disposition and to obey any reasonable instructions as to the rejected goods (*e.g.,* arrange to reship the goods). If the seller gives no instructions within a reasonable time, the buyer may ***reship*** the goods to the seller, ***store*** them for the seller's account, or ***resell*** them for the seller's account. If the buyer resells, she is entitled to recover her expenses and a reasonable commission.

3. Buyer's Right to Revoke Acceptance
Once goods are accepted, the buyer's power to reject the goods generally is terminated and the buyer is obligated to pay the price less any damages resulting from the seller's breach. However, under limited situations, a buyer may revoke an acceptance already made. A proper revocation of acceptance has the effect of a rejection.

a. When Acceptance May Be Revoked
The buyer may revoke her acceptance if the goods have a defect that ***substantially impairs*** their ***value*** to her ***and***:

(i) She accepted them on the ***reasonable belief that the defect would be cured*** and it has not been; or

(ii) She accepted them because of the ***difficulty of discovering defects*** or because of the ***seller's assurance that the goods conformed*** to the contract.

Revocation of acceptance must occur: (i) ***within a reasonable time*** after the buyer discovers or should have discovered the defects; and (ii) ***before any substantial change in the goods occurs*** that is not caused by a defect present at the time the seller relinquished possession.

4. Exceptions to the Perfect Tender Rule

a. Installment Contracts
The right to reject when a contract is an installment contract (*i.e.,* when there is to be more than one delivery) is much more limited than in a single delivery contract situation. Installment contracts follow a rule akin to the common law substantial performance doctrine. In an installment contract situation, an installment can be rejected only if the nonconformity ***substantially impairs*** the value of that installment ***and cannot be cured*** (*see* below). In addition, the whole contract is breached only if the nonconformity ***substantially impairs*** the value of the ***entire contract***.

b. Seller's Right to Cure

1) Single Delivery Contracts

a) Seller Can Cure by Notice and New Tender Within Time for Performance
If the buyer has rejected goods because of defects, the seller may within the time originally provided for performance "cure" by giving ***reasonable notice*** of her intention to do so and making a ***new tender of conforming goods*** that the buyer must then accept.

b) **Seller's Right to Cure Beyond Original Contract Time**
Ordinarily, the seller has no right to cure beyond the original contract time. However, if the buyer rejects a tender of nonconforming goods that the seller ***reasonably*** believed would be acceptable "with or without money allowance," the seller, upon a reasonable notification to the buyer, has a ***further reasonable time*** beyond the original contract time within which to make a conforming tender. A seller will probably be found to have had reasonable cause to believe that the tender would be acceptable if the seller can show that (i) trade practices or prior dealings with the buyer led the seller to believe that the goods would be acceptable, or (ii) the seller could not have known of the defect despite proper business conduct (*e.g.*, packaged goods purchased from a supplier).

2) **Installment Contracts**
Article 2 provides that a defective shipment in an installment contract cannot be rejected ***if the defect can be cured***.

D. ANTICIPATORY REPUDIATION
Recall that an anticipatory repudiation can be treated as an immediate breach of contract.

E. BREACH OF WARRANTY
Sellers give warranties as to the condition of the goods that apply even after acceptance. Failure to live up to these warranties constitutes a breach of warranty, for which a remedy is available.

IV. REMEDIES

A. NONMONETARY REMEDIES
There are two broad branches of remedies available in breach of contract situations: nonmonetary and monetary. The primary nonmonetary remedy for exam purposes is specific performance, but Article 2 has a number of other specific nonmonetary remedies for certain situations involving contracts for the sale of goods.

1. **Specific Performance**
If the ***legal remedy is inadequate***, the nonbreaching party may seek specific performance, which is an order from the court to the breaching party to perform or face contempt of court charges.

a. **Available for Land and Rare or Unique Goods**
Specific performance is always available for land sale contracts. It is also available for goods that are rare or unique at the time performance is due (*e.g.*, rare paintings, gasoline in short supply because of oil embargoes, etc.). It is ***not*** available for breach of a contract to provide ***services***, even if the services are rare or unique. This is because of problems of enforcement (it would be difficult for the court to supervise the performance) and because the courts feel it is tantamount to involuntary servitude, which is prohibited by the Constitution.

1) **Injunction as Alternate Remedy**
In contrast, a court may ***enjoin*** a breaching employee from working for a competitor

throughout the duration of the contract if the services contracted for are rare or unique.

b. **Covenant Not to Compete**
Most courts will grant an order of specific performance to enforce a contract not to compete if: (i) the services to be performed are ***unique*** (thus rendering money damages inadequate); and (ii) the covenant is ***reasonable***. To be reasonable:

1) The covenant must be reasonably necessary to protect a ***legitimate interest*** of the person benefited by the covenant (*i.e.*, an employer or the purchaser of the covenantor's business);

2) The covenant must be reasonable as to its ***geographic scope and duration*** (*i.e.*, it cannot be broader than the benefited person's customer base and typically cannot be longer than one or two years); and

3) The covenant ***must not harm the public***.

c. **Equitable Defenses Available**
In addition to standard contract defenses, an action for specific performance is subject to the equitable defenses of:

1) ***Laches***—a claim that the plaintiff has delayed bringing the action and that ***the delay has prejudiced the defendant***;

2) ***Unclean hands***—a claim that the party seeking specific performance is guilty of ***wrongdoing in the transaction being sued upon***; and

3) ***Sale to a bona fide purchaser***—a claim that the subject matter has been ***sold to a person who purchased for value and in good faith***.

2. **Nonmonetary Remedies Under Article 2**

a. **Buyer's Nonmonetary Remedies**

1) **Cancellation**
If a buyer rightfully rejects goods because they do not conform to the contract, one of her options is simply to cancel the contract.

2) **Buyer's Right to Replevy Identified Goods**

a) **On Buyer's Prepayment**
If a buyer has made at least ***part payment*** of the purchase price of goods that have been identified under a contract and the seller ***has not delivered*** the goods, the buyer may ***replevy*** the goods from the seller in two circumstances:

(i) The seller becomes ***insolvent*** within 10 days after receiving the buyer's first payment; or

(ii) The goods were purchased for ***personal, family, or household purposes.***

In either case, the buyer must ***tender*** any unpaid portion of the purchase price to the seller.

b) On Buyer's Inability to Cover

In addition, the buyer may replevy undelivered, identified goods from the seller if the buyer, after reasonable effort, is ***unable to secure adequate substitute goods*** (*i.e.,* cover).

3) Buyer's Right to Specific Performance

A right closely related to the buyer's right to replevy is her right to specific performance "where the goods are unique or in other proper circumstances." The court may order specific performance ***even where the goods have not yet been identified*** to the contract by the seller.

b. Seller's Nonmonetary Remedies

1) Seller's Right to Withhold Goods

If the buyer fails to make a payment due on or before delivery, the seller may withhold delivery of the goods. The seller may also withhold goods when the goods are sold on credit and, before the goods are delivered, the seller discovers that the buyer is insolvent. However, in such a case, the seller must deliver the goods if the buyer tenders cash for their payment.

2) Seller's Right to Recover Goods

a) Right to Recover from Buyer on Buyer's Insolvency

If a seller learns that a buyer has received delivery of goods on credit while insolvent, the seller may reclaim the goods upon demand made within 10 days after the buyer's receipt of the goods. However, the 10-day limitation does not apply if a misrepresentation of solvency has been ***made in writing*** to the particular seller ***within three months*** before delivery.

b) Right to Recover Shipped or Stored Goods from Bailee

(1) On Buyer's Insolvency

The seller may stop delivery of goods in the possession of a carrier or other bailee if he discovers that the buyer is insolvent. Of course, the seller must deliver the goods if the buyer tenders cash for their payment.

(2) On Buyer's Breach

The seller may stop delivery of carload, truckload, planeload, or larger shipments of goods if the buyer breaches the contract or the seller has a right to withhold performance pending receipt of assurances. (*See* c., *infra,* on the right to demand assurances.)

3) **Seller's Ability to Force Goods on Buyer Limited**
The seller's ability to force goods on a buyer is limited to an action for price when the seller is unable to resell the goods to others at a reasonable price. (*See* B.2.b.2), *infra.*)

c. **Right to Demand Assurances**
Under Article 2, actions or circumstances that increase the risk of nonperformance by the other party to the contract, but that do not clearly indicate that performance will not be forthcoming, may ***not*** be treated immediately as an anticipatory repudiation. Instead, if the party ***reasonably*** fears that the other party will not perform, he may demand assurances that the performance will be forthcoming at the proper time. Until he receives adequate assurances, he may suspend his own performance. If the proper assurances are not given within a reasonable time (*i.e.*, within 30 days after a justified demand for assurances), he may then treat the contract as repudiated. What constitutes an adequate assurance depends on the facts of the case.

CMR **Exam Tip** Be sure that you understand the difference between circumstances giving rise to a right to demand assurances and those constituting anticipatory repudiation. The right to demand assurances arises when there are ***reasonable grounds for insecurity***—something makes a party nervous that the other will not perform. Anticipatory repudiation requires much more than nervousness; there must be a ***clear indication*** that the other party is unwilling or unable to perform. Thus, for example, "I'm not going to perform" is an anticipatory repudiation, but "I'm not sure if I can perform" most likely is only a reason to demand assurances.

B. MONETARY REMEDY—DAMAGES

1. Types of Damages

a. **Compensatory Damages**
The usual goal of damages for breach of contract is to ***put the nonbreaching party where she would have been had the promise been performed***, so far as money can do this.

1) **"Standard Measure" of Damages—Expectation Damages**
In most cases, the plaintiff's standard measure of damages will be based on an "expectation" measure, *i.e.,* sufficient damages for her to buy a ***substitute performance***. This is also known as ***"benefit of the bargain"*** damages.

2) **Reliance Damage Measure**
If the plaintiff's expectation damages are too speculative to measure (*e.g.,* the plaintiff cannot show with sufficient certainty the profits she would have made if the defendant had performed the contract), the plaintiff may elect to recover damages based on a "reliance" measure, rather than an expectation measure. Reliance damages award the plaintiff the cost of her performance; *i.e.,* they are designed to ***put the plaintiff in the position she would have been in had the contract never been formed***.

3) **Consequential Damages**
Consequential damages consist of losses resulting from the breach that any ***reasonable person*** would have ***foreseen*** would occur from a breach at the time of

entry into the contract. Note that in contracts for the sale of goods, ***only a buyer*** may recover consequential damages.

4) **Incidental Damages—Contracts for the Sale of Goods**
In contracts for the sale of goods, compensatory damages may also include incidental damages. Incidental damages include expenses reasonably incurred by the buyer in inspection, receipt, transportation, care, and custody of goods rightfully rejected and other expenses reasonably incident to the seller's breach, and by the seller in storing, shipping, returning, and reselling the goods as a result of the buyer's breach.

b. **Punitive Damages**
Punitive damages are generally ***not*** awarded in contract cases.

c. **Nominal Damages**
Nominal (token) damages (*e.g.,* $1) may be awarded when a breach is shown but no actual loss is proven.

d. **Liquidated Damages**
The parties to a contract may stipulate what damages are to be paid in the event of a breach. These liquidated damages must be in an amount that is reasonable in view of the actual or anticipated harm caused by the breach.

1) **Requirements for Enforcement**
Liquidated damage clauses will be enforceable if the following two requirements are met:

a) Damages for contractual breach must have been ***difficult to estimate or ascertain at the time the contract was formed***; and

b) The amount agreed on must have been a ***reasonable forecast*** of compensatory damages in the case of breach. The test for reasonableness is a comparison between the amount of damages prospectively probable at the time of contract formation and the liquidated damages figure. If the liquidated damages amount is unreasonable, the courts will construe this as a ***penalty*** and will not enforce the provision.

2) **Recoverable Even If No Actual Damages**
If the above requirements are met, the plaintiff will receive the liquidated damages amount. Most courts hold this is so even if no actual money or pecuniary damages have been suffered.

2. **Contracts for Sale of Goods**

a. **Buyer's Damages**

1) **Seller Does Not Deliver or Buyer Rejects Goods or Revokes Acceptance**
The buyer's basic damages where the seller does not deliver, or the buyer properly rejects or revokes her acceptance of tendered goods, consist of the difference

between the contract price and either: (i) the market price (*i.e.,* ***benefit of the bargain*** damages) or (ii) the cost of buying replacement goods (*i.e.,* ***cover***), ***plus*** incidental and consequential damages (*see* above), if any, ***less*** expenses saved as a result of the seller's breach.

a) **Difference Between Contract Price and Market Price**
If the buyer measures damages by the difference between contract price and market price, market price usually is determined as of the time the buyer learns of the breach and at the place of tender.

CMR **Exam Tip** Note that the ***buyer's damages*** are measured as of the ***time she learns of the breach***, while the ***seller's damages*** are measured as of the ***time for delivery***. (*See* b., *infra.*)

b) **Difference Between Contract Price and Cost of Replacement Goods—"Cover"**
If the buyer chooses the cover measure (*i.e.,* difference between contract price and cost of buying replacement goods), the buyer must make a ***reasonable contract*** for substitute goods ***in good faith*** and ***without unreasonable delay***.

2) **Seller Delivers Nonconforming Goods that Buyer Accepts**

a) **Warranty Damages**
If the buyer accepts goods that breach one of the seller's warranties, the buyer may recover as damages "loss resulting in the normal course of events from the breach." The basic measure of damages in such a case is the difference between the ***value of the goods as delivered*** and the ***value they would have had if they had been according to contract***, plus incidental and consequential damages.

b) **Notice Requirement**
To recover damages for any defect as to accepted goods, the buyer must, ***within a reasonable time after she discovers or should have discovered the defect***, notify the seller of the defect. If she does not notify the seller within a reasonable time, she loses her right to sue. "Reasonable time" is, of course, a flexible standard.

3) **Seller Anticipatorily Breaches Contract**
The measure of damages when the seller anticipatorily breaches the contract is the difference between the ***market price at the time the buyer learned of the breach*** and the ***contract price***.

4) **Consequential Damages**
As noted above, a seller is liable for consequential damages arising from his breach if: (i) he had reason to know of the buyer's general or particular requirements, and (ii) the subsequent loss resulting from those needs could not reasonably be prevented by cover. Particular needs must be made known to the seller, but general requirements usually need not be.

a) **Goods for Resale**
If the buyer is in the business of reselling the goods, the seller is deemed to have knowledge of the resale.

b) **Goods Necessary for Manufacturing**
If a seller knows that the goods he provides are to be used in the manufacturing process, he should know that his breach would cause a disruption in production leading to a loss of profits.

b. Seller's Damages

1) Where Buyer Repudiates or Refuses to Accept Conforming Goods
The Code provides three measures for damages for when the buyer wrongfully repudiates or refuses to accept conforming goods. The seller can:

(i) Recover the difference between the ***market price*** (measured as of the time and at the place of delivery) ***and the contract price***;

(ii) Resell the goods and recover the difference between the ***contract price and the resale price***; or

(iii) If applicable, recover under a "***lost profits***" measure the difference between the contract price and the cost to the seller. (Note that if the seller is a dealer, his costs would be the costs incurred in obtaining the goods from the manufacturer or another dealer, whereas if the seller is a manufacturer, his costs would be the costs of manufacturing the goods.)

The seller may also recover incidental damages, such as costs of storing, shipping, and reselling the goods as a result of the buyer's breach.

Note: The Code provides that the lost profits measure may be used only when the other measures will not put the seller in as good a position as he would have been in if the buyer had not breached.

Example: Sara contracts to sell an original oil painting to Bob. Bob breaches. Sara sells the painting to Tom. If Sara uses one of the first two damages measures above, she should be fully compensated for Bob's breach; *i.e.,* she will recover what she would have made on the sale to Bob. However, if Sara is a retailer with an unlimited inventory and the contract was for a 50" TV, the result would be different. If Bob refuses to take the TV—even if Sara sells it to Tom—Sara will not be in as good a position as she would have been if Bob had performed, because if Bob had performed, Sara would have sold ***two*** TV sets. Thus, in this case, the lost profits measure is appropriate to compensate Sara for the breach.

Exam Tip Other damages measures will never be adequate if the seller is a ***lost volume seller***. To determine whether the lost profits measure is appropriate, look at the seller's ***supply***. If the seller's supply of goods is ***unlimited*** (*i.e.,* he can obtain all the goods he can sell), then he is a lost volume seller, and the lost profits measure can be used. If the seller's supply is limited (*i.e.,* he cannot obtain all the goods he can sell, as with the sale of a unique item), the lost profits measure cannot be used, and one of the other two measures must be used instead.

2) **Where Buyer Accepted Goods—Action for Price**
If the buyer has accepted the goods and has not paid, or has not accepted the goods and the seller is ***unable to resell*** them at any reasonable price, or if the goods have been lost or damaged at a time the risk of loss was on the buyer, the seller may maintain an action against the buyer for the full contract price.

3. **Contracts for Sale of Land**
The standard measure of damages for breach of land sale contracts is the difference between the ***contract price and the fair market value*** of the land.

4. **Employment Contracts**
In employment contracts, check to see whether the breach was by the employer or the employee.

a. **Breach by Employer**
Irrespective of when the breach occurs—*i.e.,* before performance, after part performance, or after full performance, the standard measure of the employee's damages is the ***full contract price*** (although such damages may be reduced if the employee fails to mitigate—*see* 8.a., *infra*).

b. **Breach by Employee**
If the employee is the breaching party, the employer is entitled to a standard measure of damages computed according to what it ***costs to replace*** the employee, *i.e.,* the difference between the cost incurred to get a second employee to do the work and the cost to the employer had the first breaching employee done the work. If the breach was unintentional (*e.g.,* due to the employee's illness), the employee may have the right to quasi-contractual recovery for the work done to date. The modern view allows employees to offset such amount whether the breach was intentional or unintentional.

5. **Construction Contracts**
If a construction contract is breached by the ***owner***, the builder will be entitled to profits that would have resulted from the contract plus any costs expended. (If the contract is breached after construction is completed, the measure is the full contract price plus interest.) If the contract is breached by the ***builder***, the owner is entitled to the cost of completion plus reasonable compensation for the delay. Most courts allow the builder to offset or recover for work performed to date to avoid unjust enrichment of the owner. (If the breach is only late performance, the owner is entitled to damages incurred because of late performance.)

6. **Contracts Calling for Installment Payments**
If a contract calls for payments in installments and a payment is not made, there is only a partial breach. The aggrieved party is limited to recovering only the missed payment, not the entire contract price. However, the contract may include an ***acceleration clause*** making the entire amount due on any late payment, in which case the aggrieved party may recover the entire amount.

7. **Certainty Rule**
The plaintiff must prove that the losses suffered were certain in their nature and ***not speculative***. Traditionally, if the breaching party prevented the nonbreaching party from setting up a new business, courts would not award lost profits from the prospective business as damages, because they were too speculative. However, modern courts may allow lost profits as damages if they can be made more certain by observing similar businesses in the area or other businesses previously owned by the same party.

8. **Avoidable Damages (Mitigation)**
The nonbreaching party cannot recover avoidable damages. Thus, she must refrain from piling up losses after she receives notice of the breach; she must not incur further expenditures or costs, and she must make reasonable efforts to cut down her losses by procuring a substitute performance at a fair price. Should she not do so, she will not be allowed to recover those damages that might have been avoided by such mitigation after the breach. Generally, a party may ***recover the expenses of mitigation***. Note the following specific contract situations:

a. **Employment Contracts**
If the employer breaches, the employee is under a duty to use ***reasonable care*** in finding a position of the same kind, rank, and grade in the same locale (although it does not necessarily have to be at the same exact pay level). However, note that the burden is on the employer to show that such jobs were available.

b. **Contracts for Sale of Goods**
If the buyer is in breach, recall that the seller generally cannot bring an action against the buyer for the full contract price unless the goods cannot be resold at a reasonable price or were damaged or lost when the risk of loss was on the buyer. (*See* 2.b.2), *supra*.)

c. **Manufacturing Contracts**
Generally, in a contract to manufacture goods, if the person for whom the goods are being manufactured breaches, the manufacturer is under a duty to mitigate by ***not continuing work*** after the breach. However, if the facts are such that completion of the manufacturing project will decrease rather than increase damages, the manufacturer has a right to continue.

d. **Construction Contracts**
A builder does not owe a duty to avoid the consequences of an owner's breach, *e.g.*, by securing other work, but does have a duty to mitigate by ***not continuing work*** after the breach. Again, however, if completion will decrease damages, it will be allowed.

CMR **Exam Tip** Keep in mind that the duty to mitigate only ***reduces*** a recovery; it does not prohibit recovery. Thus, if a fact pattern shows a clear breach and the plaintiff does not attempt to mitigate damages, she can recover for the breach, but the recovery will be reduced by the damages that would have been avoided by mitigation.

C. RESTITUTION
As an alternative to the contract damages discussed above, restitution may be available in a contract-type situation. Restitution is not really part of contract law, but rather is a distinct concept.

Restitution is based on preventing ***unjust enrichment*** when one has conferred a benefit on another without gratuitous intent. Restitution can provide a remedy not only when a contract exists and has been breached, but also when a contract is unenforceable, and in some cases when no contractual relationship exists at all between the parties.

1. Terminology

When a contract is unenforceable or no contract between the parties exists, an action to recover restitutionary damages often is referred to as an action for an ***implied in law*** contract or an action in ***quasi-contract***.

2. Measure of Damages

Generally, the measure of restitution is the ***value of the benefit conferred***. Although this is usually based on the benefit received by the defendant (*e.g.,* the increase in value of the defendant's property or the value of the goods received), recovery may also be measured by the "detriment" suffered by the plaintiff (*e.g.*, the reasonable value of the work performed or the services rendered) if the benefits are difficult to measure or the "benefit" measure would achieve an unfair result.

3. Specific Applications

a. When Contract Breached

When a contract has been breached and the nonbreaching party has not fully performed, he may choose to rescind the contract and sue for restitution to prevent unjust enrichment. Note that if the plaintiff has fully performed, he is ***limited to his damages under the contract.*** This may be less than he would have received in a restitutionary action, because a restitutionary remedy is not limited to the contract price.

1) "Losing" Contracts

A restitutionary remedy often is desirable in the case of a "losing" contract (*i.e.,* a contract in which the actual value of the services or goods to be provided under the contract is higher than the contract price), because normal contract expectation damages or reliance damages would be for a lesser amount.

2) Breach by Plaintiff

Under some circumstances, a plaintiff may seek restitution even though the plaintiff is the party who breached. If the breach was intentional, some courts will not grant the breaching party restitution; modern courts, however, will permit restitutionary recovery but limit it to the contract price less damages incurred as a result of the breach.

a) Restitution of Advance Payments or Deposit

If the buyer has paid part of the purchase price in advance and then breaches the contract, he can usually recover some of the payments. Unless the seller can prove greater damages, he may keep advance payments totaling 20% of the purchase price or $500, whichever is less. The balance must be returned to the buyer. If there is a valid liquidated damages clause, the seller need refund only the excess of the buyer's payments over the amount of liquidated damages.

b. When Contract Unenforceable—Quasi-Contract Remedy

Restitution may be available in a ***quasi-contract*** action when a contract was made but is unenforceable and unjust enrichment otherwise would result (*e.g.,* celebrity is hired to sign autographs and is paid, but dies before he performs; the other party has a restitutionary action to recover the payment).

c. When No Contract Involved—Quasi-Contract Remedy

Restitution may also be available in a ***quasi-contract*** action when there is no contractual relationship between the parties if:

1) The plaintiff has ***conferred a benefit*** on the defendant by rendering services or expending properties;

2) The plaintiff conferred the benefit with the ***reasonable expectation of being compensated*** for its value;

3) The defendant ***knew or had reason to know*** of the plaintiff's expectation; and

4) The defendant would be ***unjustly enriched*** if he were allowed to retain the benefit without compensating the plaintiff.

CMR **Exam Tip** Always keep the quasi-contract remedy in the back of your mind. ***Look first for a valid contract*** allowing the plaintiff relief. But if there is no valid contract, a quasi-contract will provide a remedy if the plaintiff has suffered a loss or rendered services.

D. RESCISSION

Rescission is a remedy whereby the original contract is considered voidable and rescinded. The parties are left as though a contract had never been made. The grounds for rescission must have occurred either ***before or at the time*** the contract was entered into. The grounds are:

(i) ***Mutual mistake*** of a material fact;

(ii) ***Unilateral mistake if the other party knew*** or should have known of the mistake;

(iii) ***Unilateral mistake if hardship by the mistaken party is so extreme*** it outweighs the other party's expectations under the contract;

(iv) ***Misrepresentation of fact or law*** by either party as to a material factor in the negotiations that was relied upon; and

(v) ***Other grounds***, such as duress, undue influence, illegality, lack of capacity, and failure of consideration.

1. Defenses

Generally, all equitable defenses (*e.g.*, laches, unclean hands) are available in a rescission action. Note that the plaintiff's negligence is not a defense.

2. Additional Relief

If the plaintiff has paid money to the defendant, she is entitled to restitution in addition to rescission.

E. REFORMATION

Reformation is the remedy whereby the writing setting forth the agreement between the parties is changed so that it conforms to the original intent of the parties. A reformation action is usually based on mutual mistake; *i.e.*, the parties agree to a set of terms and the written contract fails to reflect those terms. Reformation is also possible if there is a unilateral mistake and the party who knows of the mistake does not disclose it, and when the writing is incorrect because of misrepresentation.

1. Clear and Convincing Evidence Standard

The variance between the antecedent agreement and the writing must be established by clear and convincing evidence.

2. Parol Evidence Rule and Statute of Frauds Do Not Apply

The parol evidence rule is not applied in reformation actions. Likewise, the majority rule is that the Statute of Frauds does not apply—but many courts will deny reformation if it would add land to the contract without complying with the Statute of Frauds.

3. Defenses

In addition to the general equitable defenses, the existence of a bona fide purchaser for value is also a defense to reformation. Similarly, reformation is not permitted if the rights of third parties will be unfairly affected.

F. STATUTE OF LIMITATIONS UNDER U.C.C.

For sales contracts, the U.C.C. provides for a ***four-year statute*** of limitations. The parties may shorten the period by agreement to ***no less than one year***, but they may not lengthen the period.

1. Accrual of Action

The statutory period begins to run when a party can bring suit—*i.e.*, when breach occurs. The period begins to run regardless of whether the aggrieved party knows about the breach.

2. Breach of Warranty Actions

For a breach of warranty action, the breach occurs and the limitations period begins to run upon ***delivery*** of the goods. This is true even if the buyer does not discover the breach until much later.

a. Warranty Extends to Future Performance

If there is an ***express*** warranty that explicitly extends to future performance of the goods, the four-year period does not begin to run until the buyer should have discovered the breach.

b. Implied Warranties Breached on Delivery

Because implied warranties cannot "explicitly" extend to future performance, they are breached, if at all, upon delivery.

Contracts

Lecture Handout

barbri®

Multistate Early Bar Prep

CONTRACTS LECTURE HANDOUT

1. **APPLICABLE LAW**
2. **CONTRACT FORMATION**
3. **STATUTE OF FRAUDS**
4. **CONTRACT TERMS**
5. **PERFORMANCE**
6. **EXCUSES FOR NONPERFORMANCE**
7. **REMEDIES**
8. **THIRD-PARTY PROBLEMS**

KEY ISSUE #1: APPLICABLE LAW

A. **MULTISTATE BAR EXAM** tests on 2 kinds of contract law: the **common law** of contracts & **Article 2** of the Uniform Commercial Code (UCC). Which one applies?

1. **ARTICLE 2** applies to a ____________________ [moveable, personal property]

2. **COMMON LAW** applies to ____

B. **STATE BAR EXAM**: ____

KEY ISSUE #2: CONTRACT FORMATION

VOCABULARY

A. **CONTRACT**: A contract is a ____

An **express contract** is created by the parties' ________________ (either oral or written)

An **implied contract** is created by the parties' _____________________________

B. **QUASI-CONTRACT:** Quasi-contract protects against ________________________ whenever contract law yields an unfair result. Quasi-contract is the remedy of last resort.

Ben Affleck orally agreed to work for WB for 5 years for $20 million per film. After "Gigli" bombed, WB refused to pay Ben for the film. The Statute of Frauds bars Ben from enforcing the contract. Can Ben recover from WB in quasi-contract?

____

____

How much can Ben recover from WB in quasi-contract?

____

____

C. **BILATERAL CONTRACT**: Offer can be accepted ____________________

D. **UNILATERAL CONTRACT**: Offer can be accepted only by ____________________

1. ____

2. ____

FORMATION METHODOLOGY

A. Look first for **an agreement** (an offer that's been accepted), *then* see if the agreement is **legally enforceable** (are there any defenses against enforcement?).

B. An agreement involves **a three-step process**:

1. Was an ____________________ ever made?

2. Was the offer ____________________ before it was accepted?

3. Was the offer ____________________?

FIRST STEP OF AGREEMENT PROCESS: WAS THERE AN OFFER?

A. **OFFER**: An offer is a manifestation of an intention to be bound. On the bar exam, there are typically two kinds of offer problems: **advertisements** and **indefiniteness**.

1. **ADVERTISEMENTS**

a. **GENERAL RULE**: An advertisement is not an offer.

IHOP advertises in the Times: "Incredible offer! Breakfast special for $2.49." Offer?

____

____

b. **EXCEPTION**: unless the ad specifies a ____________________ term and who can accept.

Gap's ad reads: "**One blue dress** just like Monica's, only $1! **First come, first served**." Offer?

2. **INDEFINITENESS**: See if any of the terms are too indefinite to be enforced. Often-tested issues in this area are **requirements contracts** & **open price terms**.

a. **REQUIREMENTS CONTRACTS (Article 2)**: Requirements contracts are definite enough, even though there's no specific quantity mentioned.

Flatus Café agrees to buy **all its requirements** of beans from Seller for six years for $1/can.

Seller accepts the Café's offer. For the last three years, the Café has ordered **1,000 cans a year**. Can the Café require Seller to deliver **8,000 cans this year**?

*** b. **OPEN PRICE TERM**: An open price term is too indefinite under the **common law**, but *not* too indefinite under **Article 2**.

W sends you a letter offering to sell you his Crawford ranch, but does not state a price. Offer?

What if, instead, W sends you a letter offering to sell you **a painting** of his ranch?

SECOND STEP OF AGREEMENT PROCESS: WAS THE OFFER TERMINATED?

A. **OVERVIEW**: There are four ways an offer can be terminated: **lapse of time**; **revocation**; **rejection**; and **death before acceptance**.

B. **LAPSE**: An offer lapses after a **stated term** or after a **reasonable time** has passed.

On March 15, I offer to sell Eva my Honda for $5,000. My offer does not contain a termination date. Can Eva accept my offer **on December 22**?

____

____

C. **REVOCATION**: An offer terminates when the offeror revokes the offer.

1. **GENERAL RULE**: An offer can be revoked any time before acceptance. How?

a. **DIRECT REVOCATION**: the offeror indicates **directly to the offeree** that he has changed his mind about the deal.

*** b. **INDIRECT REVOCATION**: the **offeror engages in conduct** that indicates he's changed his mind ***and*** **the offeree is aware of the conduct**.

On January 3, I offer to sell Eva Longoria my Honda for $5,000. The next day, in the shower, I exclaim, "I do *not* want to sell my Honda to Eva." Can Eva still accept?

____

If I **sell my Honda to Teri Hatcher** on January 4, can Eva still accept my offer? [Trick Q!]

____

____

Teri tells Eva she bought the Honda from me. Can Eva still accept my offer?

____

____

2. **EXCEPTIONS**: Four situations where an offer cannot be revoked:

a. **OPTION**: An option is a promise to keep the offer open that is **paid for**.

I offer to paint Dr. House's house for $10,000 and promise to keep the offer open for a week. Can I still revoke the offer?

I offer to paint the house for $10,000 and promise to keep my offer open if House pays me $100. **House pays me $100**. Can I still revoke?

b. ***FORESEEABLE*** **RELIANCE BEFORE ACCEPTANCE** [very rare!]

I offer to sell you a painting. **Before accepting my offer**, you have an expensive frame custom-made to fit the painting. Can I still revoke my offer?

Subcontractor S submits a bid to do the electrical work on a hotel project for $250,000. Contractor C relies on S's bid in computing its own bid on the project. Can S still revoke its offer?

c. **STARTING TO PERFORM A UNILATERAL CONTRACT** [p. 2]

House offers me $10,000 to paint his house. The offer states that it can be accepted **only by painting the house**. **I start painting** the house. Can House still revoke his offer?

What if I had **bought paint**, but not yet started painting the house? Could House still revoke?

d. **FIRM OFFER (Article 2)**: In a sale of goods, if **a merchant** promises in a **signed writing** to keep an **offer open**, then the offer is irrevocable [**almost every business person is a merchant** under Article 2's broad definition].

Carmax offers to sell Homer Simpson a 1971 BMW. The offer is **in writing**, is **signed by Carmax**, and provides that **Carmax will not revoke for two weeks**. Can Carmax still revoke?

What if the writing provides that Carmax will not revoke **for six months**?

What if Carmax's promise not to revoke **does not state a time period**?

Carmax makes a signed, written offer to sell a 1971 BMW. Can Carmax still revoke? [Trick Q!]

3. **TIMING**: Revocation of an offer is effective **only on receipt**.

On Monday, I offer to sell Eva my Honda. On Tuesday, I mail her a letter revoking the offer. She receives my letter on Thursday. When is the revocation effective?

What if Eva had already accepted my offer on Wednesday?

D. **REJECTION**: An offer terminates when the offeree rejects it (“**inappropriate response**”).

1. **COUNTEROFFER**: A **counteroffer** operates as a rejection, but **mere bargaining does not**. Asking a question is considered mere bargaining.

Edie offers to sell her house on Wisteria Lane to Nina for $500,000. Nina responds, “I will only pay $460,000.” Edie refuses. Can Nina later accept Edie’s original offer?

What if Nina responded, “Will you take $460,000?”

---

2. **CONDITIONAL ACCEPTANCE**: A **conditional acceptance** operates as a rejection.

Disney sends Bill Clinton an offer to appear in the film, “Waiting to Inhale.” Bill agrees on the condition that (or “provided that”/“so long as”/“if”) he get top billing. Is there an agreement?

*** 3. **ACCEPTANCE VARYING OFFER**: An acceptance that varies the terms of the offer operates as a **rejection under the common law, but *not* under Article 2**.

a. **COMMON LAW**: Acceptance must mirror offer ("**Mirror Image Rule**")

Landlord sends Tenant a signed lease that says nothing about pets. Tenant adds, "Tenant may keep a pet," signs the lease & returns it to Landlord. Has Tenant accepted Landlord's offer?

____

____

b. **SALE OF GOODS (Article 2)**: An acceptance does **not** have to mirror the terms of the offer.

i. Under Article 2, **adding a term or changing a term does *not* prevent acceptance** (Policy: To facilitate contract formation).

ii. However, the **offeree's terms are *not* automatically included in the contract!** They become part of the contract ***only if***:

(A) Both parties are **merchants**;

(B) The term is **not a "material" change**; **and**

(C) The **offeror does not object** within a reasonable time.

Bottom line: offeree's terms ________________________ become part of the contract!

B makes a written offer to buy 100 widgets from S for $1,000. The offer does not mention any warranties. S's written acceptance **disclaims all warranties**. Is there a contract?

____

____

____

Does the contract include S's disclaimer?

____

____

____

____

What if S had not disclaimed all warranties, but had merely added "**Saturday delivery**"?

___

___

What if B had responded that Saturday delivery was **not convenient**?

___

___

E. **DEATH BEFORE ACCEPTANCE**: Death of either party before acceptance terminates a **revocable** offer.

On April 2, X makes an offer to Y. X dies on April 6. Can Y still accept X's offer?

___

On April 2, X makes an offer to Y. X promises not to revoke the offer for 7 days in exchange for $100. **Y pays X $100**. X dies on April 6. Can Y still accept X's offer?

___

THIRD STAGE OF AGREEMENT PROCESS: HAS THE OFFER BEEN ACCEPTED?

A. LANGUAGE OF THE OFFER CONTROLS

Chef Tom emails Dale a job offer that states, "You can accept this offer **only by reporting for work on Monday**." Dale emails back, "I accept!" Has he accepted the offer?

___

___

___

B faxes an order for widgets stating, "I need the widgets **shipped within 24 hours**." S faxes back: "I promise to ship the widgets within 24 hours." Has S accepted B's offer?

___

___

___

B. STARTING PERFORMANCE

1. **BILATERAL CONTRACT**: **Starting performance is acceptance** of an offer to enter a bilateral contract and carries with it an **implied promise to finish the job.**

House offers me $10,000 to paint his house. His offer does not specify how to accept [bilateral]. **I start painting the house**. Have I accepted House's offer so that I am bound to finish the job?

---

2. **UNILATERAL CONTRACT**: **Starting performance is not acceptance** of an offer to enter a unilateral contract; only **completing performance is acceptance.**

House's offer states that I can accept **only by painting the house** [unilateral contract]. **I start painting the house**. Have I accepted the offer so that I am bound to finish the job?

Once I start painting his house, **can House still revoke** his offer?

C. IMPROPER PERFORMANCE

1. **COMMON LAW**: Improper performance operates as **acceptance** *and* **breach.**

House offers me $10,000 to paint his house **white**. I paint it **maroon**. Have I accepted the offer?

---

2. **SALE OF GOODS (Article 2)**: Improper performance operates as **acceptance** *and* **breach** unless seller is sending the goods **as an accommodation** to the buyer.

B orders a Britney CD from S. S ships an Incubus CD instead. Has S accepted B's offer?

Same facts, except that S includes a note saying, "I'm out of Britney, but am sending Incubus instead **in the hope that it meets your needs**." Has S accepted?

____

____

____

D. **SILENCE:** The offeree's silence is generally not acceptance.

I leave a note on your outline at the break: "I offer to sell you my Honda for $5,000. If I don't hear from you by 9 tonight, you've accepted." You say nothing. Have you accepted my offer?

____

____

E. **TIMING OF AN ACCEPTANCE**

1. **GENERAL RULE:** Acceptance is effective **when it's mailed** ("**Mailbox Rule**"). [Policy: protects the offeree against revocation once he's mailed an acceptance].

On May 6, Borat gets a letter offering him an "awefulsome gig" for $5,000. **On May 7, he mails his acceptance**. **On May 8, he receives a letter revoking the offer**. Result?

____

____

What if Borat's acceptance letter got lost in the mail?

____

2. **EXCEPTIONS TO THE MAILBOX RULE**

a. **OFFER PROVIDES OTHERWISE**: ______________________

Captain Kirk offers to sell the Starship Enterprise to the Klingons for $5 million. His offer states, "**Your acceptance must be received by January 9**." On January 9, the Klingons mail their acceptance. **Captain Kirk receives it on January 11**. Is Captain Kirk bound?

____

____

b. **IRREVOCABLE OFFER** [rationale: if the offer is irrevocable, then the offeree doesn't need the protection of the Mailbox Rule]

Same facts, except the Klingons **paid Captain Kirk $3,000 for his promise to hold the offer open until January 9**. Is Captain Kirk bound?

____

____

c. **OFFFEROR RELIES ON *OVERTAKING* REJECTION** [where an acceptance is *sent* first, but rejection *arrives* first]

Slash gets an invitation to join the Dixie Chicks. Slash **mails an acceptance on June 8**. [MBR applies.] Slash changes his mind and **faxes a rejection on June 9**. Is his acceptance effective?

____

____

____

d. **REJECTION *SENT FIRST***: ______________________

What if Slash mails a **rejection on June 8** and then mails an **acceptance on June 9**?

____

____

____

KEY ISSUE #7: REMEDIES

A. NON-MONETARY REMEDY

1. **SPECIFIC PERFORMANCE:** Specific performance is **an equitable remedy**, available only if monetary damages are clearly inadequate to compensate the injured party. Availability depends on **the nature of the contract**.

   BAR EXAM TIP: Specific performance is **rarely the right answer** on the MBE.

   a. **REAL PROPERTY**: Specific performance is **generally available** because real property is considered unique (even if it's not really unique).

Thoreau contracts to sell **Walden Pond** to Proust. Later Thoreau has second thoughts and backs out. Proust wants Walden Pond, not money. Can Proust get specific performance?

b. **SALE OF GOODS (Article 2)**: Specific performance is available only if the goods are **unique** or there are "**other proper circumstances**" (*e.g.*, an inability to buy substitute goods in the market).

Seller contracts to sell **a rug** to Buyer. Seller breaches. Buyer sues for the rug.

c. **SERVICE CONTRACTS**: Specific performance is **not available** in service contracts, **but injunctive relief may be**.

BARBRI hires me **to lecture**. I breach. Can BARBRI get specific performance?

BARBRI hires me to lecture. I breach and go lecture for Denny Crain's Bar Review. Can BARBRI get **an injunction** barring me from lecturing for Denny Crain's Bar Review?

B. MONETARY REMEDIES (DAMAGES)

1. **PUNITIVE DAMAGES**: Punitive damages are not awarded for breach of contract because the purpose of contract damages is **to compensate, not punish**.

   BAR EXAM TIP: Don't think of "good guys" & "bad guys." The purpose of contract remedies is **to compensate** the victim, **not punish** the breaching party.

2. **LIQUIDATED DAMAGES**: Liquidated damages will be upheld if the damages were **difficult to estimate in advance** and are a **reasonable forecast of probable damages**, but liquidated damages **cannot operate as a penalty**.

Simon hires Thom to redo his office. The contract provides for damages of **$100/day** for each day Thom is late. Thom finishes 20 days late. Is the liquidated damages clause valid?

____

____

____

What if the contract provides for **$2,000 in damages** in the event that Thom is late?

____

____

Will Simon get *any* damages **if the liquidated damages clause is struck down as a penalty**?

____

3. **EXPECTATION DAMAGES**: Expectation damages put an injured party **in as good a position as full performance**. Expectation damages are the **general rule**.

a. **COMMON LAW DAMAGES**

I agree to paint House's house for **$10,000**. I breach. House pays another painter **$13,000** to paint the house. How much can House recover from me for breach of contract?

____

____

____

Same facts, except that House refuses to pay me after I have started painting his house. I have **already spent $5,000**. I expected to clear **$1,500 in profit**. What are my damages?

____

____

____

b. **SALE OF GOODS DAMAGES (Article 2):** ______________________

i. **BUYER'S DAMAGES** [three options]

(A) **COVER DAMAGES**: **cover price – contract price** if buyer **covers in good faith** [usual measure].

B contracts to buy carpeting for **$2,500**. S does not deliver. The market price for similar carpeting is $2,700. What are B's damages if B pays **$2,800** for the same carpeting?

____

____

____

(B) **MARKET DAMAGES: market price – contract price** if buyer **doesn't cover in good faith** or **doesn't cover at all.**

Same facts, except that B pays $6,000 for **much better carpeting**. Can B recover the $3,500 difference between the cover price and the contract price? If not, what are B's damages?

____

____

____

What if B does not buy any replacement carpeting at all?

____

(C) **LOSS IN VALUE**: **value as promised – value delivered** if buyer **keeps non-conforming goods.**

B contracts to buy an antique rug for $4,000. B later discovers it's not antique. **B keeps it anyway.** The rug is worth **$2,000**. Had it been antique, it would be worth **$7,000**. What are B's damages?

____

____

____

____

ii. **SELLER'S DAMAGES** [four options]

(A) **RESALE DAMAGES: contract price – resale price** if seller **resells *in good faith*** [usual measure].

I contract to sell my Toyota to Izzy for **$7,000**. Izzy breaches the contract. A week later, I sell the car to George for **$6,500**. What are my damages?

____

What if I sell the car to George for **$7,000**?

____

(B) **MARKET DAMAGES: contract price – market price** if seller **does not resell in good faith** or **does not resell** at all.

If I sell it to George for **$2,000**, can I recover the $5,000 difference from Izzy?

____

____

What if I decide not to sell the car at all?

____

*** (C) **LOST PROFIT: lost profit**, if seller is ***a lost volume dealer***.

A car dealer contracts to sell a car **out of its regular inventory** to Izzy for **$7,000**. Izzy breaches. A week later, the dealer sells **the same car** to George for **$7,000**. What are the dealer's damages?

____

____

____

____

____

BAR EXAM TIP: This is how it *always* appears on the MBE: a **dealer** resells the **same goods** for the **same price**. The bar examiners are trying to trick you into saying the dealer's damages are $0, but don't be fooled! The dealer has lost the **profit it would have made on the initial sale!**

(D) **CONTRACT PRICE**: **contract price**, if seller **is not able to resell** the goods.

I agree to buy a custom-made set of dishes featuring the Sokolow name and family crest from Spode. I breach the contract. What are Spode's damages?

4. **INCIDENTAL DAMAGES**: Incidental damages involve the cost of **transporting or caring for goods after breach** and costs associated with **arranging a substitute transaction**. Incidental damages are available to both buyer and seller.

After my breach, Spode has to store and insure the dishes, and advertises them for sale in the newspaper in an attempt to find another buyer. Can Spode recover these expenses from me?

*** 5. **CONSEQUENTIAL DAMAGES**: Consequential damages are damages that are ***special*** **to this plaintiff** and were ***reasonably foreseeable*** **by the breaching party** ***at the time of the contract*** [**note**: **not** available to a **seller** under Article 2].

Miller contracts with UPS to ship a broken mill shaft back to the manufacturer. UPS delays in shipping the shaft. **Miller does not have another shaft**. As a result, the mill is shut for nine extra days. Can Miller recover the **$20,000 in profit it lost during that nine-day period**?

House hires me to paint his beach house for **$3,000**. Before I agree, **he tells me he'll lose $500 in rent** if I don't finish the beach house by Friday. I breach. House can't get anyone else to paint by Friday and loses the rent. He later pays **$3,400** to get the job done. What are House's damages?

(a) $400 [$3,400 - $3,000] ______________________________

(b) $500 in lost rent ______________________________

(c) $900 [$400 + $500] ______________________________

(d) $3,900 [$3,400 + $500] ______________________________

____

____

6. **AVOIDABLE DAMAGES**: An injured party cannot recover damages he could have avoided ("mitigated") with reasonable effort.

Kay Pasa is fired in violation of her contract. She makes $900/week. Her former employer alleges that Kay can get a **comparable job** paying $800/week. What are Kay's damages?

____

____

____

____

____

GOOD LUCK ON THE BAR EXAM!

barbri®

Contracts

1. Ⓐ Ⓑ Ⓒ Ⓓ
2. Ⓐ Ⓑ Ⓒ Ⓓ
3. Ⓐ Ⓑ Ⓒ Ⓓ
4. Ⓐ Ⓑ Ⓒ Ⓓ
5. Ⓐ Ⓑ Ⓒ Ⓓ

6. Ⓐ Ⓑ Ⓒ Ⓓ
7. Ⓐ Ⓑ Ⓒ Ⓓ
8. Ⓐ Ⓑ Ⓒ Ⓓ
9. Ⓐ Ⓑ Ⓒ Ⓓ
10. Ⓐ Ⓑ Ⓒ Ⓓ

11. Ⓐ Ⓑ Ⓒ Ⓓ
12. Ⓐ Ⓑ Ⓒ Ⓓ
13. Ⓐ Ⓑ Ⓒ Ⓓ
14. Ⓐ Ⓑ Ⓒ Ⓓ
15. Ⓐ Ⓑ Ⓒ Ⓓ

16. Ⓐ Ⓑ Ⓒ Ⓓ
17. Ⓐ Ⓑ Ⓒ Ⓓ

CONTRACTS QUESTIONS

Question 1

On August 1, a realtor mailed a written offer to a developer for the sale of a large tract of land. The offer included the following terms:

> This offer expires on September 1, if the offeree has not caused an acceptance to be received by the offeror on or before that date.

Early on September 1, the developer sent a written acceptance by messenger but the messenger company negligently withheld delivery to the realtor until September 2. On September 4, the realtor entered into a contract for sale of the tract to another buyer but did not inform the developer of the transaction. When the developer contacted the realtor a few days later, the realtor said there was no contract between them.

Which of the following is the most correct statement?

(A) No contract between the realtor and the developer arose on September 2.

(B) A contract would have arisen if a letter of acceptance were mailed on September 1.

(C) The realtor's silence constituted an acceptance of the developer's written message on September 2.

(D) A voidable contract arose on September 1.

Question 2

A homeowner offered a landscape gardener $1,000 to trim and reshape the bushes on her property if the gardener could finish the job before her garden party on June 1. The gardener told the homeowner that he would get back to her after he had checked his calendar. The next day, the gardener phoned the homeowner, who was not at home, and left a message on her voice mail that he had the time, but could not do the job for less than $1,200. The gardener did not hear from the homeowner for several days. As June 1 drew closer, the gardener phoned the homeowner again and left another message on her voice mail stating that "I'll do the job for $1,000, this weekend, unless that would be inconvenient." The homeowner replayed the second message just as she was leaving town on a business trip and did not contact the gardener. That weekend, unbeknownst to the homeowner, the gardener took his tools to the homeowner's house and trimmed and reshaped the bushes to the homeowner's specifications. When the homeowner returned from her trip several days later, the gardener presented her with a handwritten invoice for $1,000.

If the homeowner refuses to pay the gardener, and the latter brings an action solely for breach of contract to recover the $1,000 contract amount, who will likely prevail?

(A) The gardener, because the homeowner knew of the gardener's plans to do the landscaping job over the weekend in question, putting the burden on the homeowner to call off the job if she did not want the gardener to perform.

(B) The gardener, because this was a unilateral contract, the terms of which the gardener accepted by performing his duties under the contract.

(C) The homeowner, because she revoked her offer when she ignored the gardener's subsequent phone calls agreeing to do the job at the original price.

(D) The homeowner, because she did not accept the gardener's offer to do the landscaping job for $1,000.

Question 3

A young man was planning a trip to Amsterdam to celebrate his graduation from business school. Because he had a problem with drugs in his late teens, his father was afraid that he would relapse when he got to Amsterdam, where marijuana was relatively inexpensive and legal in small amounts. Consequently, his father told him, "If you refrain from smoking marijuana during your trip to Amsterdam, I will give you $5,000 as a down payment on that car you are planning to buy." The young man said nothing but was pleased by the offer because he needed the money and had no plans to smoke marijuana in any case.

The young man went to Amsterdam and did not smoke marijuana there. Three weeks into the trip, and a week before he was due to go home, his father died suddenly of a heart attack, prompting him to cut his trip short and return home.

If the young man seeks payment of the $5,000 from his father's estate, will he likely prevail?

(A) No, because he remained silent following his father's offer and, thus, did not make a valid acceptance of the offer.

(B) No, because his father's offer to pay was terminated upon his death.

(C) Yes, because he has performed under a valid contract, and thus his father's estate must now perform.

(D) Yes, because he changed his position for the worse in reliance on his father's promise, and thus the executor is estopped from denying that the contract existed.

Question 4

A software retailer who collected vintage baseball cards as a hobby and for occasional profit had in his collection a Roger Maris baseball card, circa 1961, in pristine condition. The retailer knew that the local high school baseball coach would love to add that card to his own collection, so he told the coach that he was interested in selling it. The coach said that he would pay $2,000 for it, but would not have the money until he received his bonus from work in three weeks' time. The retailer agreed to sell the card to the coach and wrote the following on a piece of paper, which he gave to the coach: "I will sell my 1961 Roger Maris baseball card to the coach if he pays me $2,000 within the next 30 days."

Two weeks later, before the coach could purchase the baseball card from the retailer, the retailer incurred an unexpected debt and gave the baseball card to his creditor as repayment of the debt. Then the retailer called the coach to tell him that he was revoking his offer to sell the baseball card to him. The coach, who had cleared off his mantel and built a little wooden stand on which to display the card, filed suit against the retailer.

Will the coach likely be successful?

(A) Yes, because the parties have an option contract that was irrevocable for the time stated in the contract.

(B) Yes, because the agreement between the parties was for the sale of a good worth more than $500, and the revocation was not in writing.

(C) Yes, on the ground of promissory estoppel.

(D) No, because this was merely an offer for a unilateral contract that was revocable prior to acceptance.

Question 5

A seller and a buyer entered into negotiations over the telephone. They reached a general understanding that the buyer would buy widgets from the seller. Following their conversation, the seller sent the buyer a contract, already signed by the seller, agreeing to sell 1,000 widgets to the buyer for a total contract price of $10,000. Upon receipt of the contract in the mail, the buyer signed the contract and deposited an envelope containing the contract in the mailbox located in front of the buyer's office building.

Before the seller received the contract, the buyer had a change of heart. He telephoned the seller and said, "Look, I just can't make a profit on those widgets. I'm not interested in that contract we talked about." The seller replied, "That's all right, I understand. Maybe we can do business some other time." The next day, the signed contract was delivered to the seller's office. The seller, also having had a change of heart, decided that he wanted to enforce the contract.

Is the contract enforceable against the buyer?

(A) Yes, because the acceptance occurred prior to rejection.

(B) Yes, because of the parol evidence rule.

(C) No, because the offer to rescind was accepted and that discharged the original contract.

(D) No, because the rejection by telephone voided the acceptance by mail.

Question 6

A sporting goods retailer whose tent stock was running low saw a listing for the tent she wanted priced at $90 in the catalogue of a large camping goods manufacturer. The retailer phoned the manufacturer and placed her order for 10 tents on May 1. The next day, the manufacturer mailed the retailer a letter informing her that the tents were now $92 and that they would be shipped to her on May 16. The retailer received the letter on May 4, but never responded. On May 15, the retailer received a catalogue from another company showing tents similar to the ones that she ordered, but for a cost of $70. She immediately called the manufacturer to cancel her order. Nevertheless, the manufacturer shipped the tents to the retailer on May 16.

Assuming that the parties' communications were sufficient to form a contract, on what day was the contract formed?

(A) May 1, the day the retailer placed her order.

(B) May 2, the day the manufacturer sent its letter.

(C) May 4, the day the retailer received the letter.

(D) May 16, the day the tents were shipped.

Question 7

On September 15, a manufacturer of office furniture received a purchase-order form from a retailer of office furniture, ordering 100 executive leather swivel chairs for delivery no later than November 1, at a total cost of $10,000, as quoted in the manufacturer's current catalogue. Two days later, the manufacturer faxed its own purchase-order acceptance form to the retailer, who was a new customer and had never seen the form before. The purchase-order acceptance form stated that it was an acceptance of the specified order, was signed by the manufacturer's sales manager, and contained all of the terms of the retailer's form, but it also contained a clause providing for liquidated damages in the event of breach of contract.

Assuming that there were no further communications between the parties, which of the following statements best describes the status of the contract between them?

(A) There is an enforceable contract between the parties, the terms of which include the liquidated damages clause in the manufacturer's form.

(B) There is an enforceable contract between the parties, the terms of which do not include the liquidated damages clause in the manufacturer's form.

(C) There is no enforceable contract between the parties because the manufacturer's form constituted a rejection of the retailer's offer and a counteroffer by the manufacturer.

(D) There is no enforceable contract between the parties because the manufacturer's form added an additional term that materially altered the terms of the retailer's offer.

Question 8

On July 1, a rancher offered to sell his prize bull to a breeder for $15,000. On July 10, the breeder wrote the rancher as follows:

> I have decided to take the bull. A check for $15,000 is enclosed. I am leaving for Argentina for six months and will pick up the bull on January 1. I will pay you for its board and care.

The breeder's letter is:

(A) A counteroffer, because it changes the terms of the offer.

(B) A counteroffer, because it was not a definite expression of acceptance.

(C) An acceptance, and the rancher must board the bull but is entitled to the reasonable value of that service.

(D) An acceptance, and the rancher may refuse to board the bull.

Question 9

On January 1, a club owner entered into a written contract with a singer providing that the singer was to sing nightly at the club for the next six months at a set salary, commencing February 1. The club owner received no further communication from the singer until February 1, at which time he received a telegram from the singer stating: "Due to circumstances beyond my control, I will not be able to start my singing engagement at your club until February 10. I'm sorry for any inconvenience this causes you." On February 10 the singer appeared at the nightclub, ready to sing.

May the club owner cancel the contract?

(A) Yes, because the singer failed to start singing when he contracted to do so.

(B) Yes, because the singer's actions constitute a material breach.

(C) No, unless the club owner was materially prejudiced by the singer's failure to start singing on February 1.

(D) No, because the singer notified the club owner of his delay in performance in a timely fashion.

Question 10

A dealer sent a fax to a wholesaler stating "Send 500 'Granny Rocker' chairs at your usual price." The wholesaler responded, also by fax, "Will ship our last 500 'Granny Rocker' chairs at $100 per chair, our usual price. 'Granny Rocker' line is being discontinued." The wholesaler's staff immediately began the paperwork for processing the order and started preparing and packing the chairs for shipment. The dealer faxed back to the wholesaler, "Cancel order for 'Granny Rocker' chairs; your price is too high." The dealer had found a mill outlet that was the only other source of the chairs. Although the outlet's price was also $100 per chair, it was more convenient for the dealer to buy the chairs from the outlet. The day after receiving the dealer's cancellation, the wholesaler was able to sell the 500 "Granny Rocker" chairs in its stock to another party for $100 each.

If the wholesaler sues the dealer for damages, how much should the wholesaler recover?

(A) Nothing, because this was a contract between merchants and the dealer canceled within a reasonable time.

(B) Nothing, because the wholesaler was able to cover by selling the chairs at the same price it would have received from the dealer.

(C) $50,000, the full contract price, because the dealer breached the contract and $100 per chair was a fair price.

(D) The wholesaler's incidental costs of preparing the paperwork and other office costs connected with preparing and packing the chairs for shipment to the dealer.

Question 11

An automobile dealer agreed to sell a car to a buyer for $30,000, with a down payment of $6,000 due at the time the sales contract was signed and the balance payable in monthly installments over a period of five years. Under the written contract, delivery would be made within 30 days. Two weeks after making the down payment, the buyer told the dealer that he lost his job and could not afford to go through with the purchase. The dealer, which could get as many of that model of car as it required from the manufacturer for a wholesale price of $21,000, put the car in question back in its inventory but refused to return the buyer's down payment. A short time later, the dealer sold it to someone else for $28,500.

The buyer sues the dealer to get back his deposit, and the dealer counterclaims for damages. For purposes of this question, do not include incidental damages in your calculations.

Of the following choices, which is the most likely recovery?

(A) The buyer will recover $6,000.

(B) The buyer will recover $4,500.

(C) The dealer will recover $9,000.

(D) The dealer will recover $3,000.

Question 12

A sporting goods shop owner faxed an order to one of his regular suppliers for 200 12-inch leather softballs at $5 per ball, the supplier's list price, delivery within seven days. The supplier checked its inventory and discovered that it had only 180 12-inch leather softballs, which it shipped to the shop owner, along with 20 12-inch synthetic softballs. The synthetic softballs had the same list price of $5 per ball. The supplier also faxed to the shop owner the following message: "We did not have enough leather softballs in stock to fill your order. Therefore, we are sending synthetic softballs at the same list price to make up the balance of the shipment—hope you will be able to use them!"

Upon receipt of the shipment and the fax, what are the shop owner's options?

(A) The shop owner may accept the conforming part of the shipment and reject the nonconforming part, in which case he must pay the supplier $900 less any damages sustained because of the nonconforming part of the shipment.

(B) The shop owner may accept the shipment, in which case he must pay the supplier $1,000 less any damages sustained because of the nonconforming shipment.

(C) The shop owner may reject the shipment, but the supplier will not be liable for breach of contract.

(D) The shop owner may reject the shipment, in which case he may recover against the supplier for breach of contract.

Question 13

A hotelier planning to build a new hotel estimated that first year profits would be about $10,000 per day. To encourage its contractor to work in a timely manner, the hotelier included in their contract a liquidated damages clause, providing that the contractor would be liable to pay the hotelier $100,000 per day for each day that the contractor is late in completion of the project. During the project, the contractor failed to place an order for the hotel's elevators in a timely manner. As a result of that oversight, the elevators were installed late and the hotel consequently opened 30 days later than scheduled.

The hotelier sued the contractor for damages. At trial, an expert witness testified that the hotel would have received $300,000 in income during that 30-day period and would have expended $200,000, leaving a total profit of $100,000.

How much should the contractor be required to pay to the hotelier in damages?

(A) $100,000, representing the hotelier's lost profits.

(B) $300,000, representing the hotelier's lost income.

(C) $3 million, representing damages provided in the contract.

(D) $3.1 million, representing damages provided in the contract plus lost profits.

Question 14

A small parish hired a contractor to build a school wing onto its church for a cost of $200,000 by August 31. The parties entered into a written contract that provided for five progress payments of $40,000 each at various stages of completion. On July 18, after the contractor had spent $160,000 on performance and received $120,000 in progress payments, he notified the parish that he was quitting the project because a more lucrative job came up. The parish hired some local laborers who did construction work for a living to finish the job by August 31 for $120,000, which was a reasonable price given the short notice.

Which of the following statements regarding the parties' remedies is correct?

(A) The parish can recover $80,000, the difference between the contract price and the total amount that was expended in construction of the wing.

(B) The parish can recover $40,000, the difference between the contract price and the total amount that the parish paid for construction of the wing.

(C) The contractor can recover $40,000, the difference between the amount it expended on performance and the amount it was paid, to prevent the parish's unjust enrichment.

(D) Neither party can recover anything, because the $40,000 extra that the parish had to pay to complete construction of the wing is offset by the $40,000 difference between the contractor's expenditures and the payments that the parish made to the contractor.

Question 15

On August 1, a buyer contracted to purchase a parcel of land from a seller at a price of $100,000. The written agreement required that the buyer deposit 5% of the purchase price (*i.e.,* $5,000) with the seller on August 1 and that, should the buyer fail to tender the remainder of the purchase price on or before September 15 (the appointed closing date), the $5,000 would be forfeited to the seller. On September 15, the buyer told the seller that he was no longer interested in purchasing the parcel and demanded a refund of his $5,000. The seller refused and sold the parcel the next day to a third party for $100,000. The buyer filed suit against the seller to recoup the $5,000 he had given the seller on August 1.

If the court rules in favor of the seller, it will be because:

(A) $5,000 constitutes reasonable damages for breach.

(B) The provision allowing the seller to keep the $5,000 was a valid penalty clause.

(C) The buyer's breach left him with no further rights in the $5,000.

(D) The risk of loss is on the buyer.

Question 16

A homeowner contracted with a builder for the remodeling of the homeowner's bathroom and kitchen at a cost of $10,000. The contract was in writing and specified that the work was to be completed within two months after the date of execution of the contract. Two weeks after entering into the contract with the homeowner, the builder was offered an extremely lucrative job that would take all of his time and effort for several months. The builder told the homeowner that he was not going to perform.

The homeowner diligently called many other contractors over a period of several weeks and none of them could offer a price anywhere near as low as $10,000 for the remodeling work that he wanted done. Two months after entering into the contract with the builder, the homeowner sued the builder for specific performance.

What is the likely result of the suit?

(A) The court will order specific performance, because the homeowner was ready and able to perform his part of the contract.

(B) The court will order specific performance, because, despite diligent efforts, the homeowner could find no one who could perform the desired services at a competitive price.

(C) The court will not order specific performance, because the doctrine of laches applies.

(D) The court will not order specific performance, because the remedy at law is adequate.

Question 17

A homeowner purchased a large recreational vehicle. Local ordinances in the homeowner's suburb prohibited residents from parking recreational vehicles on the street or in an open driveway, so the homeowner contacted a local contractor and explained his requirements for a garage. The contractor measured the vehicle and then entered into a written contract to build a garage for the homeowner at a price of $5,000, payable on completion of the job. When the garage was finished but before the contractor was paid, the homeowner drove the vehicle into the garage, only to discover that the garage was three inches too short to accommodate the vehicle. The homeowner was told that it would cost $4,000 to partially dismantle the garage and rebuild it to fit the vehicle. The homeowner refused to pay the contractor anything for the job. The contractor consulted with several independent real estate appraisers, and they all agreed that the garage had enhanced the value of the homeowner's property by $6,000.

If the contractor sues the homeowner, the contractor is likely to recover:

(A) $5,000, because a three-inch variation in length is, at most, a minor breach.

(B) $2,000, measured by the difference between the amount that the garage enhanced the value of the property and the cost to rebuild the garage to specifications.

(C) $1,000, measured by the difference between the contract price and the amount it would cost to rebuild the garage to specifications.

(D) Nothing, because the three-inch error was a material breach, and the contractor will be unable to successfully claim substantial performance.

CONTRACTS ANSWERS

Answer to Question 1

(A) No contract arose on September 2 because the realtor's offer expired on September 1, when the realtor did not receive the developer's acceptance. If a period of acceptance is stated in an offer, the offeree must accept within that period to create a contract. Failure to timely accept terminates the power of acceptance in the offeree (*i.e.*, a late acceptance will not be effective and will not create a contract). Under the mailbox rule, an acceptance generally is effective upon dispatch (*i.e.*, the acceptance creates a contract at the moment it is mailed or given to the delivery company). However, the mailbox rule does not apply where the offer states that acceptance will not be effective until received. In the latter case, acceptance is effective only upon receipt. Here, the realtor's offer specifically stated that the acceptance must be received by September 1 to be effective. Thus, the realtor opted out of the mailbox rule and no contract was created by delivery of the acceptance on September 2. Note that the developer will not be able to successfully argue that the acceptance was valid since the late delivery was the messenger company's fault. This would be a valid argument if the mailbox rule applied here, because the acceptance would have been effective on September 1, when the message was given to the messenger company. However, by opting out of the mailbox rule, the realtor put the burden of any negligence in delivery on the developer. Thus, there was no valid acceptance. (B) is incorrect because of the requirement that acceptance be ***received*** by September 1. This requirement obviates the general "mailbox rule," so that the mere mailing of a letter (or sending of a message) does not operate as an effective acceptance. (C) is incorrect because the realtor was not obligated to respond in any way to the message received on September 2. Once the specified time passed without receipt of acceptance, the offer (as well as the developer's power of acceptance) was terminated. Thus, receipt of the message on September 2 created neither a contract nor an obligation on the part of the realtor to respond to the message. (D) is incorrect because no contract, voidable or otherwise, arose on September 1. As explained above, there could be no contract because acceptance of the offer was not received as specified by the offer. Also, the facts do not indicate circumstances under which a contract is usually held to be voidable. A voidable contract is a contract that one or both parties may elect to avoid (*e.g.*, contracts of infants). The facts of this question provide no basis for concluding that any contract that might have arisen between these parties would be voidable.

Answer to Question 2

(D) The homeowner will likely prevail on the breach of contract claim because she did not enter into a contract with the gardener. To form a contract, there must be a valid offer and acceptance. The homeowner made an offer, but the gardener rejected the offer the next day with his first phone call. Once an offer is rejected, the offeree's power of acceptance is destroyed. Thus, the gardener's second call was not an acceptance, but rather a counteroffer. The homeowner did nothing to accept the gardener's counteroffer, and this is not the type of case where silence will be deemed to be an acceptance (*e.g.*, where the parties have so agreed or where that has been their course of dealing). Thus, there was no acceptance and no contract to breach. (A) is incorrect because an offeree cannot be forced to speak under penalty of having silence treated as an acceptance. If an offeree silently takes offered benefits, the courts will often find acceptance, especially if prior dealings between the parties, or trade practices known to both parties, create a commercially reasonable expectation by the offeror that silence represents an acceptance; in such cases, the offeree is under a duty to notify the offeror if she does not intend to accept. As discussed above, the gardener rejected the initial offer and made a counteroffer, putting the homeowner in the position of offeree. The homeowner's silence cannot be construed as acceptance absent a showing of prior dealings between the parties or trade practices known to both. Moreover, the gardener's last phone call to the homeowner was somewhat ambiguous, and the homeowner could argue that she did not know with certainty that the gardener would still perform the job after getting no response. Further, she was not home that weekend and, therefore, did not stand idly by and knowingly accept the gardener's work. (B) is incorrect because this was not a unilateral contract. A unilateral contract exists only when an offeror makes acceptance possible only by performing a stipulated act, whereas a bilateral contract contemplates an exchange of promises. Here, the homeowner asked the gardener whether he would perform an act and expected a reply from the gardener; indeed, the gardener told the homeowner that he would telephone her with his answer the next day, which he did (in effect, rejecting the offer). Thus, this was not a unilateral contract that could properly be accepted through performance. (C) is incorrect because the gardener's power of acceptance was destroyed when he rejected the homeowner's offer, as discussed above, and once that occurred, the offer was gone and could not be revoked.

Answer to Question 3

(C) The young man will prevail because he has performed under a valid contract. The parties entered into a valid unilateral contract: The father offered to give his son $5,000 if he did not smoke marijuana during his trip to Amsterdam; the son accepted by giving up something that he had a legal right to do under Amsterdam law. Thus, there was consideration on both sides. Because the young man performed his duties under the contract by refraining from smoking marijuana while in Amsterdam, the father's estate is bound to perform its duties and pay the young man. (A) is incorrect because a unilateral contract such as this one is accepted by performance rather than by a promise. (B) is incorrect because an offer will not be terminated by the death of the offeror if the offeror's power to revoke is limited by law, such as in the case of a valid unilateral contract. Here, the young man had begun performance (by refraining from smoking marijuana), making the offer irrevocable during the time he was given to complete performance. (D) is incorrect because it contemplates promissory estoppel, a remedy that is relied on to make a promise enforceable when it would otherwise be unenforceable because of insufficient consideration. Because there was sufficient consideration between the young man and his father, as discussed above, a promissory estoppel argument would not be appropriate here.

Answer to Question 4

(D) No, the coach will not be successful in his suit, because this was merely an offer for a unilateral contract that was revocable prior to acceptance, and the retailer did, in fact, revoke his offer before the retailer accepted. An offer for a unilateral contract is a promise to perform in exchange for a requested performance, and acceptance is achieved by that requested performance rather than by a return promise. Here, the retailer promised to sell the baseball card to the coach if the coach performed by tendering $2,000. Thus, the contract is unilateral and revocable prior to the offeree's performance. (A) is incorrect because the coach did not receive an option. An option is a promise to keep an offer open for an agreed-upon time and requires consideration except when the seller is a merchant. A merchant's signed writing giving assurances that the offer would be held open is not revocable during the time stated (or, if no time is stated, for a reasonable time not to exceed three months), even absent consideration. Under Article 2 of the U.C.C., a "merchant" is one who deals in the type of goods involved in the transaction, or who through his occupation has specialized knowledge of the business practices involved. Here, no consideration was given for the retailer's promise to keep the offer open, and the retailer is not a merchant.

Although he sells goods for a living, the retailer sells software, not baseball cards, and thus would not qualify as a merchant for purposes of this proposed sale. (B) is incorrect because termination of an offer does not have to be in writing. The reference to a sale of goods valued at more than $500 suggests that the Statute of Frauds is implicated here, but the Statute of Frauds requires a writing only for the sale contract and not for a revocation of the contract. (C) is incorrect because there is no ground for promissory estoppel here. Under the Second Restatement, a promise is enforceable (but limited as justice requires) if the promisor should reasonably expect to induce action or forebearance, and such action or forebearance is in fact induced. Here, the coach relied on the retailer's promise to sell him the baseball card only to the extent that he cleared off his mantel and built a little wooden stand on which to display the card. These actions involve an insignificant amount of effort and cost which, in any case, the retailer would not have foreseen. Thus, promissory estoppel is not applicable.

Answer to Question 5

(A) The contract is enforceable because the "mailbox rule" applies here. Acceptance by mail creates a contract at the ***moment of posting***, properly addressed and stamped, unless the offer stipulates that acceptance is not effective until received, or an option contract is involved. If the offeree sends an acceptance and then rejects the offer, the mailbox rule applies; *i.e.,* a contract is created upon dispatch of the acceptance. Because no option contract is involved here, and the seller's offer did not state that the buyer's acceptance would only be effective when received, the buyer's acceptance was effective the moment he placed the envelope containing the contract in the mailbox. The buyer's attempt to reject occurred after acceptance took place. Thus, a valid contract was formed and the seller may enforce it. (B) is incorrect because nothing in the parol evidence rule would serve to validate the contract. Ostensibly, this choice implies that there is a contract because the parol evidence rule will prevent the buyer from introducing evidence of the oral rescission. However, as discussed below, the rescission is ineffective because there was no meeting of the minds. The parol evidence rule would not prevent introduction of the rescission if it were otherwise valid. (C) is incorrect because there is no "meeting of the minds" concerning the rescission. A contract may be discharged by an express agreement between the parties to rescind; the agreement to rescind is itself a binding contract. Because the seller did not know that the buyer had accepted the contract, the seller's statement that "that's all right" cannot be construed as acceptance of the buyer's offer to rescind. Therefore, a contract to rescind was not formed. (D) is incorrect because the telephone rejection did not void the acceptance by mail. As discussed above, if the offeree sends an acceptance first, followed by a rejection, the mailbox rule applies; *i.e.,* a contract is created upon dispatch of the acceptance. Because the buyer's telephone rejection took place after his acceptance by mail, his acceptance was effective and a contract was created when the letter was mailed. While an ***offeree*** will be estopped from enforcing the contract if the offeror receives the rejection first and changes his position in reliance on it, the seller is the one wanting to enforce the contract here.

Answer to Question 6

(B) The contract was formed on May 2. An offer to buy goods for shipment is generally construed as inviting acceptance either by a promise to ship or by shipment. Here, the letter constitutes a promise to ship and thus is an acceptance. The rule for acceptances is that they are effective as soon as they are dispatched, which was May 2. Thus, (B) is correct, and (C) is wrong. (A) is wrong because the order was an offer, not an acceptance of the catalogue listing. Catalogues containing price quotations are generally construed as invitations to offer rather than offers. (D) is wrong because acceptance occurred before shipment; it occurred when the manufacturer sent its ***promise to ship***.

Answer to Question 7

(B) The manufacturer and the retailer have a contract without the liquidated damages clause. In contracts for the sale of goods, a definite expression of acceptance operates as an acceptance even if it states additional terms. Between merchants, additional terms proposed by the offeree in an acceptance automatically become part of the contract unless (i) they ***materially*** alter the original terms of the offer (*e.g.*, they change a party's risk or the remedies available); (ii) the offer expressly limits acceptance to the terms of the offer; or (iii) the offeror objects to the additional terms within a reasonable time. Here, a clause was added by the manufacturer (the offeree) providing for liquidated damages in the event of a breach. This additional term significantly changed the remedies available, and thus materially altered the original terms of the offer. Therefore, the liquidated damages clause would not become part of the contract. (A) is therefore incorrect. (C) is incorrect because it reflects the common law "mirror image" rule, which the U.C.C. has rejected in sale of goods cases. (D) is incorrect because under the U.C.C., the inclusion of a material additional term does not prevent formation of a contract; instead, a contract is formed without the inclusion of that additional term.

Answer to Question 8

(D) The breeder's letter is an acceptance, and the rancher may refuse to board the bull. The U.C.C. applies because the parties are merchants with respect to the sale of the bull. Under U.C.C. section 2-207, proposed new terms in a deal between merchants do not terminate the offer (*i.e.*, do not constitute a counteroffer) and they become part of the deal unless (i) the offer is limited to its own terms, (ii) the new terms materially alter the deal, or (iii) the offeror objects within a reasonable time. (D) is correct and (C) is incorrect because the breeder's proposal would materially alter the terms of the contract. (A) and (B) are wrong because the letter is not a counteroffer; it was an acceptance despite the additional terms.

Answer to Question 9

(C) While the singer clearly breached the contract, because he was under an absolute duty to perform and failed to do so, the club owner would only be entitled to cancel the contract if the breach is material (*i.e.,* if the nonbreaching party did not receive the substantial benefit of his bargain). If the breach is only minor, the nonbreaching party is not entitled to cancel the contract (although he will have an action for any damages suffered). Six factors that courts look at to determine materiality of breach are: (i) the amount of benefit the nonbreaching party received, (ii) adequacy of damages remedy, (iii) extent of part performance by breaching party, (iv) hardship to the breaching party, (v) whether the breaching party's behavior was negligent or willful, and (vi) likelihood of the breaching party's completing performance. Although the singer has not yet begun performance, his delay was only for 10 days and the contract was for a period of six months; also, the club owner has an adequate remedy for damages for the 10-day period. The singer's conduct does not appear to be negligent or willful, and he appears ready to perform the remainder of his contract. Thus, in the absence of facts indicating that the club owner was materially prejudiced by the singer's delay, the breach would be minor and the club owner could not cancel the contract. (A) is incorrect because it just establishes that a breach occurred. Whether the club owner may cancel depends on whether the breach is material or minor. (B) is incorrect because it goes too far. In the absence of the additional circumstance in choice (C), it appears that the breach was not material. (D) is incorrect not only because it is not entirely true (*i.e.,* notification on the same day performance was to begin probably did not give the club owner time to procure a substitute performance), but also because notification of delay, while perhaps indicating absence of willful behavior, is not itself one of the factors courts consider in determining materiality of breach.

Answer to Question 10

(D) The wholesaler will recover only its incidental damages, *i.e.,* the costs of preparing to ship the chairs. An offer calling for shipment of goods, such as the offer here, may be accepted by prompt shipment with notice or by a promise to ship. Acceptance forms a contract. Here, the wholesaler accepted the dealer's offer by promising to ship (the warning that the wholesaler had no more chairs was unimportant surplusage since it could fill the dealer's order), and a contract was formed. The dealer breached the contract by canceling its order. When a buyer breaches by repudiating its offer, as the dealer did here, the seller has a right to recover its incidental damages plus either the difference between the contract price and the market price or the difference between the contract price and the resale price of the goods. If neither measure is adequate to put the seller in as good a position as performance would have, she may recover lost profits. Here, the contract price was the same as both the resale price and the market price; thus, that measure of damages is not useful. Lost profits are not possible here because the wholesaler sold the chairs and they were the last ones it had and would have, since the line was discontinued. Therefore, the wholesaler lost no profits. It made what it would have made if the sale with the dealer had gone through. Thus, the wholesaler would be limited to its incidental damages under the first two measures of damages. (A) is incorrect because there is no rule under the U.C.C., which governs the contract here, that makes contracts between merchants cancelable within a reasonable time. (B) is incorrect because, as indicated above, the U.C.C. allows the seller to recover incidental damages. (C) is incorrect because the U.C.C. seeks only to put the nonbreaching party in as good a position as it would have been in had the other party performed, and here, awarding the wholesaler lost profits would put it in a better position than performance would have, since it would give the wholesaler a double recovery for selling the same goods. (The result would be different, however, if the wholesaler had had more chairs to sell, because in that case, the breach would have cost the wholesaler additional sales—*i.e.,* the wholesaler could have sold to the dealer ***and*** to the other party.)

Answer to Question 11

(D) The dealer will recover $3,000, which is the difference between its lost profits and the buyer's down payment. When the buyer repudiates or refuses to accept goods, the usual measure of the seller's damages is the difference between the contract price and the market price or the difference between the contract price and the resale price of the particular goods. However, neither of those measures of damages gives adequate compensation for the buyer's breach where the seller has an unlimited supply of the goods (*i.e.,* a lost volume seller), because, but for the buyer's breach, the seller would have made two sales instead of one. In this type of case, lost profit is measured by the contract price less the cost to the seller. Here, the dealer could have made two sales of that model of car because it could get as many as it needed from the manufacturer. Hence, it lost a profit of $9,000 as a result of the buyer's breach. This amount is offset against the amount of the down payment that the buyer made, resulting in a net recovery of $3,000 by the dealer. (A) is incorrect because the dealer did suffer damages as a result of the buyer's breach. (B) is wrong because it represents the down payment minus the difference between the contract price and the resale price for the goods. As discussed above, that does not adequately compensate the dealer for its damages from the buyer's breach. (C) is incorrect because $9,000 constitutes the dealer's lost profits from the buyer's breach, but it must be offset against the down payment that the dealer received from the buyer.

Answer to Question 12

(C) Under Article 2 of the U.C.C., an offer to buy goods for current or prompt shipment is construed as inviting acceptance either by a promise to ship or by current or prompt shipment. A shipment of nonconforming goods ordinarily is an acceptance creating a bilateral contract as well as a breach of that contract. The result is different if the seller seasonably notifies the buyer that a shipment of nonconforming goods is offered only as an accommodation to the buyer; in that case, the shipment is a counteroffer, not an acceptance and breach, and the buyer is free to accept it or reject it. (A) is incorrect because, as discussed above, the shipment constituted a counteroffer by the supplier, which the shop owner was obligated to wholly accept or reject. Choices (B) and (D) are incorrect because, without a valid contract, the shop owner cannot recover any damages from the supplier.

Answer to Question 13

(A) The hotelier will be able to recover $100,000, its lost profits. The purpose of contract damages is to put the nonbreaching party into as good a position as it would have been had the breaching party fully performed. This would be represented here by the hotelier's lost profits, which is its income ($300,000) minus its expenses ($200,000), or $100,000. The liquidated damages provision will not apply because it is unreasonable (*see* below). (B) is incorrect because giving the hotelier its $300,000 income would put it in a better position than it would have been in if the contractor had performed, because such an award does not take into account the expenses that the hotelier avoided by not being in operation. (C) is incorrect because a court would not uphold the liquidated damages clause here. Liquidated damages clauses are enforceable only if damages were difficult to estimate at the time the contract was formed, and the amount agreed upon is a reasonable forecast of the damages that would result from a breach. Here, the damages may have been difficult to predict when the contract was formed because it is not known just how well a new hotel will do; however, the amount agreed upon is too high. The facts indicate that a reasonable estimate at the time of the contract was about $10,000 per day, but since the liquidated damages amount ($100,000 per day) is 10 times that amount, this amount was unreasonable. (D) is incorrect because it seeks to combine the actual damages with the liquidated damages. Regardless of whether the liquidated damages clause will be enforced here, this measure is improper because a party may recover either liquidated damages, or, if not available, the actual damages, but not both.

Answer to Question 14

(B) The parish can recover $40,000, which is the amount above the contract price that it cost the parish to get the wing completed. In construction contracts, when the builder breaches after partially performing, the standard measure of damages to which the owner is entitled is the cost of completion plus reasonable compensation for any delay in performance (unless completion would involve undue economic waste). In addition, most courts allow the builder to offset or recover for work performed to date if necessary to avoid the unjust enrichment of the owner. Here, the cost of completion (the amount above the contract price that it cost to get the building completed) is $40,000, which was reasonable considering the deadline. No offset will be allowed for the reasons discussed in (C) and (D) below. Hence, the parish can recover $40,000. (A) is incorrect because the cost of completion is determined from the perspective of the owner, *i.e.*, how much additional money did the owner have to pay to have construction completed? Here, the owner (the parish) paid $40,000 more to have the wing completed than it would have paid had the contract been performed to completion. The parish would be unjustly enriched if it could recover another $40,000 beyond the damages it suffered. (C) and (D) are incorrect because the parish was not unjustly enriched by the additional amount that the contractor expended in performance over the progress payments that it received. The parish still had to pay $40,000 more than the contract amount for completion of the wing because of the contractor's breach. Thus, the parish received no windfall as a result of the contractor's additional expenditures.

Answer to Question 15

(A) The provision providing for forfeiture of the $5,000 is a liquidated damages provision. It will be enforceable if it is ***not*** a "penalty" but rather a reasonable estimate of damages for breach. (B) is incorrect because, if the provision is indeed a penalty, it will ***not*** be enforceable. (C) is incorrect because, although the buyer is in breach, the liquidated damages provision would not be enforceable if it were an invalid penalty; rather, the seller would recover only actual damages, which, on the facts, seem to be nil. (D) is incorrect because this is not a risk of loss problem. There is no "loss" in the sense of damage to the property or its value; rather, the issue is the enforceability of the liquidated damages provision in the contract.

Answer to Question 16

(D) Specific performance is available only when monetary damages are inadequate. The court will not order specific performance merely because the builder had a much lower price than anyone else. Instead, the court will require the nonbreaching party to hire a different contractor, and the builder would be liable for the difference between the new price for remodeling and the original $10,000 price. It should be noted that nothing indicates that the builder was hired for his unique talents; even if he were, specific performance would not be granted because of difficulties of supervision and a reluctance to force one person to work for another. Thus, (A) and (B) are incorrect. (C) is also incorrect. Laches is a defense that would be asserted by the builder, contending that the homeowner had not filed suit demanding specific performance in a timely fashion. However, the facts tell us that the homeowner diligently called other contractors for many weeks and sued the builder two months after the initial contract. Thus, the defense of laches does not apply.

Answer to Question 17

(C) The contractor will recover $1,000 in a restitution or quasi-contract action. Despite having built a garage, the contractor has breached the contract here. He was to build a garage that would fit the homeowner's recreational vehicle and the garage that he built is too short. Moreover, the breach was material, even though the garage was a mere three inches short, because the homeowner did not receive the substantial benefit of his bargain—a place for his vehicle. Therefore, the contractor cannot recover in contract and (A) is incorrect. Nevertheless, courts agree that where the breach is not willful, the contractor can recover on the failed contract in restitution or quasi-contract to prevent unjust enrichment. Here, it is clear that the breach was not willful. (D) is therefore incorrect. Regarding the amount of recovery, most courts would limit the recovery to the contract price (rather than the benefit received by the nonbreaching party), offset by the damages to the nonbreaching party (here, the $4,000 cost of rebuilding the garage as bargained for). Thus, (C) is correct and (B) is incorrect.

Criminal Law

Elements of a Crime
Accomplice Liability
Inchoate Offenses
Defenses
Property Offenses
Habitation Offenses

CRIMINAL LAW

INTRODUCTION: GENERAL APPROACH

The Multistate Examination directs examinees to answer questions according to "the generally accepted view" unless otherwise noted. In Criminal Law, the examiners may tell you the law to apply if there is no prevailing view. For example:

(i) The call of a question might tell you that the common law applies or that the state follows the Model Penal Code ("M.P.C.") approach;

(ii) A fact pattern may also include a statute that you are to apply to the facts;

(iii) Finally, a question might reference a well-known legal doctrine (*e.g.,* the Wharton rule or the *M'Naghten* test).

Note that if the examiners do not tell you whether the common law or a statutory version of the crime applies, it likely means that specific elements of the crime are not relevant to the question—for example, the question may concern whether voluntary intoxication is a defense to a crime, in which case the relevant factor is what type of mental state the crime requires, not other elements of the crime that may vary from jurisdiction to jurisdiction.

I. JURISDICTION AND GENERAL MATTERS

A. JURISDICTION

Generally, a state has jurisdiction over a crime if: any act constituting an element of the offense was committed in the state, an act outside the state caused a result in the state, the crime involved the neglect of a duty imposed by the law of the state, there was an attempt or conspiracy outside the state plus an act inside the state, or there was an attempt or conspiracy inside the state to commit an offense outside the state.

B. SOURCES OF CRIMINAL LAW

There is no federal common law of crimes; all federal crimes are statutory. A majority of the states retain common law crimes. The modern trend is to abolish common law crimes either expressly by statute or impliedly by the enactment of comprehensive criminal codes.

C. THEORIES OF PUNISHMENT

Theories justifying criminal punishment include incapacitation of the criminal, special deterrence of the criminal, general deterrence of others, retribution, rehabilitation, and education of the public.

D. CLASSIFICATION OF CRIMES

There are two classes of crimes: felonies and misdemeanors. Felonies are generally punishable by ***death or imprisonment for more than one year***; other crimes are misdemeanors.

E. VAGUENESS AND OTHER CONSTITUTIONAL LIMITATIONS

Due process requires that a criminal statute not be vague. There must be (i) ***fair warning*** (*i.e.,* a person of ordinary intelligence must be able to discern what is prohibited), and (ii) ***no arbitrary***

and discriminatory enforcement. The Constitution places two substantive limitations on both federal and state legislatures—no ex post facto laws and no bills of attainder.

F. INTERPRETATIONS OF CRIMINAL STATUTES

Criminal statutes are construed strictly in favor of defendants. If two statutes address the same subject matter but dictate different conclusions, the more specific statute will be applied rather than the more general. The more recently enacted statute will control an older statute. Under new comprehensive codes, crimes committed prior to the effective date of the new code are subject to prosecution and punishment under the law as it existed at the time the offense was committed.

G. MERGER

1. Common Law

At common law, if a person engaged in conduct constituting both a felony and a misdemeanor, she could be ***convicted*** only of the felony. The misdemeanor merged into the felony.

2. Modern Law—No Merger

There is no longer any merger ***except*** that one who solicits another to commit a crime may not be convicted of ***both the solicitation and the completed crime*** (if the person solicited does complete it). Similarly, a person who completes a crime after attempting it may not be convicted of ***both the attempt and the completed crime***. Conspiracy, however, does not merge with the completed offense (*e.g.,* one can be convicted of both robbery and conspiracy to commit robbery).

3. Rules Against Multiple Convictions for Same Transaction

Double jeopardy prohibits trial or conviction of a person for a lesser included offense if he has been put in jeopardy for the greater offense. However, a court can impose multiple punishments at a single trial where the punishments are for two or more statutorily defined offenses specifically intended by the legislature to carry ***separate punishments***, even though the offenses arise from the same transaction and constitute the same crime.

II. ESSENTIAL ELEMENTS OF A CRIME

A. ELEMENTS OF A CRIME

A crime almost always requires proof of a physical act (actus reus) and a mental state (mens rea), and concurrence of the act and mental state. It may also require proof of a result and causation (*i.e.,* that the act caused the harmful result).

B. PHYSICAL ACT

Defendant must have either performed a ***voluntary*** physical act or failed to act under circumstances imposing a legal duty to act. An act is a ***bodily movement***.

CMR **Exam Tip** Remember that the act must be ***voluntary***. In the past, the bar examiners have set up very unlikely scenarios to test this point—*e.g.,* they have an unconscious person shoot a victim. Don't be fooled by these odd facts; if the facts tell you that the defendant was unconscious, the act was not voluntary, and thus defendant cannot be convicted of a crime based on this act. (The

only exception to this rule would be if the defendant knew he was likely to become unconscious and commit the act, but this situation would have to be presented in the facts.)

1. **Omission as an "Act"**
Failure to act gives rise to liability only if:

(i) There is a ***specific duty to act*** imposed by law;

(ii) The ***defendant has knowledge*** of the facts giving rise to the duty to act; and

(iii) It is ***reasonably possible to perform*** the duty.

A legal duty to act can arise from a statute, contract, relationship between the defendant and the victim (*e.g.,* a parent has a duty to protect child from harm), voluntary assumption of care by the defendant for the victim, or the creation of peril for the victim by the defendant.

CMR Exam Tip For an omission to be a criminal act, there must be a ***duty*** to act. There is no general Good Samaritan law requiring people to help others in trouble. Thus, a defendant is not liable for the failure to help or rescue another person unless he has a duty to do so—no matter how easy it would have been to render help. Your moral outrage is not enough for a criminal conviction.

2. **Possession as an "Act"**
Criminal statutes that penalize the possession of contraband generally require only that the defendant have control of the item for a long enough period to have an opportunity to terminate the possession. Possession need not be exclusive to one person, and possession also may be "constructive," meaning that actual physical control need not be proved when the contraband is located in an area within the defendant's "dominion and control."

a. **State of Mind Requirement**
Absent a state of mind requirement in the statute, the defendant must be aware of his possession of the contraband, but he need not be aware of its illegality. However, many statutes add a state of mind element (*e.g.,* "knowingly") to possession crimes. Under such statutes, the defendant ordinarily must know the identity or nature of the item possessed. On the other hand, a defendant may not consciously avoid learning the true nature of the item possessed; knowledge or intent may be inferred from a combination of suspicion and indifference to the truth.

C. MENTAL STATE

1. **Specific Intent**
A crime may require not only the doing of an act, but also the doing of it with a specific intent or objective. The existence of a specific intent cannot be conclusively imputed from the mere ***doing*** of the act, but the ***manner*** in which the crime was committed may provide circumstantial evidence of intent. The major specific intent crimes and the intents they require are as follows:

a. ***Solicitation***: Intent to have the person solicited commit the crime.

b. ***Attempt***: Intent to complete the crime.

c. ***Conspiracy***: Intent to have the crime completed.

d. ***First degree premeditated murder***: Premeditation.

e. ***Assault***: Intent to commit a battery.

f. ***Larceny and robbery***: Intent to permanently deprive the other of his interest in the property taken.

g. ***Burglary***: Intent to commit a felony in the dwelling.

h. ***Forgery***: Intent to defraud.

i. ***False pretenses***: Intent to defraud.

j. ***Embezzlement***: Intent to defraud.

CMR **Exam Tip** Never forget that attempt is a ***specific intent*** crime—even when the crime attempted is not. Thus, although murder does not require a specific intent to kill (*i.e.,* recklessly disregarding a high risk to human life would be enough), attempted murder requires the specific ***intent to kill***. Without that intent, a defendant is not guilty of attempted murder.

Examples: 1) D intends to kill V but only wounds him. D had the requisite specific intent (*i.e.,* the intent to kill) and is guilty of attempted murder.

2) D intends to scare V by shooting V's hat off his head. If D's shot kills V, D is guilty of murder; but if V is merely wounded, D is not guilty of attempted murder. (D may, of course, be guilty of battery.)

2. Malice—Common Law Murder and Arson

The intent necessary for malice crimes (common law murder and arson) sounds like specific intent, but it is not as restrictive; it requires only a reckless disregard of an obvious or high risk that the particular harmful result will occur. Defenses to specific intent crimes (*e.g.,* voluntary intoxication) do not apply to malice crimes.

3. General Intent—Awareness of Factors Constituting Crime

Almost all crimes require at least "general intent," which is an awareness of all factors constituting the crime; *i.e.*, defendant must be aware that she is acting in the proscribed way and that any required attendant circumstances exist. The defendant need not be certain that all the circumstances exist; it is sufficient that she is aware of a high likelihood that they will occur.

a. Inference of Intent from Act

A jury may infer the required general intent merely from the doing of the act.

b. Transferred Intent

The defendant can be liable under the doctrine of transferred intent where she intends the harm that is actually caused, but to a different victim or object. Defenses and mitigating circumstances may also usually be transferred. The doctrine of transferred intent applies to homicide, battery, and arson. It does not apply to attempt.

Exam Tip A person found guilty of a crime on the basis of transferred intent is usually guilty of two crimes: the completed crime against the actual victim and attempt against the intended victim. Thus, if D intends to shoot and kill X, but instead shoots and kills V, D can be guilty of the murder of V (under the transferred intent doctrine) and the attempted murder of X.

c. **Motive Distinguished**
Motive is the reason or explanation for the crime; it is different from intent to commit the crime. Motive is immaterial to substantive criminal law.

4. **Strict Liability Offenses**
A strict liability or public welfare offense is one that does not require awareness of all of the factors constituting the crime; *i.e.,* the defendant can be found guilty from the mere fact that she committed the act. Common strict liability offenses are selling liquor to minors and statutory rape. Certain defenses, such as mistake of fact, are not available.

5. **Model Penal Code Analysis of Fault**
The M.P.C. eliminates the common law distinctions between general and specific intent and adopts the following categories of intent:

a. **Purposely, Knowingly, or Recklessly**
When a statute requires that the defendant act purposely, knowingly, or recklessly, a ***subjective standard*** is used.

1) **Purposely**
A person acts purposely when his ***conscious object*** is to engage in certain conduct or cause a certain result.

2) **Knowingly**
A person acts knowingly when he is ***aware*** that his conduct is of a particular nature or ***knows*** that his conduct will necessarily or very likely cause a particular result. Knowing conduct satisfies a statute requiring willful conduct.

3) **Recklessly**
A person acts recklessly when he ***knows*** of a ***substantial and unjustifiable risk*** and ***consciously disregards*** it. Mere realization of the risk is not enough. Thus, recklessness involves both objective ("unjustifiable risk") and subjective ("awareness") elements. Unless the statute specifies a different degree of fault or is a strict liability offense, the defendant must have acted at least recklessly to be criminally liable.

Exam Tip A criminal law question often asks you to interpret a statute. Check the language of the statute carefully for the mental state required for each material element of the crime, because whether a defendant is guilty often turns on that mental state. For example, if the statute requires that a defendant act "knowingly" (such as "knowingly selling guns to a felon"), the defendant will not be guilty if she did not have that knowledge (*e.g.,* did not know the purchaser was a felon). In interpreting a statute, also keep in mind that "willfully" is equivalent to "knowingly."

b. **Negligence**
A person acts negligently when he ***fails to be aware of a substantial and unjustifiable***

risk, where such failure is a substantial deviation from the standard of care. To determine whether a person acted negligently, an ***objective standard*** is used. However, it is not just the reasonable person standard that is used in torts. The defendant must have taken a very unreasonable risk.

6. Vicarious Liability Offenses

A vicarious liability offense is one in which a person without personal fault may nevertheless be held liable for the criminal conduct of another (usually an employee). The trend is to limit vicarious liability to regulatory crimes and to limit punishment to fines.

7. Enterprise Liability—Liability of Corporations and Associations

At common law, a corporation does not have capacity to commit crimes. Under modern statutes, corporations may be held liable for an act performed by: (i) an agent of the corporation acting within the scope of his office or employment; or (ii) a corporate agent high enough in hierarchy to presume his acts reflect corporate policy.

D. CONCURRENCE OF MENTAL FAULT WITH PHYSICAL ACT

The defendant must have had the intent necessary for the crime at the time he committed the act constituting the crime, and the intent must have actuated the act. For example, if D is driving to V's house to kill him, he will lack the necessary concurrence for murder if he ***accidentally*** runs V over before reaching the house.

E. CAUSATION

Some crimes (*e.g.,* homicide) require result and causation.

III. ACCOMPLICE LIABILITY

A. PARTIES TO A CRIME

1. Common Law

At common law, parties to a crime included the ***principal in the first degree*** (person who actually engaged in the act or omission that constitutes the offense or who caused an innocent agent to do so), ***principal in the second degree*** (person who aided, commanded, or encouraged the principal and was present at the crime), ***accessory before the fact*** (person who assisted or encouraged but was ***not present***), and ***accessory after the fact*** (person who, with knowledge that the other committed a felony, assisted him to escape arrest or punishment). At common law, conviction of the principal was required for conviction of an accessory and the charge must have indicated the correct theory of liability (*i.e.,* as principal or accessory).

2. Modern Statutes

Most jurisdictions have abolished the distinctions between principals in the first degree and principals in the second degree or accessories before the fact. All such "parties to the crime" can be found guilty of the principal offense. For convenience, however, think of the one who actually engages in the act (either personally or through an innocent agent) or omission as the principal and the other parties as accomplices.

Note: An accessory after the fact (one who assists another knowing that he has committed a felony in order to help him escape) is still treated separately. Punishment for this crime usually bears no relationship to the principal offense.

B. MENTAL STATE—INTENT REQUIRED

To be guilty as an accomplice, most jurisdictions require that the person give aid, counsel, or encouragement to the principal with the ***intent*** to encourage the crime. In the absence of a statute, most courts would hold that ***mere knowledge*** that a crime will result is not enough, at least where the aid given is in the form of the sale of ordinary goods at ordinary prices (*e.g.,* a gas station attendant will not be liable for arson for knowingly selling a gallon of gasoline to an arsonist). However, procuring an illegal item or selling at a higher price because of the buyer's purpose (*e.g.,* charging the arsonist $100 for the gallon of gas) may constitute a sufficient "stake in the venture" to constitute intent.

C. SCOPE OF LIABILITY

An accomplice is responsible for the crimes he did or counseled ***and*** for any other crimes committed in the course of committing the crime contemplated to the same extent as the principal, as long as the other crimes were ***probable or foreseeable***.

1. Inability to Be Principal No Bar to Accomplice Liability

One who may not be convicted of being a principal may be convicted of being an accomplice. *Example:* At common law a woman cannot be convicted of being the principal in a rape but can be found guilty as an accomplice if she aids the principal.

2. Exclusions from Liability

a. Members of the Protected Class

Members of the class protected by a statute are excluded from accomplice liability. *Example:* A woman transported across state lines cannot be an accomplice to the crime of transporting women across state lines for immoral purposes, since she is within the class protected.

b. Necessary Parties Not Provided For

A party necessary to the commission of a crime, by statutory definition, who is not provided for in the statute is excluded from accomplice liability. *Example:* If a statute makes the sale of heroin illegal, but does not provide for punishment of the purchaser, he cannot be found guilty under the statute as an accomplice to the seller.

c. Withdrawal

A person who effectively withdraws from a crime before it is committed cannot be held guilty as an accomplice. Withdrawal must occur ***before*** the crime becomes unstoppable.

(i) ***Repudiation*** is sufficient withdrawal for mere encouragement.

(ii) ***Attempt to neutralize*** assistance is required if participation went beyond mere encouragement.

Notifying the police or taking other action to prevent the crime is also sufficient.

IV. INCHOATE OFFENSES

A. SOLICITATION

1. Elements

Solicitation consists of ***inciting*, *counseling*, *advising*, *urging*, *or commanding*** another to commit a crime, with the ***intent that the person solicited commit the crime***. It is not necessary that the person solicited respond affirmatively.

2. Defenses

It is not a defense that the person solicited is not convicted, nor that the offense solicited could not in fact have been successful. In most jurisdictions, it is not a defense that the solicitor renounces or withdraws the solicitation. The M.P.C. recognizes renunciation as a defense if the defendant prevents the commission of the crime, such as by persuading the person solicited not to commit the crime. However, it ***is a defense*** that the solicitor could not be found guilty of the completed crime because of a legislative intent to exempt her (*e.g.,* a woman cannot be found guilty of soliciting a man to transport her across state lines for immoral purposes).

3. Merger

If the person solicited commits the crime solicited, both that person and the solicitor can be held liable for that crime. If the person solicited commits acts sufficient to be liable for attempt, both parties can be liable for attempt. If the person solicited agrees to commit the crime, but does not even commit acts sufficient for attempt, both parties can be held liable for conspiracy. However, under the doctrine of merger, the solicitor ***cannot be punished for both*** the solicitation and these other offenses.

B. CONSPIRACY

A conspiracy is an agreement between two or more parties to commit a crime.

1. Elements

A conspiracy requires (i) an ***agreement*** between two or more persons; (ii) an ***intent to enter into the agreement***; and (iii) an ***intent*** by at least two persons ***to achieve the objective of the agreement***. A majority of states now also require an ***overt act***, but an act of mere preparation will suffice.

CMR **Exam Tip** Conspiracy is probably the most tested inchoate crime. One important thing for you to remember is that it takes two to conspire at common law. Make sure that the facts of a question show at least two "guilty minds"—two people who intend to agree ***and*** intend that the crime be committed. Thus, if the defendant and an undercover police officer "agree" to commit a crime, there is no conspiracy at common law because only the defendant intended that the crime be committed. Similarly, if the defendant and another person "agree" but the facts show that the other person merely pretended to go along and really meant to warn the police, there is no conspiracy.

a. Agreement Requirement

The parties must agree to accomplish the same objective by mutual action. However, the agreement need not be express; it may be inferred from joint activity.

1) Implications of Requirement of Two or More Parties

A conspiracy at common law must involve a "meeting of minds" between at least two independent persons. This requirement presents the following issues:

a) **Husband and Wife**
At common law, a husband and wife could not conspire together, but this distinction has been abandoned in most states.

b) **Corporation and Agent**
There can be no conspiracy between a corporation and a single agent acting on its behalf. There is a split of authority as to whether the agents of a corporation can be deemed co-conspirators with the corporation.

c) **Wharton Rule**
Under the Wharton Rule, where two or more people are necessary for the commission of the substantive offense (*e.g.*, adultery, dueling), there is no crime of conspiracy unless ***more parties participate*** in the agreement than are necessary for the crime (*e.g.,* because it takes two people to commit adultery, it takes three people to conspire to commit adultery). *Exception:* The Wharton Rule does not apply to agreements with "necessary parties not provided for" by the substantive offense; both parties may be guilty of conspiracy even though both are necessary for commission of the substantive offense.

d) **Agreement with Person in "Protected Class"**
If members of a conspiracy agree to commit a crime designed to protect persons within a given class, persons within that class cannot be guilty of the crime itself or of conspiracy to commit that crime. Likewise, the nonprotected person cannot be guilty of conspiracy if the agreement was with the protected person only.

e) **Effect of Acquittal of Some Conspirators**
Under the traditional view, the ***acquittal*** of all persons with whom a defendant is alleged to have conspired precludes conviction of the remaining defendant. In some jurisdictions following the traditional view, a conviction for conspiracy against one defendant is allowed to stand when the alleged co-conspirator is acquitted in a ***separate trial***.

CMR Exam Tip Acquittal is the key here. If the defendant and others allegedly conspired and only the defendant is charged and tried (*e.g.,* the other parties are not apprehended or not prosecuted), the defendant can be convicted. But if the defendant is charged and tried and ***all the others have been acquitted***, the defendant cannot be convicted. (The acquittals show that there was no one with whom the defendant could conspire.)

f) **Model Penal Code Unilateral Approach**
Under the M.P.C. "unilateral" approach, the defendant can be convicted of conspiracy regardless of whether the other parties have all been acquitted or were only feigning agreement.

b. **Mental State—Specific Intent**
Conspiracy is a specific intent crime. Parties must have: (i) the intent to ***agree*** and (ii) the intent to ***achieve the objective*** of the conspiracy.

c. **Overt Act**
At common law, the conspiracy was complete when the agreement with the requisite intent was reached. Most states now require that an act in furtherance of the conspiracy be performed. An act of mere preparation is usually sufficient.

2. **Liability for Co-Conspirators' Crimes**
A conspirator may be held liable for crimes committed by other conspirators if the crimes (i) were committed ***in furtherance*** of the objectives of the conspiracy and (ii) were ***foreseeable.***

3. **Termination of Conspiracy**
The point at which a conspiracy terminates is important because acts and statements of co-conspirators are admissible against a conspirator only if they were done or made in furtherance of the conspiracy. A conspiracy usually terminates ***upon completion of the wrongful objective***. Unless agreed to in advance, acts of concealment are ***not*** part of the conspiracy. Note also that the government's defeat of the conspiracy's objective does not automatically terminate the conspiracy.

4. **Defenses**

a. **Factual Impossibility**
Factual impossibility is ***not*** a defense to conspiracy.

b. **Withdrawal**
Generally, withdrawal from the conspiracy is ***not*** a defense ***to the conspiracy***, because the conspiracy is complete as soon as the agreement is made and an act in furtherance is performed. Withdrawal ***may*** be a defense to ***crimes committed in furtherance*** of the conspiracy, including the substantive target crime of the conspiracy.

1) **When Withdrawal Effective**
To withdraw, a conspirator must perform an affirmative act that notifies all members of the conspiracy of her withdrawal. Notice must be given in time for the members to abandon their plans. If she has also provided assistance as an accomplice, she must try to neutralize the assistance.

CMR **Exam Tip** Withdrawal from a conspiracy is another important test issue. You must be careful here not to let your feelings get in the way of a correct answer. Remember that a conspiracy is complete upon the agreement with the requisite intent and an overt act. Since the overt act can be a preparatory act, the conspiracy is usually complete very soon after the agreement. If the crime is complete, the defendant is ***guilty of conspiracy***—even if the facts show that she had second thoughts, told her co-conspirators that she was backing out, warned the police, hid the weapons, etc. These actions come too late; defendant is guilty of conspiracy. (Such actions may relieve defendant of criminal liability for her co-conspirators' acts after this withdrawal, but they have no effect on the crime of conspiracy.)

5. **Punishment—No Merger**
Conspiracy and the completed crime are distinct offenses; *i.e.*, there is no merger. A defendant may be convicted of and punished for both.

6. **Number of Conspiracies in Multiple Party Situations**
In complex situations, there may be a large conspiracy with a number of subconspiracies. In

such situations, it is important to determine whether members of one subconspiracy are liable for the acts of another subconspiracy. The two most common situations are:

a. **Chain Relationship**
A chain relationship is a single, large conspiracy in which all parties to subagreements are interested in the single large scheme. In this case, all members are liable for the acts of the others in furtherance of the conspiracy.

b. **Hub-and-Spoke Relationship**
In a hub-and-spoke relationship a number of independent conspiracies are linked by a common member. Although the common member will be liable for all of the conspiracies, members of the individual conspiracies are not liable for the acts of the other conspirators.

C. ATTEMPT

1. Elements
Attempt is an act, done with ***intent to commit a crime***, that ***falls short of completing*** the crime.

a. **Mental State**
To be guilty of attempt, the defendant must intend to perform an act and obtain a result that, if achieved, would constitute a crime. Regardless of the intent necessary for the completed offense, an attempt ***always requires a specific intent*** (*i.e.,* the intent to commit the crime). *Example:* To be guilty of attempt to commit murder, defendant must have had the specific ***intent to kill*** another person, even though the mens rea for murder itself does not necessarily require a specific intent to kill.

Exam Tip Attempt to commit a crime defined as the negligent production of a result (*e.g.,* negligent homicide) is logically impossible because a person does not intend to be negligent. Thus, there can be no attempted negligent homicide, etc.

b. **Overt Act**
Defendant must commit an act ***beyond mere preparation*** for the offense. Traditionally, most courts followed the "***proximity***" ***test***, which requires that the act be "dangerously close" to successful completion of the crime (*e.g.,* pointing a loaded gun at an intended victim and pulling the trigger, only to have the gun not fire or the bullet miss its mark is sufficient). However, today most state criminal codes (and the Model Penal Code) require that the act or omission constitute a "***substantial step*** in a course of conduct planned to culminate in the commission of the crime" that strongly corroborates the actor's criminal purpose.

Exam Tip Note that the overt act required for attempt is much more substantial than the overt act required for conspiracy.

2. Defenses

a. **Impossibility of Success**
Legal impossibility arises only when the defendant did, or intended to do, acts that

would not constitute a crime under any circumstances. So defined, ***all*** states (and the M.P.C.) will recognize this as a defense. ***Factual impossibility***—that it would be factually impossible for the defendant to complete his plan (*e.g.,* a robbery victim who has no property)—is not a defense.

CMR **Exam Tip** If you get stumped on a question that asks you to decide whether impossibility is a defense, ask yourself: "If the defendant were able to complete all of the acts that he intended to do, and if all of the attendant circumstances actually were as the defendant believed them to be, would the defendant have committed a crime?" The answer usually will be yes, in which case the impossibility is factual and not a defense. In the unusual case where the answer is no, the defendant most likely has a legal impossibility defense.

b. Abandonment

Abandonment is ***not*** a defense at common law. If the defendant had the intent and committed an overt act, she is guilty of attempt despite the fact that she changed her mind and abandoned the plan before the intended crime was completed. The M.P.C. provides that a ***fully voluntary*** and ***complete*** abandonment is a defense.

3. Prosecution for Attempt

A defendant charged only with a completed crime may be found guilty of the completed crime ***or*** an attempt, but a defendant charged only with attempt may ***not*** be convicted of the completed crime.

V. RESPONSIBILITY AND CRIMINAL CAPACITY

A. INSANITY

There are several formulations of the test to be applied to determine whether, at the time of the crime, the defendant was so mentally ill as to be entitled to acquittal.

1. *M'Naghten* Rule

Under this rule, a defendant is entitled to acquittal only if he had a mental disease or defect that caused him to either: (i) ***not know that his act would be wrong***; or (ii) ***not understand the nature and quality of his actions***. Loss of control because of mental illness is no defense.

2. Irresistible Impulse Test

Under this test, a defendant is entitled to acquittal only if, because of a mental illness, he was ***unable to control his actions or conform his conduct to the law***.

3. *Durham* (or New Hampshire) Test

Under this test, a defendant is entitled to acquittal if the ***crime was the product of his mental illness*** (*i.e.,* crime would not have been committed but for the disease). The *Durham* test is broader than either the *M'Naghten* test or the irresistible impulse test.

4. A.L.I. or Model Penal Code Test

Under the M.P.C. test (which represents the "modern trend"), a defendant is entitled to acquittal if he had a mental disease or defect, and, as a result, he ***lacked the substantial capacity*** to either:

(i) ***Appreciate the criminality*** of his conduct; or

(ii) ***Conform his conduct*** to the requirements of law.

CMR **Exam Tip** It is important to know these separate insanity tests because questions may ask you about a specific test (*e.g.,* "If the jurisdiction has adopted the M.P.C. test for determining insanity, what is defendant's best argument for acquittal on this ground?"). To answer this type of question, you must know the requirements for that particular test. A shorthand way to remember the test is:

M'Naghten—defendant does ***not know right from wrong***;

Irresistible Impulse—(as the name says) an ***impulse*** that defendant ***cannot resist***;

Durham—***but for the mental illness***, defendant would not have done the act;

A.L.I. or M.P.C.—***combination*** of *M'Naghten* and irresistible impulse.

5. Procedural Issues

a. Burdens of Proof
All defendants are presumed sane; the defendant must raise the insanity issue. There is a split among the jurisdictions as to whether the defendant raising the issue bears the burden of proof.

b. When Defense May Be Raised
Although the insanity defense may be raised at the arraignment when the plea is taken, the defendant need not raise it then. A simple "not guilty" at that time does not waive the right to raise the defense at some future time.

c. Pretrial Psychiatric Examination
If the defendant does ***not*** raise the insanity issue, he ***may*** refuse a court-ordered psychiatric examination to determine his competency to stand trial. If the defendant ***raises*** the insanity issue, he may ***not*** refuse to be examined by a psychiatrist appointed to aid the court in the resolution of his insanity plea.

6. Post-Acquittal Commitment to Mental Institution
In most jurisdictions, a defendant acquitted by reason of insanity may be committed to a mental institution until cured. Confinement may exceed the maximum period of incarceration for the offense charged.

7. Mental Condition During Criminal Proceedings
Under the Due Process Clause of the United States Constitution, a defendant may not be tried, convicted, or sentenced if, as a result of a mental disease or defect, he is unable (i) to understand the nature of the proceedings being brought against him; or (ii) to assist his lawyer in the preparation of his defense. A defendant may not be executed if he is incapable of understanding the nature and purpose of the punishment.

8. Diminished Capacity

Some states recognize the defense of "diminished capacity" under which defendant may assert that as a result of a mental defect short of insanity, he did not have the mental state required for the crime charged. Most states allowing the diminished capacity defense limit it to specific intent crimes, but a few states allow it for general intent crimes as well.

B. INTOXICATION

Intoxication may be caused by any substance (*e.g.,* drugs, alcohol, medicine). It may be raised whenever intoxication negates one of the elements of the crime. The law usually distinguishes between voluntary and involuntary intoxication.

1. Voluntary Intoxication

Intoxication is voluntary if it is the result of the intentional taking without duress of a substance known to be intoxicating.

a. Defense to Specific Intent Crimes

Evidence of "voluntary" intoxication may be offered by defendant only if the crime requires ***purpose* (*intent*) *or knowledge***, and the intoxication prevented the defendant from formulating the purpose or obtaining the knowledge. Thus, it is often a good defense to ***specific intent*** crimes. The defense is not available if the defendant purposely becomes intoxicated in order to establish the defense.

b. No Defense to Other Crimes

Voluntary intoxication is no defense to crimes involving malice, recklessness, negligence, or strict liability. For this reason, voluntary intoxication will not reduce second degree murder (requiring criminal recklessness) to manslaughter.

2. Involuntary Intoxication

Intoxication is involuntary only if it results from the taking of an intoxicating substance ***without knowledge*** of its nature, ***under direct duress*** imposed by another, or ***pursuant to medical advice*** while unaware of the substance's intoxicating effect. Involuntary intoxication may be treated as a mental illness, and the defendant is entitled to acquittal if she meets the jurisdiction's insanity test.

3. Relationship to Insanity

Continuous, excessive drinking or drug use may bring on actual insanity and thus a defendant may be able to claim both an intoxication defense and an insanity defense.

C. INFANCY

At common law, there could be no liability for an act committed by a child under age seven. For acts committed by a child between ages seven and 14, there was a rebuttable presumption that the child was unable to understand the wrongfulness of his acts. Children age 14 or older were treated as adults. Modern statutes often modify this and provide that no child can be convicted of a crime until a stated age is reached, usually 13 or 14. However, children can be found to be delinquent in special juvenile or family courts.

VI. PRINCIPLES OF EXCULPATION

A. JUSTIFICATION

The justification defenses arise when society has deemed that although the defendant committed a proscribed act, she should not be punished because the circumstances justify the action.

Exam Tip The right to self-defense or other justification defenses depends on the immediacy of the threat; a threat of future harm is not sufficient. Thus, if someone threatens the defendant by saying, "Tomorrow I'm going to kill you," the defendant is ***not justified*** in killing the person to "protect" himself.

Exam Tip It is crucial to determine the level of force that the defendant used in committing the proscribed act. As a rule of thumb, ***nondeadly force*** is justified where it appears necessary to avoid imminent injury or to retain property; ***deadly force*** is justified only to prevent death or serious bodily injury.

1. Self-Defense

a. Nondeadly Force

A person without fault may use such force as ***reasonably appears necessary*** to protect herself from the imminent use of unlawful force upon herself. There is no duty to retreat.

b. Deadly Force

A person may use deadly force in self-defense if (i) she is without fault; (ii) she is confronted with "unlawful force"; and (iii) she is threatened with imminent death or great bodily harm.

Exam Tip If the defendant kills in self-defense but not all three of the requirements for the use of deadly force are met, some states would find the defendant guilty of manslaughter rather than murder under the "imperfect self-defense" doctrine.

1) Retreat

Generally, there is no duty to retreat before using deadly force. The minority view requires retreat before using deadly force if the victim can safely do so, ***unless***: (i) the attack occurs in the victim's home, (ii) the attack occurs while the victim is making a lawful arrest, or (iii) the assailant is in the process of robbing the victim.

c. Right of Aggressor to Use Self-Defense

If one is the aggressor in the altercation, she may use force in defense of herself only if (i) she ***effectively withdraws*** from the altercation and ***communicates*** to the other her desire to do so, ***or*** (ii) the victim of the initial aggression ***suddenly escalates*** the minor fight into a deadly altercation and the initial aggressor has no chance to withdraw.

2. Defense of Others

A defendant has the right to defend others if she reasonably believes that the person assisted has the legal right to use force in his own defense. All that is necessary is the ***reasonable appearance*** of the right to use force. Generally, there need be no special relationship between the defendant and the person in whose defense she acted.

3. **Defense of a Dwelling**
Nondeadly force may be used to prevent or terminate what is reasonably regarded as an unlawful entry into or attack on the defender's dwelling. ***Deadly force*** may be used only to prevent a violent entry made with the intent to commit a personal attack on an inhabitant, or to prevent an entry to commit a felony in the dwelling.

CMR **Exam Tip** As a practical matter, deadly force usually is justified in repelling a home invader but the basis for the right to use such force is ***not*** to protect the dwelling, but to protect the safety of the inhabitants of the dwelling.

4. **Defense of Other Property**

   a. **Defending Possession**
   Deadly force may never be used in defense of property. ***Nondeadly force*** may be used to defend property in one's possession from unlawful interference, but may not be used if a request to desist or refrain from the activity would suffice.

   b. **Regaining Possession**
   Force ***cannot*** be used to regain possession of property wrongfully taken unless the person using force is in immediate pursuit of the taker.

5. **Crime Prevention**
Nondeadly force may be used to the extent that it reasonably appears necessary to prevent a felony or serious breach of the peace. ***Deadly force*** may be used only to terminate or prevent a dangerous felony involving risk to human life.

6. **Use of Force to Effectuate Arrest**
Nondeadly force may be used by police officers if it reasonably appears necessary to effectuate an arrest. ***Deadly force*** is reasonable only if it is necessary to prevent a felon's escape ***and*** the felon threatens death or serious bodily harm.

   a. **Private Persons**
   A private person has a privilege to use ***nondeadly force*** to make an arrest if a ***crime was in fact committed*** and the private person has ***reasonable grounds to believe*** the person arrested has in fact committed the crime. A private person may use ***deadly force only if*** the person harmed was ***actually guilty*** of the offense for which the arrest was made.

7. **Resisting Arrest**
Nondeadly force may be used to resist an improper arrest even if a known officer is making that arrest. ***Deadly force*** may be used, however, only if the person does not know that the person arresting him is a police officer.

8. **Necessity**
It is a defense to a crime that the person ***reasonably believed*** that commission of the crime was necessary to avoid an imminent and greater injury to society than that involved in the crime. The test is objective; a good faith belief is not sufficient.

   a. **Limitation—Death**
   Causing the death of another person to protect property is ***never justified***.

b. **Limitation—Fault**
The defense of necessity is not available if the defendant is at fault in creating the situation requiring that he choose between two evils.

c. **Duress Distinguished**
Necessity involves pressure from natural or physical forces; duress involves a human threat (*see* B., *infra*).

9. **Public Policy**
A police officer (or one assisting him) is justified in using reasonable force against another, or in taking property, provided the officer acts pursuant to a law, court order, or process requiring or authorizing him to so act.

10. **Domestic Authority**
The parents of a minor child, or any person "in loco parentis" with respect to that child, may lawfully use reasonable force upon the child for the purpose of promoting the child's welfare.

B. **EXCUSE OF DURESS**
It is a defense to a crime ***other than a homicide*** that the defendant reasonably believed that another person would imminently inflict death or great bodily harm upon him or a member of his family if he did not commit the crime.

C. **OTHER DEFENSES**

1. **Mistake or Ignorance of Fact**
Mistake or ignorance of fact is relevant to criminal liability only if it shows that the defendant ***lacked the state of mind required*** for the crime; thus, it is irrelevant if the crime imposes "strict" liability.

a. **Reasonableness**
If mistake is offered to "disprove" a ***specific intent***, the mistake ***need not be reasonable***; however, if it is offered to disprove any other state of mind, it ***must have been reasonable*** mistake or ignorance.

CMR **Exam Tip** Don't confuse the defense of mistake of fact with the issue of factual impossibility, discussed earlier. Even though in both situations defendant is mistaken about certain facts, the results are different. ***Mistake*** is usually raised as a defense to a crime that has been completed; mistake of fact may negate the intent required for the crime. ***Impossibility*** arises only when defendant has ***failed*** to complete the crime because of his mistaken belief about the facts, and is being charged with an ***attempt*** to commit the crime; factual impossibility is ***not*** a defense to attempt.

2. **Mistake or Ignorance of Law—No Defense**
Generally, it is not a defense that the defendant believed that her activity would not be a crime, even if that belief was reasonable and based on the advice of an attorney. However, if the reliance on the attorney negates a necessary mental state element, such reliance can demonstrate that the government has not proved its case beyond a reasonable doubt.

a. **Exceptions**
The defendant has a defense if: (i) the statute proscribing her conduct was not published or made reasonably available prior to the conduct; (ii) there was reasonable reliance on a statute or judicial decision; or (iii) in some jurisdictions, there was reasonable reliance on official interpretation or advice.

b. **Ignorance of Law May Negate Intent**
If the defendant's mistake or ignorance as to a collateral legal matter proves that she lacked the state of mind required for the crime, she is entitled to acquittal. The ignorance or mistake must involve the ***elements*** of the crime, ***not the existence*** of a statute making the act criminal. For example, a defendant cannot be found guilty of selling a gun to a known felon if she thought that the crime the buyer had been found guilty of was only a misdemeanor.

3. **Consent**
Unless the crime requires the lack of consent of the victim (*e.g.,* rape), consent is usually ***not*** a defense. Consent is a defense to minor assaults or batteries if there is no danger of serious bodily injury. Whenever consent may be a defense, it must be established that: (i) the consent was ***voluntarily and freely given***; (ii) the party was ***legally capable*** of consenting; and (iii) ***no fraud*** was involved in obtaining the consent.

4. **Condonation or Criminality of Victim—No Defense**
Forgiveness by the victim is no defense. Likewise, the nearly universal rule is that illegal conduct by the victim of a crime is no defense.

5. **Entrapment**
Entrapment exists only if (i) the ***criminal design originated with law enforcement officers*** and (ii) the defendant was ***not predisposed*** to commit the crime prior to contact by the government. Merely providing the opportunity for a predisposed person to commit a crime is not entrapment.

a. **Unavailable—If Private Inducement or If Material for Crime Provided by Government Agent**
A person cannot be entrapped by a private citizen. Under federal law, an entrapment defense cannot be based on the fact that a government agent provided an ingredient for commission of the crime (*e.g.,* ingredients for drugs), even if the material provided was contraband.

Exam Tip Entrapment is a difficult defense to establish in court and so too on the MBE. In fact, on the exam, the defendant is usually predisposed to commit the crime and thus entrapment usually is a wrong choice.

VII. PROPERTY OFFENSES

A. LARCENY
Larceny consists of:

(i) ***A taking*** (obtaining control);

(ii) ***And carrying away*** (asportation);

(iii) ***Of tangible personal property*** (excluding realty, services, and intangibles, but including written instruments embodying intangible rights such as stock certificates);

(iv) ***Of another*** with possession;

(v) ***By trespass*** (without consent or by consent induced by fraud);

(vi) ***With intent to permanently deprive*** that person of her interest in the property.

1. Possession

The property must be taken from the possession of another. If the ***defendant*** had possession of the property at the time of the taking, the crime is not larceny, but may be embezzlement.

a. Custody vs. Possession

Possession involves a greater scope of authority to deal with the property than does custody. Ordinarily, low level employees have only custody of an employer's property and so are guilty of larceny for taking it. A bailee, on the other hand, has a greater scope of authority over an owner's property and so is not guilty of larceny for taking it, but may be guilty of embezzlement.

2. Intent to Permanently Deprive

Generally, larceny requires that ***at the time of the taking*** defendant intended to permanently deprive a person of her property.

a. Sufficient Intent

An intent to create a substantial risk of loss, or an intent to sell or pledge the goods to the owner, is sufficient for larceny.

b. Insufficient Intent

Where the defendant believes that the property she is taking is hers or where she intends only to borrow the property or to keep it as repayment of a debt, there is no larceny.

c. Possibly Sufficient Intent

There ***may be*** larceny where the defendant intends to pay for the goods (***if*** the goods were not for sale) or intends to collect a reward from the owner (***if*** there is no intent to return the goods absent a reward).

CMR Exam Tip For a larceny question, be sure that the defendant had the intent to permanently deprive ***when she took the property***. If not, there is no larceny (unless it is a continuing trespass situation (*see* 4., *infra*)). Many questions turn on this one small point.

3. Abandoned, Lost, or Mislaid Property

Larceny can be committed with lost or mislaid property or property that has been delivered by mistake, but not with abandoned property.

4. "Continuing Trespass" Situation

If the defendant ***wrongfully*** takes property ***without*** the intent to permanently deprive (*e.g.,* without permission borrows an umbrella), and later decides to keep the property, she is guilty of larceny when she decides to keep it. However, if the original taking was ***not wrongful*** (*e.g.,* she took the umbrella thinking it was hers) and she later decides to keep it, it is not larceny.

B. EMBEZZLEMENT

Embezzlement is:

(i) The ***fraudulent***;

(ii) ***Conversion*** (*i.e.,* dealing with the property in a manner inconsistent with the arrangement by which defendant has possession);

(iii) Of ***personal property***;

(iv) Of ***another***;

(v) By a person ***in lawful possession*** of that property.

1. Distinguish from Larceny

Embezzlement differs from larceny because in embezzlement the defendant misappropriates property while it is in his rightful possession, while in larceny the defendant misappropriates property not in his possession.

2. Fraudulent Intent

Defendant must intend to defraud.

a. Intent to Restore

If the defendant intends to restore the ***exact*** property taken, it is ***not*** embezzlement. However, if the defendant intends to restore similar or substantially identical property, it is embezzlement, even if it was money that was initially taken and other money—of identical value—that he intended to return.

b. Claim of Right

As in larceny, embezzlement is not committed if the conversion is pursuant to a claim of right to the property. Whether defendant took the property openly is an important factor.

C. FALSE PRETENSES

The offense of false pretenses is:

(i) Obtaining ***title***;

(ii) To ***personal property of another***;

(iii) By an ***intentional false statement*** of past or existing ***fact***;

(iv) With ***intent to defraud*** the other.

1. **"Larceny by Trick" Distinguished**
If the victim is tricked—by a misrepresentation of fact—into giving up mere ***possession*** of property, the crime is larceny by trick. If the victim is tricked into giving up ***title*** to property, the crime is false pretenses.

2. **The Misrepresentation Required**
The victim must actually be deceived by, or act in reliance on, the misrepresentation, and this must be a major factor (or the sole cause) of the victim passing title to the defendant. A misrepresentation as to what will occur in the future is not sufficient. A false promise, even if made without the present intent to perform, is also not sufficient.

D. ROBBERY
Robbery consists of:

(i) A ***taking***;

(ii) Of ***personal property of another***;

(iii) ***From the other's person or presence*** (including anywhere in his vicinity);

(iv) ***By force or threats of immediate death or physical injury*** to the victim, a member of his family, or some person in the victim's presence;

(v) With the ***intent to permanently deprive*** him of it.

Exam Tip For a defendant to be guilty of robbery, the victim must give up her property because she feels threatened. If she gives up her property for another reason (*e.g.*, she feels sorry for the defendant, or she wants the defendant to go away), the defendant will not be guilty of robbery. He may, however, be guilty of attempted robbery.

1. **Distinguish Larceny**
Robbery differs from larceny because robbery requires that the defendant use ***force or threats*** to obtain or retain the victim's property. Thus, pickpocketing generally would be larceny, but if the victim notices the attempt and resists, the taking would be robbery.

E. EXTORTION
Common law extortion consists of the corrupt collection of an unlawful fee by an officer under color of office. Under modern statutes, extortion (blackmail) often consists of obtaining property ***by means of threats*** to do harm or to expose information. Under some statutes, the crime is complete when threats are made with the intent to obtain property; *i.e.,* the property need not be obtained.

1. **Distinguish Robbery**
Extortion differs from robbery because in extortion the threats may be of future harm and the taking does not have to be in the presence of the victim.

F. RECEIPT OF STOLEN PROPERTY
Receipt of stolen property consists of:

(i) Receiving ***possession and control***;

(ii) Of ***"stolen" personal property***;

(iii) ***Known*** to have been obtained in a manner constituting a criminal offense;

(iv) ***By another person***;

(v) With the ***intent to permanently deprive*** the owner of his interest in it.

1. "Possession"
Manual possession is not necessary. The defendant possesses the property when it is put in a location designated by her or she arranges a sale for the thief to a third person (*i.e.*, "fencing").

2. "Stolen" Property
The property must be stolen property ***at the time the defendant receives it***.

CMR **Exam Tip** In analyzing receipt of stolen property questions, carefully check the property's status at the time defendant receives it. If the police have already recovered the property and use it ***with the owner's permission***, it is no longer stolen, and the defendant cannot be convicted of receipt of stolen property. Note, however, that the defendant ***can*** be convicted of ***attempted*** receipt of stolen property if she intended to receive the property believing it to be stolen.

G. THEFT
Under many modern statutes and the M.P.C., some or all of the above property offenses are combined and defined as the crime of "theft."

H. FORGERY
Forgery consists of the following:

(i) ***Making or altering*** (by drafting, adding, or deleting);

(ii) A ***writing*** with apparent legal significance (*e.g.*, a contract, not a painting);

(iii) So that it is ***false***; *i.e.*, representing that it is something that it is not, not merely containing a misrepresentation (*e.g.*, a ***fake*** warehouse receipt, but not an ***inaccurate*** real warehouse receipt);

(iv) With ***intent to defraud*** (although no one need actually have been defrauded).

1. Fraudulently Obtaining Signature of Another
If the defendant fraudulently causes a third person to sign a document that the third person does not realize he is signing, forgery has been committed. But if the third person realizes he is signing the document, forgery has not been committed even if the third person was induced by fraud to sign it.

2. Uttering a Forged Instrument
Uttering a forged instrument consists of: (i) ***offering as genuine***; (ii) an ***instrument*** that may be the subject of forgery and is ***false***; (iii) with ***intent to defraud***.

I. MALICIOUS MISCHIEF
Malicious mischief consists of:

(i) The ***malicious***;

(ii) ***Destruction*** of or damage to;

(iii) The ***property of another***.

Malice requires no ill will or hatred. It does, however, require that the damage or destruction have been ***intended or contemplated*** by the defendant.

VIII. OFFENSES AGAINST THE HABITATION

A. BURGLARY

Common law burglary consists of:

(i) A ***breaking*** (creating or enlarging an opening by at least minimal force, fraud, or intimidation; if defendant had the resident's consent to enter, the entry is not a breaking);

(ii) And ***entry*** (placing any portion of the body or any instrument used to commit the crime into the structure);

(iii) ***Of a dwelling*** (a structure used with regularity for sleeping purposes, even if used for other purposes such as conducting a business);

(iv) ***Of another*** (ownership is irrelevant; occupancy by someone other than defendant is all that is required);

(v) ***At nighttime***;

(vi) ***With the intent to commit a felony in the structure*** (felony need not be carried out to constitute burglary).

Modern statutes often eliminate many of the "technicalities" of common law burglary, including the requirements of a breaking, that the structure be a dwelling, that the act occur at nighttime, and that the intent be to commit a felony (*i.e.,* intent to commit misdemeanor theft is often enough).

CMR **Exam Tip** The intent to commit a felony within must be present ***at the time of entry***; a later-acquired intent is not sufficient. This technicality is tested; remember it.

B. ARSON

Arson at common law consists of:

(i) The ***malicious*** (*i.e.*, intentional or with reckless disregard of an obvious risk);

(ii) ***Burning*** (requiring some damage to the structure caused by fire);

(iii) ***Of the dwelling***;

(iv) ***Of another.***

Like statutory changes for burglary, modern arson statutes (including the M.P.C.) have modified the common law rules, usually to expand potential criminal liability. Most states have expanded the definition of arson to include damage caused by explosion, and expanded the types of property that may be destroyed to include commercial structures, cars, trains, etc.

CMR **Exam Tip** Although common law arson requires a burning of a ***dwelling***, MBE questions testing on other arson issues often assume, without specifically stating, that arson extends to structures other than dwellings. Many statutes so provide.

1. Damage Required

Destruction of the structure, or even significant damage to it, is not required to complete the crime of arson. Mere blackening by smoke or discoloration by heat (scorching) is not sufficient, but mere ***charring is sufficient***.

2. Related Offense—Houseburning

The common law misdemeanor of houseburning consisted of: (i) a malicious; (ii) burning; (iii) of one's own dwelling; (iv) if the structure is situated either in a city or town, or so near to other houses as to create a danger to them.

Criminal Law

Lecture Handout

barbri®

Multistate Early Bar Prep

CRIMINAL LAW LECTURE HANDOUT

I. INTRODUCTION

A. SOURCES OF LAW FOR THE MULTISTATE BAR EXAMINATION

1. ______________________________

2. ______________________________

3. ______________________________

B. OVERVIEW: CRIMINAL LAW TOPICS

1. **ESSENTIAL ELEMENTS OF CRIMES**

   a) ______________ c) ______________

   b) ______________ d) ______________

2. **SPECIFIC CRIMES**

   a) ______________ b) ______________

3. **LIABILITY FOR THE CONDUCT OF OTHERS**

   a) ______________

4. **INCHOATE ("Incomplete") OFFENSES**

   a) ______________ c) ______________

   b) ______________

5. **DEFENSES**

   a) ______________ d) ______________

   b) ______________ e) ______________

   c) ______________ f) ______________

II. THE ESSENTIAL ELEMENTS OF CRIMES

A. PHYSICAL ACT …

B. MENTAL STATES

1. **COMMON LAW MENTAL STATES:** There are **four** common law mental states.

   a) **Mental State #1:** ______________________________

      (1) **Definition:** When the crime requires not just the desire to do the *act*, but also the desire to achieve a ______________________________________

      (2) **The 11 Specific Intent Crimes**

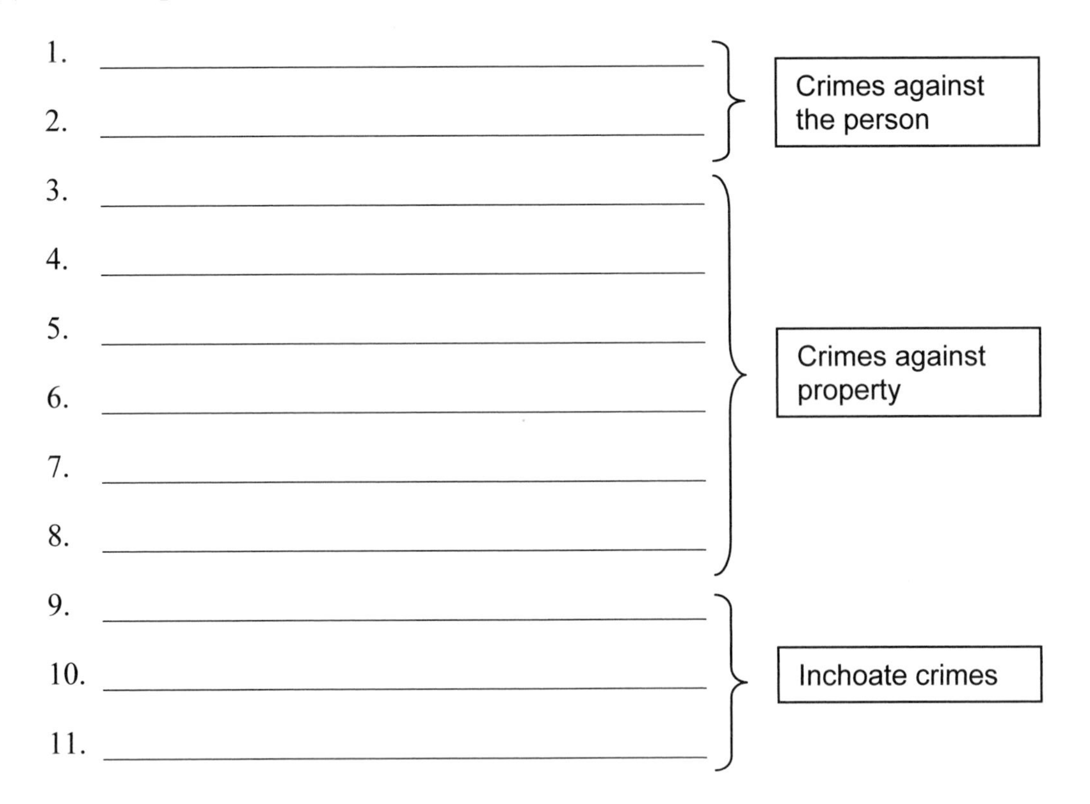

1. ________
2. ________
3. ________
4. ________
5. ________
6. ________
7. ________
8. ________
9. ________
10. ________
11. ________
Crimes against the person
Crimes against property
Inchoate crimes

b) **Mental State #2:** ______________________________

(1) **Definition:** When a defendant acts ______________________ or with

__________________________________ of an obvious or known risk.

(2) **Common Law Malice Crimes**

(a) _________________________

(b) _________________________

c) **Mental State #3:** ______________________________

(1) **Definition:** The defendant need only be ___________________

_________________ of the factors constituting the crime; he need not intend a specific result.

(**Note**: The jury can usually infer the general intent simply from the doing of the act.)

(2) **Examples of General Intent Crimes**

(a) _________________________

(b) _________________________

(c) _________________________

(d) _________________________
(All crimes against the person.)

d) **Mental State #4:** ______________________________

(1) **Definition:** When the crime requires simply doing the act; no mental state is needed.

(2) **Two Types of Strict Liability Crimes**

(a) ______________________________________: Regulatory or morality offenses that typically carry small penalties. Examples:
1) Selling alcohol to a minor
2) Selling contaminated food
3) Corrupting the morals of a minor

(b) ______________________________________: Having sex with someone who is under the age of consent.

2. COMMON LAW MISTAKE

a) Mistake of Fact

(1) **The Rule:** Whether a defendant's mistake of fact will be a defense depends upon the mental state for the crime and whether the mistake is reasonable or unreasonable. So, if the mental state is –

(a) ______________________________, then ***any*** mistake (even an unreasonable one) will be a defense.

(b) ______________________________, then ***only*** a reasonable mistake will be a defense.

(c) ______________________________, then a mistake will ***not*** (ever) be a defense.

(2) **The Same Rule** (stated another way)

(a) A ______________________________ mistake will be a defense to ***any*** crime, except a crime of strict liability.

(b) An ______________________________ mistake will be a defense ***only*** to specific intent crimes.

b) Mistake of Law

(1) **The Rule:** Mistake of law is ______________________________

(2) **The Exceptions**

(a) If the statute specifically makes knowledge of the law an element of the crime (*e.g.*, "selling a gun to a known felon").

(b) Others …

3. **MODEL PENAL CODE ("MPC") MENTAL STATES:** The MPC and many states no longer use the common law mental states, but instead have defined **five** mental states–

a) **Purposely:** When it is the defendant's ______________________________ to accomplish a particular result. (In other words, that is what the defendant ______________ to do.)

b) **Knowingly:** When the defendant is ____________ of what he is doing.

c) **Recklessly:** When the defendant is ____________ of a substantial and unjustifiable risk, and ____________________________________ that risk.

d) **Negligently:** When the defendant ______________________________ about a substantial and unjustifiable risk.

e) **Strict Liability:** No mental state required (similar to the common law).

4. **MPC MISTAKE DOCTRINE**

a) **Mistake of Fact**

(1) **The Rule:** Under the MPC, a mistake of fact will be a defense if the mistake negates the required mental state.

(2) **Application**

(a) **For crimes of purpose, knowledge, or recklessness,** a mistake of fact (even an unreasonable one) will often be a defense.

(b) **For crimes of negligence,** only a ____________________ mistake will be a defense.

(c) **For strict liability crimes,** a mistake of fact will _________ be a defense, no matter how reasonable it is.

b) **Mistake of Law:** Mistake of law is ___________ a defense. (Similar to the common law.)

C. CAUSATION ...

D. CONCURRENCE

1. **THE RULE:** The defendant must have the ______________________________ at the same time as he engages in ___________________

2. **APPLICATION:** Concurrence issues arise most frequently with two crimes:

a) __________________________, and

b) __________________________

III. CRIMES AGAINST THE PERSON: ASSAULT AND BATTERY ...

IV. CRIMES AGAINST THE PERSON: HOMICIDE ...

V. CRIMES AGAINST THE PERSON: CONFINEMENT OFFENSES AND SEX OFFENSES ...

VI. CRIMES AGAINST PROPERTY: THEFT-RELATED OFFENSES

A. COMMON LAW THEFT CRIMES

1. LARCENY

a) **Definition:** *The trespassory taking and carrying away of the personal property of another, with the intent to steal.*

(1) **"Trespassory":** ____________________

(2) **"Taking and Carrying Away":** ____________________

(3) **"Personal Property *of Another*":** Key is ____________________

(a) If D validly possesses property, he *cannot* be guilty of larceny for taking it (even if D doesn't own it).

(b) Conversely, D *can* be guilty of larceny for taking his own property, if someone else had valid possession of it.

(4) **"With the Intent to Steal":** ____________________
So, if D intends to give the property back, the taking is not larceny. If D erroneously thinks the property is his, the taking is not larceny.

b) **The Erroneous Takings Rule:** A taking under a ____________________

____________________ is never larceny.

HYPO 1. Is Dudley guilty of larceny?

1(a) Dudley picks up Victor's cell phone, mistakenly believing that the phone is his.

1(b) Dudley knowingly takes Victor's cell phone from Victor's bag without Victor's permission, planning to return the cell phone once he's finished using it.

1(c) Dudley leases his car to Victor for a one-year term. Two months into the one-year lease, Dudley has a change of heart and takes the car back without Victor's permission, knowing that doing so violates the lease agreement.

HYPO 2. Dudley knowingly takes Victor's cell phone from Victor's bag without Victor's permission, planning to return the cell phone once he's finished with it. After using it, however, Dudley decides that Victor's phone is so nice, he's going to keep it. Is Dudley guilty of larceny?

c) **Continuing Trespass:** If a defendant *wrongfully* takes property, but *without* the intent to steal, he will not be guilty of larceny. But, if the defendant *later* forms the intent to steal, the initial trespassory taking is considered to have "continued," and he will be guilty of larceny.

2. EMBEZZLEMENT

a) **Definition:** *Conversion of the personal property of another by a person already in lawful possession of that property, with the intent to defraud.*

b) **Mental State:** ______________________

Note: If the defendant intends to give the *exact* property back in the *exact* form, he will not have the intent to defraud (**but** money is not fungible).

c) **Key Difference from Larceny:** D must already have lawful ______________ of the property before a taking can be considered embezzlement.

d) **Possession vs. Custody:** Possession involves more than mere custody. It requires the authority to exercise some discretion over the property.

HYPO 3. Have the following defendants committed larceny, embezzlement, or neither?

3(a) A lawyer holds $10,000 in trust for one of his clients. Without his client's permission, the lawyer takes the money to Las Vegas where he uses it to purchase gambling chips. The lawyer's plan is to double the money playing blackjack, and then return it with interest. Unfortunately, the lawyer loses all the money.

3(b) A bank president wrongfully writes himself a check on the bank's account.

3(c) A bank teller wrongfully takes $1,000 from the cash drawer.

3. FALSE PRETENSES

a) **Definition:** *Obtaining title to the personal property of another by an intentional false statement, with the intent to defraud.*

b) **Key Difference from Larceny:** In larceny, the defendant gets only

possession; in false pretenses, the defendant gets _______________

c) **"False Statement":** Must be of a ___________________________________ (not a future promise).

HYPO 4. Is Dudley guilty of false pretenses?

4(a) Dudley says to Victor: "If you give me your cell phone, I will write you a $100 check on my new checking account." Dudley knows that the checking account is empty. Victor agrees to the deal and gives Dudley the cell phone in return for a $100 check …

4(b) Dudley says to Victor: "If you give me your cell phone, I will give you $100 cash tomorrow." Dudley has no intention of paying the money. Victor agrees to the deal and gives Dudley the cell phone …

4(c) Dudley says to Victor: "If you lend me your cell phone for one week, I will write you a $20 check on my new checking account." Dudley knows that the checking account is empty. Victor agrees to the deal and lends Dudley the cell phone in return for a $20 check …

4. LARCENY BY TRICK:

If the defendant obtains only _____________________ (not title) as a result of the intentional false statement, the crime is "larceny by trick," not false pretenses.

5. ROBBERY

a) Elements

(1) A ____________________

(2) from another's ________________ or ____________________

(3) by ________________ or threat of ____________________ injury.

b) Mental State: ________________________________ (specific intent)

c) "Presence": Includes from V's vicinity or from V's house while V is in it.

d) "Force": Sufficient to overcome resistance.

(1) Picking a pocket: ________________________________

(2) Snatching a chain: ________________________________

e) Threats

(1) Immediate Injury: ________________________
("your money or your life")

(2) Future Injury: ________________________
("give me your money, or I'll break your legs tomorrow")

(3) Embarrassment: ________________________
("give me your money, or I'll post those pictures of you")

B. MODERN STATUTORY APPROACHES TO THEFT CRIMES

1. CONSOLIDATION: The MPC and most states have consolidated the common law property crimes of larceny, embezzlement, false pretenses, or larceny by trick

into a single offense typically known as ______________

2. GRADING: Under these statutory approaches, the seriousness of the offense will be determined by the value of the property stolen.

C. Miscellaneous Theft-Related Offenses

1. RECEIPT/POSSESSION OF STOLEN PROPERTY

a) Receiving ____________________________

b) of ________________________ property …

c) **Mental State:** … with ___________________________ that it was stolen.

Note: "Knowledge" is the mental state for most possession crimes.

2. FORGERY

a) ________________________ or ______________________ a writing

b) so that it is ________________________ …

c) **Mental State:** … with ____

3. UTTERING

a) ________________________ as genuine

b) a _________________________ instrument…

c) **Mental State:** … with ____

4. MALICIOUS MISCHIEF

a) ________________________ or ______________________ someone else's property

b) **Mental State:** … with ____

HYPO 5. What crimes has Dudley committed?

5(a) Dudley needs $100 fast, so he takes Victor's checkbook, writes out a $100 check to himself, and signs Victor's name to the check …

5(b) … he takes the check to the local check cashing store and hands it to the clerk behind the window …

5(c) … and he receives $100 from the clerk.

VII. Crimes Against Property: Habitation Offenses

A. Burglary

1. **COMMON LAW BURGLARY:** *Breaking and entering the dwelling of another at night with the intent to commit a felony inside.*

   a) **"Breaking":** Creating or enlarging an opening ____________________

      (1) **Includes:** breaking a window, opening a window, opening a door.

      (2) **Does Not Include:** climbing through an already open window, entering with permission.

   b) **"Entry":** Some part of the defendant's body must enter the building.

   c) **"Dwelling":** A structure where someone ____________________

   d) **"Of Another":** You can't burglarize your own house.

   e) **"At Night":** Self-explanatory.

   f) **"Intent to Commit a Felony Inside":** ____________________ (intent to steal, rob, rape, assault, kill, etc.)

HYPO 6. Is Dudley guilty of burglary?

6(a) Dudley mistakenly believes that Victor has stolen his laptop computer. So Dudley breaks into Victor's house at night and takes Victor's laptop.

6(b) Dudley, who is homeless, breaks into Victor's house to get warm …

6(c) … while inside the house, Dudley sees Victor's laptop computer, decides to steal it, and absconds with the laptop.

2. **MODERN STATUTORY CHANGES:** Many states have eliminated the technical requirements of common law burglary (especially "breaking," "at night," and "dwelling").

B. Arson

1. **COMMON LAW ARSON**

   a) **Definition:** *The malicious burning of a building.*

   b) **State of Mind:** ______________________________

   c) **"Burning":** Requires the ____________________ of the structure ("scorching" is not enough; some part of the building must actually be burned up).

2. **STATUTORY DEVELOPMENTS**

   a) **"Dwelling":** Traditionally, arson was limited to "dwellings," but most states have now extended arson to all buildings.

   b) **"Of Another":** Traditionally, a defendant could not commit arson on his own property; most states have eliminated that restriction.

VIII. LIABILITY FOR THE CONDUCT OF OTHERS: ACCOMPLICE LIABILITY

A. DEFINITIONS

1. **THE PERSON WHO COMMITS THE CRIME** is called the __________

2. **THE PERSON WHO HELPS** is called the ______________

   a) **Act:** ___________ or ______________ the principal,

   b) **Mental State:** with the __________ that the crime be committed.

B. SCOPE OF ACCOMPLICE LIABILITY

1. **THE RULE:** The accomplice is guilty of –

   a) all crimes that he _______ or ____________ (just as if he did it),

   and

   b) all other ____________ crimes committed along with the aided crime.

2. **THE UNPROSECUTED PRINCIPAL:** If the principal is not prosecuted or has an individual defense (*e.g.*, insanity), the accomplice is _______________

3. PERSONS WHO ARE NOT ACCOMPLICES

a) ______________________________ does not make someone an accomplice (must actually help).

b) ______________________________ does not make someone an accomplice (must actually intend to aid or encourage).

c) ______________________________: The *victim* of the crime cannot be an accomplice.

4. WITHDRAWAL: What happens when an accomplice changes his mind? It depends upon what the accomplice did –

a) Encourager: An accomplice who only "encouraged" the principal may

withdraw simply by __________________ the crime (before it is committed).

b) Aider: An accomplice who actually helped the principal must either

_____________________ the assistance or ____________________ the

crime from happening (including notifying the authorities).

HYPO 7. Penny complains to her friend Dudley that she is short on money. Dudley responds, "I know just the opportunity for you. The drug dealer who used to operate at the corner of Center and Main was arrested yesterday. Why don't you set up shop there and start selling drugs." If Penny takes his advice and starts selling drugs, will Dudley be guilty of a crime? What must Dudley do to avoid criminal liability?

HYPO 8. What if, in addition to advising Penny to sell drugs, Dudley also gave her a supply of small plastic baggies, a stamp to brand the baggies with a trademark, and an untraceable cell phone? What must Dudley do now to avoid liability as an accomplice to drug dealing?

C. ACCESSORY AFTER THE FACT

1. **ACCESSORY AT COMMON LAW:** To commit the separate common law offense of being an "accessory," a defendant must-

   a) ____________________ a principal who has committed a felony

   b) with ____________________ that the crime has been committed, **and**

   c) with the __________________ to help the principal avoid arrest or conviction.

2. **MODERN STATUTORY APPROACHES:** Typically called "obstruction of justice," "harboring a fugitive," or "hindering prosecution."

IX. INCHOATE OFFENSES

A. THE THREE INCHOATE OFFENSES

1. **SOLICITATION**

   a) The Definition: __________ someone to commit a crime, with the __________ that the crime be committed.

   b) Mental State: ____

   c) Completion Unnecessary: The crime is in the ___________________________ (**Note:** It doesn't matter whether the other person agrees or whether the crime is actually committed.)

2. **CONSPIRACY**

   a) Definition: An ____________________ between two or more people to commit a crime, plus an ____________________ in furtherance of the crime.

   b) "Overt Act": *Any* act of ___________________ (minimal requirement). Traditionally, the common law did not require an overt act, but the majority of states now do.

   c) Mental State: ______________________ to accomplish the conspiracy's objective.

   d) Completion Unnecessary: The crime is in the ____________________ (plus the overt act).

e) **Can You Have a One-Person Conspiracy?**

(1) **Common Law:** NO. There must be at least ______________________, both of whom actually agree to accomplish the conspiracy's objectives.

(a) **Related Common Law Rule:** If all other parties to the agreement are

______________, the last remaining defendant cannot be convicted.

(2) **MPC:** YES. Under the _______________ approach, a defendant may be guilty of conspiracy even if the other parties are acquitted or were just pretending to agree.

HYPO 9. Dudley and Donnie agree to kill Victor, their business partner. Unbeknownst to Dudley, however, Donnie is actually an undercover FBI agent. Dudley is arrested while he is preparing to kill Victor. Is Dudley guilty of conspiracy to commit murder?

9(a) Under the Common Law?

9(b) Under the MPC?

f) **Vicarious Liability:** In addition to conspiracy, a defendant will be liable for *other* crimes committed by his co-conspirators, so long as those crimes –

(1) were in __________________ of the conspiracy's objective, **and**

(2) were __________________________

HYPO 10. Dudley and Alex agree to rob a bank. As they are making their preparations, Alex says, "I'll go steal us a gun so we can use it to rob the bank." That night, Alex breaks into Victor's house and steals Victor's gun. Dudley and Alex later use the gun to rob the bank. What crimes may Dudley be convicted of?

3. ATTEMPT

a) The Act

(1) **The Common Law Test:** Conduct that gets ______________________ to the commission of the crime (sometimes called the "dangerous proximity test").

(2) **The MPC/Majority Test:** Conduct that is a ______________________

__________ towards the crime and ____________________________

__________________________________ of a criminal purpose.

HYPO 11. Dudley wants to kill Victor. His plan is to shoot Victor as Victor is walking home from work. At what point has Dudley engaged in enough conduct to be guilty of attempted murder?

11(a) Dudley buys an untraceable gun from an illegal gun dealer ….

Common Law:

MPC:

11(b) Dudley takes the loaded gun and drives along the route that Victor typically uses when he walks home from work, but can't find Victor ….

Common Law:

MPC:

11(c) Two days later, Dudley tries again. This time, he sees Victor walking down the street. Dudley raises the gun, takes aim at Victor, and fires. The bullet misses ….

Common Law:

MPC:

---

b) <u>Mental State</u>: The ________________________ to commit the crime.

HYPO 12. Dudley, intending to kill Victor, fires a gun at Victor. What crime if …

12(a) … the bullet hits Victor killing him?

12(b) … the bullet misses and Victor is unharmed?

HYPO 13. Dudley, intending to burn down Victor's house, throws a lit incendiary device at the house while Victor is in it. What crime if …

13(a) … the house burns down?

13(b) … the house is not burned?

HYPO 14. Dudley, intending to show off his marksmanship skills, covers his eyes, spins around three times, and tries to shoot an apple off Victor's head. What crime if …

14(a) … the bullet strikes Victor killing him?

14(b) … the bullet misses and Victor is unhurt?

(1) The Rule: You can't attempt ____________________ crimes. That means, there are no attempt versions of-

(a) ______________________________, or

(b) ______________________________, or

(c) ______________________________

(2) It is possible to attempt malice, general intent, or strict liability crimes, **but only if** the D specifically intends to commit the crime.

c) <u>Impossibility</u>

(1) Factual Impossibility

(a) **Definition:** The claim that it was impossible to complete the crime because of some circumstance beyond the defendant's control.

(b) **The Rule:** Factual impossibility is _________ a defense to attempt.

HYPO 15. Dudley, intending to pick Victor's pocket, surreptitiously puts his hand into Victor's pocket, but the pocket is empty.

15(a) Is Dudley guilty of larceny?

15(b) Is Dudley guilty of attempted larceny?

HYPO 16. Dudley, intending to distribute cocaine, buys and resells a bag of white powdery substance. Unbeknownst to Dudley, however, the substance is a mixture of baby powder and sugar.

16(a) Is Dudley guilty of distributing cocaine?

16(b) Is Dudley guilty of attempting to distribute cocaine?

(2) Legal Impossibility

(a) **Definition:** The claim that it was impossible to complete the crime because what the defendant was trying to do was not illegal.

(b) **The Rule:** Legal impossibility _________ a defense to attempt.

HYPO 17. Dudley buys and sells a bag containing baby powder and sugar. Dudley believes that it is a crime to distribute a baby powder-sugar mixture.

17(a) Is Dudley guilty of distributing an illegal substance?

17(b) Is Dudley guilty of attempting to distribute an illegal substance?

B. Inchoate Offense Doctrines

1. **WITHDRAWAL/RENUNCIATION/ABANDONMENT:** What happens when a solicitor, co-conspirator, or attempter changes his mind?

   a) **Common Law:** Withdrawal is ______________________________ a defense.

      (1) **One Wrinkle:** Once D withdraws from a conspiracy he will no longer be

      ______________________________ for crimes committed by his

      co-conspirators after he left the conspiracy (D is still guilty of conspiracy).

   b) **MPC:** Withdrawal can be a defense, but ***only*** if

      (1) the D ____________________ and ____________________ renounces

      the solicitation, conspiracy, or attempt, **and**

      (2) the renunciation is based on a "change of heart," not a fear of failing or being caught.

2. **MERGER:** When can a defendant be convicted of multiple crimes for the same conduct?

   a) **The Rule for Lesser Included Offenses**

      (1) **Definition:** A "lesser included offense" is an offense that is *necessarily* part of the greater offense. In other words, every element of the lesser offense is also an element of the greater offense.

      (2) **Examples**

         (a) Is larceny a lesser included offense of robbery? __________

         (b) Is larceny a lesser included offense of burglary? __________

      (3) **The Rule:** A lesser included offense will merge with the greater offense.

   b) **The Rules for Inchoate Offenses**

      (1) ______________________ and ______________________ merge with the completed crime (and with each other);

      (2) ______________________ does not merge.

3. INCHOATE OFFENSES: REVIEW

HYPO 18. Dudley wants to kidnap Victor, but he doesn't want to be recognized. So he decides to recruit someone else to do it ....

18(a) Is Dudley guilty of a crime? ____________________

Dudley asks his friend Alex to do the kidnapping ....

18(b) Is Dudley guilty of a crime? ____________________

Alex says: "Sure, I'll do it." Dudley then gives Alex a photograph of Victor.

18(c) Is Dudley guilty of another crime? ____________________

18(d) Is Dudley still guilty of solicitation? ____________________

Alex tries to commit the kidnapping. He hides in the bushes outside Victor's house waiting for Victor to come home from work. When Victor arrives, however, he is accompanied by a bodyguard. So Alex decides to wait.

18(e) Is Dudley guilty of another crime? ____________________

18(f) Is Dudley still guilty of conspiracy? ____________________

Alex returns the next day, and kidnaps Victor.

18(g) Is Dudley guilty of another crime? ____________________

18(h) Is Dudley still guilty of attempt? ____________________

18(i) Is Dudley still guilty of conspiracy? ____________________

X. DEFENSES ...

barbri®

Criminal Law

1. Ⓐ Ⓑ Ⓒ Ⓓ
2. Ⓐ Ⓑ Ⓒ Ⓓ
3. Ⓐ Ⓑ Ⓒ Ⓓ
4. Ⓐ Ⓑ Ⓒ Ⓓ
5. Ⓐ Ⓑ Ⓒ Ⓓ

6. Ⓐ Ⓑ Ⓒ Ⓓ
7. Ⓐ Ⓑ Ⓒ Ⓓ
8. Ⓐ Ⓑ Ⓒ Ⓓ
9. Ⓐ Ⓑ Ⓒ Ⓓ
10. Ⓐ Ⓑ Ⓒ Ⓓ

11. Ⓐ Ⓑ Ⓒ Ⓓ
12. Ⓐ Ⓑ Ⓒ Ⓓ
13. Ⓐ Ⓑ Ⓒ Ⓓ
14. Ⓐ Ⓑ Ⓒ Ⓓ
15. Ⓐ Ⓑ Ⓒ Ⓓ

16. Ⓐ Ⓑ Ⓒ Ⓓ
17. Ⓐ Ⓑ Ⓒ Ⓓ

CRIMINAL LAW QUESTIONS

Question 1

The defendant sent an email with a malicious program attached to an acquaintance at a large company. Once the acquaintance opened the email, the program would download to the acquaintance's workstation, so that the defendant could use the acquaintance's workstation as a zombie computer to send spam email to others. If it worked as the defendant thought it would, the acquaintance would never realize that the program was downloaded to his workstation. Unfortunately, the program did not work as the defendant thought it would—it damaged the hard drive on the acquaintance's workstation and required repairs that cost the company $507.

The jurisdiction in which this occurred has a statute making it a criminal offense to "knowingly cause more than $500 in damage to another's property."

Can the defendant be found guilty under the statute?

(A) No, because the defendant did not know that the program would cause damage to the computer.

(B) No, because the defendant did not intend to cause the damage to the computer.

(C) Yes, because the defendant knew that he was sending an unauthorized program to the acquaintance's computer.

(D) Yes, because the defendant should have been aware that the program could cause damage to the computer.

A music teacher purchased a piano from his neighbor for $1,500. The teacher wrote the neighbor a check for the purchase price, even though he had only about $200 in his checking account at the time. The teacher believed that he would easily be able to sell the piano for $3,000 and deposit the money in the checking account in time to cover the check he had written to the neighbor. However, the teacher was unable to sell the piano and never deposited funds sufficient to cover the check he had written to the neighbor. The teacher was arrested and charged with issuing a check against insufficient funds with intent to defraud.

If, at the trial, the jury believed the teacher's story to be correct, it should find him:

(A) Guilty, because the check was not paid.

(B) Guilty, because at the time the teacher wrote the check, the money in his account was insufficient to cover it, and he knew it was insufficient.

(C) Not guilty, but only if the jury finds that the teacher's expectation of being able to sell the piano was reasonable.

(D) Not guilty, even if the jury finds that the teacher's expectation of being able to sell the piano was unreasonable.

A state statute prohibited, under criminal penalties, "lewd conduct with a minor." A minor is defined as a person younger than 16 years of age. A hotel clerk called the police when an adult male, who had previously rented a room and left, returned accompanied by a female who appeared to be a teenager. The police went to the room and knocked on the door. After a minute, they were let in by a partially disrobed female. When the police entered the room, they saw an adult male, also partially disrobed, quickly climbing down the fire escape. The police determined that the female was in fact 15 years old, and that she had engaged in conduct that would be considered "lewd conduct" under the statute. The adult escaped apprehension. The minor is now being prosecuted under the statute as having aided and abetted the adult in violation of the statute.

Which of the following is her best argument in defense?

(A) She cannot be convicted as an aider and abettor unless the principal is first convicted.

(B) She cannot be convicted as an aider and abettor of violating a statute designed to protect the class of which she is a member—minors.

(C) She cannot be convicted of aiding and abetting any crime because she is a minor.

(D) She cannot be convicted alone of committing a crime that requires at least two parties to commit a violation.

Question 4

In an effort to fix a longstanding rodent problem, a city enacted a statute that, in subsection one, required that all food waste be stored in lidded containers made of plastic or metal and, in subsection two, prohibited the outdoor use of any waste container that did not have a lid. Violation of the statute was considered to be a misdemeanor, and the statute provided for a fine of $50 for each violation. The defendant knew about the statute, as its enactment was well-publicized, but he misread the statute and believed that subsection two applied only to food waste. In the course of cleaning out his home office, the defendant put many old files into cardboard boxes without lids, which he then left on his curb for his trash collector to pick up that same day. The defendant was promptly fined $50.

Did the defendant commit any offense?

(A) No, because he had no intent to violate the statute.

(B) No, because the mistake of law was reasonable, given that the first subsection only applied to food items.

(C) Yes, because the defendant's mistake of fact that the statute applied only to food items is not a defense.

(D) Yes, because the defendant's mistake of law as to the application of the statute is not a defense.

Question 5

A gang member decided to burn down a rival's home. After finding out his address and writing it down, the gang member bought several cans of gasoline and drove to his rival's neighborhood; however, when he wrote down his rival's address, he had transposed two numbers. He began to pour gasoline over the porch of his rival's neighbor, but he was apprehended before he could light the fire.

If tried for attempted arson, the gang member should be:

(A) Acquitted, because he did not have the specific intent to burn the neighbor's home.

(B) Acquitted, because the transferred intent doctrine does not apply to attempt crimes.

(C) Convicted, because he performed a substantial step in committing the arson.

(D) Convicted, because factual impossibility is no defense to the crime of attempt.

Question 6

A homeowner decided to burn down his own home for the insurance proceeds, which constituted the crime of arson in the jurisdiction. The homeowner hired an arsonist to commit the crime so that he could establish an alibi elsewhere. On the night of the planned crime, a neighbor alerted police after seeing the arsonist pour gasoline all over the defendant's front porch, and the police apprehended the arsonist before he could start the fire. The arsonist implicated the homeowner and agreed to testify against him in exchange for the charges of conspiracy to commit arson and attempted arson being dropped against the arsonist.

Which of the following best states the crimes for which the homeowner may be convicted?

(A) Solicitation, attempted arson, and conspiracy to commit arson.

(B) Attempted arson and conspiracy to commit arson.

(C) Solicitation and attempted arson.

(D) Attempted arson only.

Question 7

A career burglar and his friend planned to steal money from a retail store's safe by renting an apartment above the store and drilling through the floor to gain access to the store. They progressed with their drilling to the point that the only thing left to do was kick the floor to open the hole. However, on the evening that they were going to break into the store, the friend got cold feet. He told the burglar that he was not going through with the plan and left the apartment. The burglar decided to go through with the plan anyway, but he was caught by store security while he was trying to break open the safe. The jurisdiction follows the modern rules for attempt liability.

If the burglar and the friend are charged with conspiracy and attempted larceny, the likely result will be:

(A) The burglar will be convicted of both conspiracy and attempted larceny, and the friend will be convicted of conspiracy only.

(B) The burglar and the friend will be convicted of both conspiracy and attempted larceny.

(C) The burglar and the friend will be convicted of attempted larceny only.

(D) The burglar and the friend will be convicted of conspiracy only.

Question 8

A student took a personal check from his roommate's checkbook, with the intent of later forging his roommate's signature in order to cash it for money. However, he realized that he probably would not get away with his plan and ripped the check up before filling it out.

The student is:

(A) Guilty of attempted forgery.

(B) Guilty of larceny.

(C) Guilty of both larceny and attempted forgery.

(D) Guilty of neither crime.

Question 9

A defendant planned to hold up his neighborhood market. He waited at the bus stop across the street from the market until he saw that the market was empty. He went into the market and walked up to the counter with his hand in his jacket pocket to simulate a gun. Before the clerk could turn around to see what the defendant wanted, a shopper entered the market, startling the defendant, who turned and ran out the door. The defendant jumped into the shopper's car, which was standing unlocked with the motor running outside the market, and sped off to the nearby bus station. The shopper's car was recovered at the bus station and the defendant was later arrested in another town.

If the defendant is charged with the theft of the shopper's car, he should be found:

(A) Guilty of larceny, because it was taken to aid in the commission of an inherently dangerous felony.

(B) Guilty of larceny, because using the car for his escape subjected it to a substantial risk of loss.

(C) Not guilty of larceny, because he only intended to use it for his escape.

(D) Not guilty of larceny, because the shopper was grossly negligent in leaving it unlocked and running.

Question 10

A man who was heavily in debt asked his neighbor, who was going out of town for a week, whether he could borrow her car because his was undergoing repairs in a local body shop. In fact his car was working fine and was in his garage. The neighbor agreed and the man drove her to the airport and promised to take good care of the car. Two days later, the man drove the neighbor's car across the state line and entered the car in a "demolition derby." He had concluded that he would have a better chance to win the $10,000 prize awarded to the last car left running with his neighbor's car because it was heavier and bigger than his car. The man had never driven in a demolition derby and wrecked the car in a matter of minutes. When the neighbor returned, the man admitted what he had done, and the neighbor had him arrested.

If the man is convicted, it will most likely be for:

(A) Common law larceny.

(B) Embezzlement.

(C) False pretenses.

(D) Larceny by trick.

Question 11

The defendant rented a room for two nights at a hotel. The room was equipped with a large color television set. The defendant decided to steal the set, pawn it, and keep the proceeds. To conceal his identity as the thief, he contrived to make his room look as if it had been burglarized. However, he was traced through the pawnbroker and arrested.

The defendant is guilty of:

(A) Embezzlement.

(B) False pretenses.

(C) Larceny.

(D) Larceny by trick.

Question 12

A student wanting to purchase marijuana was told that he could make a purchase from a store clerk. The student approached the clerk for that purpose, but the clerk was suspicious and told the student that a single marijuana cigarette would cost $50. The student did not have this much money, but he knew that he had a counterfeit $50 bill, and he gave this to the clerk. The clerk then gave the student a "marijuana cigarette," which was in fact only an ordinary tobacco cigarette.

As the student left the store, he lit the cigarette. He was immediately apprehended by the police, who had been keeping the clerk under surveillance.

Based on his dealings with the student, the clerk could be convicted of:

(A) Larceny by trick.

(B) False pretenses.

(C) Embezzlement.

(D) No theft offense.

Question 13

A gunman came up behind a pedestrian, stuck a gun in his back, and said, "Your money or your life!" The pedestrian turned around, saw the gun, and fainted. The gunman lifted the pedestrian's wallet and stuck it in the back pocket of his pants. The gunman took off at a trot, but after he had traveled about 10 feet from the pedestrian, the wallet slipped out of the gunman's pocket and fell to the ground. The gunman did not realize this until he arrived home and found the wallet missing. When the pedestrian revived, he found the wallet with all its contents intact. He reported the crime to the police and identified a mugshot of the gunman, who was subsequently arrested.

The gunman should be convicted of:

(A) Larceny only.

(B) Robbery only.

(C) Larceny and robbery.

(D) Neither larceny nor robbery.

Question 14

A pickpocket lifted a man's wallet from his rear pants pocket while the man was distracted by the pickpocket's confederate, and the pickpocket began walking away. When the man noticed that his wallet was gone a few seconds later, he turned and started after the pickpocket, but the confederate grabbed him momentarily, allowing the pickpocket to escape.

If the pickpocket and the confederate are subsequently arrested and charged with robbery, the likely result will be:

(A) Only the pickpocket will be guilty of robbery because he stole the wallet.

(B) Only the confederate will be guilty of robbery because he used force against the man.

(C) Both the pickpocket and the confederate will be guilty of robbery.

(D) Neither the pickpocket nor the confederate will be guilty of robbery.

Question 15

A homeowner and his neighbor, who both enjoyed woodworking as a hobby, kept all of their woodworking equipment in the neighbor's garage, which was not attached to the house and much larger than the homeowner's. The homeowner had a key and equal access to the garage so that he could work on his carpentry projects any time he wished.

One evening the homeowner engaged in a sexual act in the garage with a 16-year-old babysitter, using his key to gain access to the garage. When the babysitter left, she impulsively took the neighbor's CD player from the garage, unbeknownst to the homeowner.

Assume that the jurisdiction in which these events took place maintains the common law definitions of property crimes, and that the state statutes define the "age of consent" for statutory rape, which is a felony in the jurisdiction, as 17 years of age.

Which of the following best describes the criminal liability, if any, of the homeowner and the babysitter?

(A) The homeowner is guilty of burglary, and the babysitter is guilty of larceny.

(B) Both the homeowner and the babysitter are guilty of burglary, and the babysitter is guilty of larceny.

(C) The homeowner is not guilty of burglary, but the babysitter is guilty of larceny.

(D) Neither the homeowner nor the babysitter is guilty of larceny or burglary.

Question 16

A man intending to play a practical joke on his friend broke into his house one night when he knew that he was out of town on a business trip. He proceeded to nail or otherwise attach his friend's furniture to the ceiling of his living room and glued knickknacks, books, and magazines to the surfaces of the upsidedown tables. He then got a beer from the refrigerator, drank it, and then drank several more beers, intending to replace them the next time he came to visit the friend. As he was staggering out of the kitchen on his way out of the house, the man noticed a framed, autographed photo of the coach of his friend's college football team. Being an alumnus of a rival college, the man impulsively took out his cigarette lighter and set the photo aflame as it hung on the wall. The ensuing blaze completely destroyed the friend's house. The jurisdiction has not altered the common law crimes in any way.

If the man is prosecuted for arson and larceny, he should be convicted of:

(A) Arson only.

(B) Both arson and larceny.

(C) Larceny only.

(D) Neither arson nor larceny.

Question 17

A college student was the sole lifetime beneficiary under a large trust administered by a banker, whose office was in another city. The student received a large monthly distribution from the trust, and whenever he ran short, he simply called the banker for extra funds, because the trust provided that the student was to receive whatever he needed from income or principal.

The student's roommate found out about the trust arrangement and decided to see if he could make it pay off for him. The roommate sent a telegram to the banker, which appeared to be from the student, and which read as follows:

> Have to go into hospital tomorrow for emergency surgery; am short of funds and need at least $5,000 to cover medical bills; am sending my roommate to pick up money; please give him $5,000.

The next day, the roommate showed up at the banker's office and obtained $5,000 on the promise that he would take the money to the student. The roommate absconded with the funds.

When the roommate sent the telegram to the banker, he committed:

(A) No common law crime.

(B) No completed crime, but a criminal attempt.

(C) Solicitation.

(D) Forgery and uttering.

CRIMINAL LAW ANSWERS

Answer to Question 1

(A) The defendant cannot be found guilty of violating the statute because he did not know that his act would cause the damage to the acquaintance's workstation that it did. Under the Model Penal Code fault standards adopted by modern criminal codes, a person acts "knowingly" with respect to the nature of his conduct when he is aware that his conduct is of that nature or that certain circumstances exist. He acts knowingly with respect to the result of his conduct when he knows that his conduct will necessarily or very likely cause such a result. When a statute establishes a culpable state of mind without indicating to which material elements of the offense it is to apply, the statute will be interpreted as requiring that state of mind for every material element of the offense. In this case, the statute requires that the defendant "knowingly cause more than $500 in damage to another's property." The requirement that the damage caused be over $500 is a material element of the offense because it defines the harmful result that will trigger criminal liability under the statute. Thus, the defendant must have known that his act of sending the computer program would necessarily or very likely cause over $500 in damage to the workstation to be liable under the statute in this case. (B) is incorrect because intent is not required by the statute for the defendant to be liable. Under modern criminal codes, intent is equated with purpose, which is defined as having a conscious object to engage in certain conduct or cause a certain result. Here, the defendant could be guilty under the statute even if he did not have the objective of causing that damage to the workstation, as long as he knew that it was at least very likely to occur. (C) is incorrect because the fact that the defendant knew that he was sending a program is not enough to establish guilt. As discussed above, the statute also requires that he know that his conduct will or is very likely to cause over $500 in damage to the workstation. (D) is incorrect because, even if the defendant knew that there was a small chance that this damage ***might*** occur, he has not acted with the required degree of culpability under the statute. The defendant must have known, at a minimum, that his conduct was very likely to cause the damage to the workstation. Being aware that such damage could occur in a very small percentage of cases may establish that the defendant acted recklessly, but it does not establish that he acted knowingly.

(D) If the jury believes the teacher's story, he would be found not guilty because he did not have the ***intent to defraud.*** The statute under which the teacher was charged requires the issuing of a check against insufficient funds with the intent to defraud. Intent to defraud is similar to intent to steal; it must be established that the defendant intended to permanently deprive another of his property through fraud. As the teacher intended to cover the check, he did not possess the intent to defraud necessary for this criminal charge. The teacher may have acted very foolishly and very recklessly, but he did not act with the intent to defraud required by the criminal statute. (A) is wrong because it would make guilt hinge entirely on the fact that the check was not paid, but more is required to commit the crime; the teacher must have had the necessary intent. (B) is wrong. The teacher might be guilty of another crime, such as "knowingly issuing a check against insufficient funds," but he would not be guilty of "issuing a check against insufficient funds with intent to defraud." (C) is wrong. If the teacher honestly believed that he would cover the check, he would not have the intent to defraud even if his belief were an unreasonable one. To avoid criminal liability for some crimes, a reasonable mistake or belief must be established. However, when the criminal charge requires a specific intent, such as intent to defraud, even an unreasonable mistake will negate liability if it eliminates the requisite intent.

Answer to Question 3

(B) Her best argument is that she is a member of the class that the statute is designed to protect. One who aids, counsels, commands, or encourages another in the commission of a crime and who is present when the crime is committed is generally guilty of aiding and abetting (under the common law, a principal in the second degree). Because the statute makes lewd conduct with a minor illegal, the minor conceivably could be found guilty of aiding and abetting under the general rule. However, there are exceptions to the general rule, including an exception for members of the class sought to be protected by the statute that has been violated. Because the statute speaks in terms of "lewd conduct with a minor," without creating any punishment for the minor, it probably was intended for the protection of minors, and a legislative exemption for those same minors can be presumed that overrides principles of aiding and abetting. (A) is incorrect because in most jurisdictions an aider and abettor can be convicted even if the principal cannot be convicted, and this was true even under the common law as to principals in the second degree (aiders and abettors), such as the minor. (C) is an incorrect statement of law; there is no aiding and abetting exception for minors in general, and minors over age 14 can generally be found guilty of committing a crime. (Minors under age 14 may have the benefit of a presumption that they lack the necessary mental state.) (D) is an incorrect statement of law, and closely akin to (A); the adult violated the law and the minor can be convicted as an aider and abettor even though the adult is never apprehended or convicted, unless some superseding principle intervenes, as in (B).

Answer to Question 4

(D) The defendant's mistaken belief that the statute only applied to food items provides no defense to the crime charged. It is not a defense to a crime that the defendant was unaware that his acts were prohibited by the law or that he mistakenly believed that his acts were not prohibited, even if such ignorance or mistake was reasonable. Here, the defendant knew that he was storing garbage in a container that did not have a lid, but was unaware that this constituted a violation of subsection two. Such ignorance of law will not be a defense to the misdemeanor charge, even if such ignorance was reasonable. (A) is incorrect because the crime here appears to be a strict liability crime because it is a regulatory offense with a relatively low penalty; thus, the defendant's intent to violate the statute is irrelevant. (B) is also incorrect. Even if the defendant reasonably believed the statute applied only to the disposal of food items, his mistake of law would not provide a defense, as explained above. The statute is clear in its terms, and was reasonably available for the collector's perusal. (C) is incorrect because defendant's mistake is one of law, not fact.

Answer to Question 5

(C) The gang member should be convicted because he has committed an attempt. An attempt has two elements: (i) a specific intent to commit the target crime, and (ii) an overt act in furtherance of the crime. In the instant case, the gang member drove to the neighbor's home, poured gasoline over the neighbor's porch, and was about to light the gasoline. These acts show his intent to burn the neighbor's home and satisfy the overt act requirement. He intended to burn a particular house (that of the neighbor) and set out to do so. (A) is incorrect. The fact that he was mistaken as to whose house he was burning is irrelevant. As stated above, the defendant did have the intent to burn the neighbor's house—he was just mistaken as to the owner of the house. The evidence that the gang member intended to burn a rival's home would provide a motive for the crime; however, proof of motive generally is not an element of any substantive crime. (B) is also incorrect. Although the transferred intent doctrine does not apply to attempt crimes, it is not needed under these facts for the reasoning described above. (D) is incorrect. Factual impossibility does not apply here. Factual impossibility arises when it would be impossible for the defendant to complete the intended crime. Here, there are no facts indicating that it would have been impossible for the gang member to burn the neighbor's home.

Answer to Question 6

(B) The homeowner may be convicted of attempted arson and conspiracy to commit arson. The homeowner is liable for attempted arson under the principles of accomplice liability because he solicited the arsonist to commit arson with the intent that his house be burned. If the person solicited proceeds far enough to be liable for attempt, the solicitor will be a party to that attempt. Here, the arsonist has proceeded far enough to constitute an attempt—the pouring of the gasoline is an overt act that has proceeded beyond mere planning. Therefore, the homeowner can be found criminally liable for attempted arson based on an accomplice theory. The homeowner also can be convicted of conspiracy, which is an agreement between two or more persons to commit an unlawful act, because he agreed with the arsonist to commit the crime of arson. Further, the arsonist's conduct satisfies the overt act requirement for conspiracy. Note that under the majority rule, conspirators may be convicted of both the criminal conspiracy and the crime they committed pursuant to the conspiracy; *i.e.,* there is no merger. (A) and (C) are incorrect because, unlike conspiracy, solicitation merges into the completed crime. (An attempt will be considered a completed crime for purposes of merger.) Thus, the homeowner cannot be convicted of both solicitation and attempted arson, as those choices state. (D) is incorrect because, as discussed above, conspiracy does not merge into the completed crime. Additionally, the fact that the charge of conspiracy was dropped against the arsonist does not preclude the homeowner's conviction for conspiracy. Although an acquittal of the other party to a conspiracy, as a general rule, precludes the conviction of the remaining party, this rule does not apply if the other party is charged with a lesser offense or is no longer being prosecuted.

Answer to Question 7

(A) The burglar and the friend are guilty of conspiracy. At common law, conspiracy was an agreement between two or more persons to commit an unlawful act or to commit a lawful act in an unlawful manner. Most states also require some overt act in furtherance of the conspiracy. Additionally, some jurisdictions recognize withdrawal as a defense to a conspiracy charge, but even those jurisdictions require that the co-conspirator somehow act to thwart the conspiracy. Withdrawal, however, does act as a defense to the subsequent crimes committed by the co-conspirators in furtherance of the conspiracy. When the burglar and the friend agreed to burglarize the store and began to carry out their plan, they committed common law conspiracy. Hence, (C) is incorrect. Given that the friend did nothing to thwart the conspiracy, his withdrawal provides no defense to the conspiracy charge, but it does immunize him from the subsequent crimes of the burglar. The burglar also committed an attempted larceny, but the friend did not. An attempt has two elements: (i) a specific intent to commit the target crime; and (ii) an overt act in furtherance of the crime. Under the modern M.P.C. approach, a ***complete and fully voluntary*** abandonment of the crime is a defense to an attempt charge. The abandonment must not be a temporary abandonment of the criminal purpose, nor may it be to find a different victim. In the instant case, both the burglar and the friend had the specific intent to commit the crime and performed overt acts in furtherance of the crime (*e.g.,* drilling into the floor). Had they been caught at that time, both could be convicted of attempt. However, the friend voluntarily and fully abandoned the crime before completion. Thus, abandonment provides him with a defense to the attempt charge. Thus, (A) is correct and (B) is incorrect. (D) is incorrect because the burglar can be convicted of attempted larceny, as described above.

Answer to Question 8

(B) The student is guilty of larceny. Larceny is the taking and carrying away of tangible personal property of another by trespass with the intent to permanently (or for an unreasonable time) deprive that person of her interest in the property. Although the student abandoned the plan to forge the check, he actually took a check and intentionally ripped it up, thus permanently depriving his roommate of the interest in the printed check, which has some value in and of itself. Thus, the student is guilty of larceny, making (B) correct and (D) incorrect. (A) and (C) are incorrect because the student did not proceed far enough to have committed an attempt. An attempt has two elements: (i) a specific intent to commit the target crime, and (ii) an overt act in furtherance of the crime. The act must constitute a substantial step in the course of carrying out the crime rather than mere preparation, as well as be strong corroboration of the actor's criminal purpose. Here, the only act the student took was removing a check from his roommate's checkbook. While that may be corroborative of an intent to commit forgery, it likely is not a substantial enough step to satisfy the overt act requirement.

Answer to Question 9

(C) Because the defendant only intended to use the shopper's car briefly (to get to the bus station), he lacked the intent to permanently deprive the shopper of the car. Larceny consists of a taking and carrying away of the tangible personal property of another by trespass, with intent to permanently (or for an unreasonable time) deprive the person of her interest in the property. If the defendant intends to deal with the property in a manner that involves a substantial risk of loss, this intent is sufficient for larceny. Although the defendant wrongfully took and carried away the shopper's car, he did not have the requisite intent for larceny. The defendant intended only to use the shopper's car as a means of getting to the bus station, where he would leave the car and where it could easily be recovered. Therefore, the defendant lacked the requisite intent for larceny. (A) is incorrect because the taking of property to aid in the commission of an inherently dangerous felony does not in and of itself constitute larceny. (A) implies the existence of a "felony larceny" rule, similar to felony murder. There is no such rule. Therefore, it must be shown that the defendant possessed the requisite intent before he will be found guilty of larceny. (B) is wrong because, as discussed above, there is no indication that the circumstances of the escape were such that there existed a substantial risk of loss of the car. The defendant was not going to drive the car a great distance, nor was he going to abandon it in some dangerous or obscure location. Admittedly, there may have been ***some*** risk of loss involved in the defendant's use of the car. However, the risk was not so substantial as to indicate that the defendant possessed the intent to deprive that is required for larceny. (D) is incorrect because the negligence of the owner of property does not constitute a defense to a charge of larceny. Although it may have been unwise for the shopper to leave her car unlocked with the motor running, a taking of the car without her consent would still be wrongful.

Answer to Question 10

(D) The man is guilty of larceny by trick because he obtained possession of the neighbor's car by means of misrepresentation. Larceny is the taking and carrying away of tangible personal property of another by trespass, with intent to permanently (or for an unreasonable time) deprive the person of her interest in the property. The taking must be without the consent of the person in possession of the property. If such consent is induced by a misrepresentation, the consent is not valid. The resulting larceny is called larceny by trick. Here, the man obtained possession of the neighbor's car with her consent. However, this consent was obtained by means of the man's statement concerning the unavailability of his own car. This was a false statement as to present facts, made with the intent that the neighbor rely on it. Thus, it was a misrepresentation that was used to induce the neighbor's consent. At the time of this taking, the man intended to deal with the car in a manner that involved a substantial risk of loss. This suffices as intent to permanently deprive. Therefore, all the elements are in place for larceny by trick. (A) is not as good a choice as (D) because the taking in this case is better characterized as larceny by trick rather than larceny, given that the man induced the neighbor to consent to his taking possession of the car. (C) is incorrect because the man obtained only possession of the car, not title. False pretenses differs from larceny by trick in what is obtained. If the defendant obtains only possession of the property, the offense is larceny by trick, whereas the obtaining of title means that false pretenses has been committed. What the victim intended to convey to the defendant is determinative. The neighbor intended only to let the man borrow her car for the week she was to be away, not to convey title to him. Consequently, the only thing the man obtained was possession of the car. Because title to the car was not obtained, there can be no conviction of false pretenses. Regarding (B), embezzlement is the fraudulent conversion of property of another by a person in lawful possession of that property. In embezzlement, misappropriation occurs while the defendant has lawful possession of the property, while in larceny, it occurs generally at the time the defendant obtains wrongful possession of the property. Here, as detailed above, the man's taking possession of the car was trespassory due to the manner in which he obtained the neighbor's consent to such possession. The crime of larceny was complete upon the man's taking possession with the requisite intent to permanently deprive. Thus, at the time the car was wrecked, the man had already misappropriated the car and was not in lawful possession of it. As a result, there can be no conviction for embezzlement.

Answer to Question 11

(C) The defendant is guilty of larceny because, while having mere custody of the television set, he carried it away from the hotel intending to permanently deprive the hotel owner of his interest in the set. Larceny consists of the taking and carrying away of tangible personal property of another by trespass, with intent to permanently (or for an unreasonable time) deprive the person of his interest in the property. Property must be taken from someone who has a possessory interest superior to that of the defendant. If the defendant has custody of the property, rather than possession, his misappropriation of the property is larceny. Possession involves a much greater scope of authority to deal with the property than does custody. Here, the defendant only had the authority to use the television set for viewing purposes while he was staying at the hotel. Thus, the defendant had only enough authority to deal with the set as to indicate that he had custody of it rather than possession. Consequently, the hotel owner had a possessory interest in the set superior to that of the defendant. The defendant took the set by trespass (without the consent of the owner) and carried it away with the intent to permanently deprive the owner of his interest in the set. Thus, the defendant is guilty of larceny. (D) is incorrect because larceny by trick occurs when the victim consents to the defendant's taking possession of the property but such consent has been induced by a misrepresentation. Here, the hotel owner never consented to give the defendant possession of the television set, through misrepresentation or otherwise. Instead, the defendant simply took the set without the consent of the owner. Therefore, this is not larceny by trick. (B) is incorrect for a similar reason. The offense of false pretenses consists of obtaining title to the property of another by an intentional (or knowing) false statement of past or existing fact, with intent to defraud the other. The defendant made no misrepresentations to the hotel owner, nor did the owner convey title to the television set to the defendant. Thus, the defendant is not guilty of false pretenses. (A) is incorrect because embezzlement requires the fraudulent conversion of property of another by a person in lawful possession of that property. The defendant never had lawful possession of the television set. The taking of the set without the consent of the hotel owner was trespassory. Thus, the defendant has not committed embezzlement.

Answer to Question 12

(B) The clerk has committed false pretenses because his misrepresentation concerning the contents of the cigarette induced the student to convey title to the counterfeit $50 bill. The offense of false pretenses consists of obtaining title to the property of another by an intentional (or knowing) false statement of past or existing fact, with intent to defraud the other. The clerk falsely represented to the student that the cigarette he gave him contained marijuana, intending that the student would rely upon such misrepresentation by paying money for the cigarette. The student, acting in reliance upon this misrepresentation, conveyed to the clerk title to the counterfeit $50 bill. Although the bill was counterfeit, it still constitutes property for purposes of a prosecution for false pretenses, because it is personal property capable of being possessed and having some value. Despite its counterfeit nature, the bill has value because its apparent genuineness allows its owner to pass it off as real money. Thus, all of the elements of false pretenses are present in the clerk's dealings with the student. Because the clerk has committed false pretenses, which is a theft offense, (D) is incorrect. (A) is incorrect because the clerk obtained title to the counterfeit bill rather than mere possession. If a victim consents to someone's taking possession of property, but such consent is induced by a misrepresentation, the consent is not valid. The resulting offense is larceny by trick. False pretenses differs from larceny by trick in what is obtained. If the victim intends to convey only possession of the property, the offense is larceny by trick. However, if the victim intends to convey title, the offense is false pretenses. Here, the student intended to convey title to the counterfeit bill, acting in reliance upon the clerk's false representation that the cigarette contained marijuana. Because the clerk obtained title, the offense of which he can be convicted is false pretenses rather than larceny by trick. (C) is incorrect because embezzlement consists of the fraudulent conversion of property of another by a person in lawful possession of that property. In embezzlement, misappropriation of the property occurs while the defendant has lawful possession of it. Here, the clerk did not convert the counterfeit bill while he was in lawful possession of it; rather, he obtained title to the bill by means of a misrepresentation. Because the clerk did not have lawful possession of the bill, he has not committed embezzlement.

Answer to Question 13

(B) The gunman should be convicted of robbery but cannot also be convicted of larceny because larceny is a lesser included offense of robbery. Robbery consists of a taking of the personal property of another from the other's person or presence, by force or intimidation, with the intent to permanently deprive him of it. The gunman took the pedestrian's personal property (his wallet) from his person at gunpoint, intending to permanently deprive him of his property. Although the pedestrian fainted, this taking was accomplished by force, because the gunman's threat of shooting the pedestrian precipitated his fainting. Thus, the gunman can be convicted of robbery. Larceny consists of a taking and carrying away of the tangible personal property of another by trespass, with intent to permanently deprive the person of his interest in the property. Although the gunman carried the pedestrian's wallet only 10 feet before it slipped out of his pocket, this is a sufficient carrying away for purposes of larceny. Thus, the gunman could be convicted of larceny. However, one may not be convicted of both a greater offense and a lesser included offense. A lesser included offense is one that consists entirely of some, but not all, elements of the greater crime. Larceny is a lesser included offense of robbery because larceny consists of all the elements of robbery except for force or intimidation. Indeed, robbery can be considered an aggravated form of larceny, in which the taking is accomplished by force or threat of force. Thus, the gunman cannot be convicted of ***both*** larceny and robbery. Therefore, (C), which would allow conviction of both crimes, is wrong. (A) is wrong because it would preclude a conviction for robbery and, as has been explained, the gunman can be convicted of robbery. (D) is wrong because the gunman can be convicted of robbery.

Answer to Question 14

(D) Neither the pickpocket nor the confederate would likely be convicted of robbery. The elements of robbery are: (i) a taking (ii) of the personal property of another, (iii) from the other's person or presence (iv) by force or intimidation (v) with the intent to permanently deprive him of it. Here, no force or intimidation was used to take the man's wallet. Force was only used by the confederate to prevent the man from apprehending the pickpocket ***after*** the taking. The force is not part of the robbery unless the force is used ***immediately*** after the possession has been accomplished to prevent the victim from regaining the property. Hence, (A), (B), and (C) are incorrect because neither defendant has committed robbery.

Answer to Question 15

(C) The babysitter is guilty of larceny for having taken the CD player. However, the elements of burglary are not present. At common law, burglary consists of a breaking and entry of the dwelling of another at nighttime, with the intent of committing a felony therein. While the homeowner may have had the intent to commit the felony of statutory rape when he entered the garage, he did not commit a "breaking" because he had access to the garage at any time. Also, to the extent the common law elements apply, the garage is not a "dwelling," *i.e.,* a structure regularly used for sleeping. Hence, it follows that there was no burglary committed on these facts. Larceny is the taking and carrying away of tangible personal property of another by trespass with intent to permanently (or for an unreasonable time) deprive the person of his interest in the property. The babysitter took the CD player when she left the garage. In doing so, the babysitter obtained control of the property and moved it without the consent of the person in possession of the property, with the intent to permanently deprive the owner of his property at the time of the taking. Thus, the requisite elements of larceny are present, and the babysitter is guilty of this crime. (A) is incorrect because, although the babysitter is guilty of larceny, the homeowner (as detailed above) is not guilty of burglary. (B) is similarly incorrect. (D) is incorrect because, although the homeowner is not guilty of either crime listed, the babysitter is guilty of larceny.

Answer to Question 16

(A) The man can be convicted of arson only. Arson is the ***malicious*** burning of the dwelling of another. To have acted with malice, the man must have either intended the burning that actually took place or have shown a reckless disregard of an obvious risk that the structure would burn. Here, the man probably acted with a reckless disregard of an obvious risk that the structure would burn by lighting the picture on fire while it was still attached to the wall. Thus, (C) and (D) should be eliminated. At common law, larceny consists of a taking and carrying away (asportation) of the tangible personal property of another by trespass with the intent to permanently (or for an unreasonable time) deprive the person of his interest in the property. Here, the issue is whether the man had the necessary intent to permanently deprive the friend of his property (the beer), given that the man intended to replace the beer. The man would not be convicted of larceny of the beer because the better view is that intent to return equivalent property is a defense to larceny if the defendant has the present ability to replace the property and the property is such that it is unlikely to matter to the owner whether he has the original or its equivalent. Thus, (B) is incorrect, and (A) is correct.

Answer to Question 17

(D) The roommate committed forgery and uttering when he sent the telegram. Forgery consists of the making of a false writing or the altering of an existing writing with intent to defraud. Uttering consists of offering as genuine an instrument that may be the subject of forgery and is false, with intent to defraud. Any writing that has apparent legal significance is a potential subject of forgery. The writing must represent itself to be something that it is not. The telegram sent by the roommate had apparent legal significance, because it appeared to be a request by the student for a disbursement of funds from the trust, which the banker was required to comply with according to the trust terms. Also, the telegram appeared to set forth an agency relationship between the student and the roommate, at least for purposes of picking up the money. In addition, the telegram was false, because it represented itself to be a request for disbursement of trust funds by one with authority to make such request. The roommate made out this telegram with intent to defraud the trust and the sole lifetime beneficiary of $5,000. Consequently, the roommate is guilty of forgery. When the roommate sent the telegram to the banker, the roommate offered the false instrument as genuine, again with the intent to defraud. This constituted uttering. (A) is incorrect because the roommate has committed forgery and uttering, which are common law crimes. (B) is incorrect because the crimes of forgery and uttering were completed upon sending the telegram. Therefore, the roommate's acts went beyond a mere attempt. (C) is incorrect because solicitation consists of inciting, counseling, advising, inducing, urging, or commanding another to commit a felony with the specific intent that the person solicited commit the crime. Here, the roommate sent the telegram, not as a means of inducing the banker to commit an offense, but rather as part of the roommate's plan to trick the banker into giving him the money. The banker was totally unaware of the scheme concocted by the roommate. Thus, the roommate did not commit solicitation.

Evidence

Hearsay

EVIDENCE

I. THE HEARSAY RULE

A. STATEMENT OF THE RULE

The Federal Rules define hearsay as "a statement, other than one made by the declarant while testifying at the trial or hearing, offered in evidence to prove the truth of the matter asserted." If a statement is hearsay, and no exception to the rule applies, the evidence must be excluded upon appropriate objection. The reason for excluding hearsay is that the adverse party was denied the opportunity to cross-examine the declarant.

CMR **Exam Tip** An out-of-court statement that incorporates other hearsay within it ("hearsay within hearsay" or "double hearsay") is admissible only if ***both*** the outer hearsay statement and the inner hearsay statement fall within an exception to the hearsay rule.

1. "Statement"

For purposes of the hearsay rule, a "statement" is: (i) an oral or written assertion, or (ii) nonverbal conduct intended as an assertion (*e.g.,* nod of the head).

2. "Offered to Prove the Truth of the Matter"

If the out-of-court statement is introduced for any purpose other than to prove the truth of the matter asserted, there is no need to cross-examine the declarant; so the statement is not hearsay. The following out-of-court statements are ***not hearsay***:

a. ***Verbal acts or legally operative facts*** (*e.g.,* words of contract; defamatory words);

b. Statements offered to show their ***effect on the hearer or reader*** (*e.g.,* to prove notice in a negligence case); and

c. Statements offered as ***circumstantial evidence of declarant's state of mind*** (*e.g.,* evidence of insanity or knowledge).

CMR **Exam Tip** Do not confuse statements offered as circumstantial evidence of declarant's state of mind, which are almost always offered as evidence of insanity or knowledge, with statements that reflect directly on declarant's state of mind, which are usually offered to establish intent. The former is not hearsay, while the latter is hearsay subject to a specific exception.

CMR **Exam Tip** In deciding whether evidence is hearsay, ask yourself whether we are relying on the declarant's credibility; *i.e.,* does it matter whether the declarant is telling the truth? If not, the evidence is not hearsay.

3. Nonhuman Declarations

There is no such thing as ***animal*** or ***machine*** hearsay; there must be an out-of-court statement by a ***person***. Thus, testimony about what a radar gun "said" or what a drug-sniffing dog did is not hearsay (but still must be relevant and authenticated to be admitted).

B. STATEMENTS THAT ARE NONHEARSAY UNDER THE FEDERAL RULES

Despite meeting the common law definition of hearsay, the following statements are not hearsay under the Federal Rules and are, therefore, admissible as substantive evidence:

1. Prior Statements by Witness

Under the Federal Rules, a prior statement by a witness is not hearsay if:

a. The prior statement is ***inconsistent*** with the declarant's in-court testimony and was ***given under oath*** at a prior proceeding;

b. The prior statement is ***consistent*** with the declarant's in-court testimony and is ***offered to rebut*** a charge that the witness is ***lying or exaggerating*** because of some motive (and the statement was made before any motive to lie or exaggerate arose); or

c. The prior statement is one of ***identification*** of a person made after perceiving him.

2. Admissions by Party-Opponent

An admission is a statement made or act that amounts to a prior acknowledgment by one of the parties of one of the relevant facts. Admissions of a party-opponent are not hearsay under the Federal Rules. To be an admission, the statement need not have been against the declarant's interest when made, and may even be in the form of an opinion. Personal knowledge is not required; the admission may be predicated on hearsay. The following types of admissions merit special attention.

a. Judicial and Extrajudicial Admissions

Formal judicial admissions (*e.g.,* in pleadings, stipulations, etc.) are conclusive. ***Informal*** judicial admissions made during testimony and ***extrajudicial*** (evidentiary) admissions are not conclusive and can be explained.

b. Adoptive Admissions

A party may make an admission by expressly or impliedly adopting or acquiescing in the statement of another.

1) Silence

If a reasonable person would have responded, and a party remains silent in the face of accusatory statements, his silence may be considered an implied admission. Silence is treated as an admission only if:

(i) The party ***heard and understood*** the statement;

(ii) The party was physically and mentally ***capable of denying*** the statement; and

(iii) A ***reasonable person would have denied*** the accusation.

Note that silence in the face of accusations by police in a ***criminal case*** is almost never considered an admission of a crime.

c. Vicarious Admissions

1) **Co-Parties**
Admissions of a party are not receivable against her co-parties merely because they happen to be joined as parties.

2) **Authorized Spokesperson**
The statement of a person authorized by the party to speak on its behalf (*e.g.,* statement by a company's press agent) can be admitted against the party as an admission.

3) **Principal-Agent**
Statements by an agent concerning any matter within the scope of her agency, made while the employment relationship exists, are not hearsay and are admissible against the principal.

4) **Partners**
After a partnership is shown to exist, an admission of one partner relating to matters within the scope of the partnership business is binding upon her co-partners.

5) **Co-Conspirators**
Admissions of one conspirator, made to a third party in furtherance of a conspiracy to commit a crime or civil wrong at a time when the declarant was participating in the conspiracy, are admissible against co-conspirators. However, testimonial admissions of a conspirator are admissible against another conspirator only if there was an opportunity to cross-examine the hearsay declarant.

6) **Privies in Title and Joint Tenants—State Courts Only**
In most state courts, admissions of each joint owner are admissible against the other, and admissions of a former owner of real property made at the time she held title are admissible against those claiming under her (grantees, heirs, etc.). These statements are not considered admissions under the Federal Rules, but may be admissible under one of the hearsay exceptions (*e.g.,* statement against interest).

7) **Preliminary Determinations**
Before admitting a hearsay statement as a vicarious admission, the court must make a preliminary determination of the declarant's relationship with the party against whom the statement is offered. In making such a determination, the court ***must consider the contents of the statement***, but the statement alone is not sufficient to establish the required relationship.

C. HEARSAY EXCEPTIONS—DECLARANT UNAVAILABLE

There are five important exceptions to the hearsay rule that condition admissibility of the hearsay statement on the present unavailability of the declarant to testify.

1. "Unavailability"

A declarant is unavailable if he:

a. Is exempt from testifying because of ***privilege***;

b. ***Refuses to testify*** concerning the statement despite a court order;

c. Testifies to ***lack of memory*** of the subject matter of the statement;

d. Is unable to testify due to ***death or physical or mental illness***; or

e. Is ***absent*** (beyond the reach of the court's subpoena), and the proponent is unable to procure his attendance by reasonable means.

2. Former Testimony

The testimony of a now-unavailable witness, given at another hearing or deposition, is admissible if:

a. The party against whom the testimony is offered or (in a civil case) the party's predecessor in interest was a ***party in the former action*** ("predecessor in interest" includes grantor-grantee and other privity relationships);

b. The former action involved the ***same subject matter*** (causes of action need not be identical);

c. The testimony was given ***under oath***; and

d. The party against whom the testimony is offered had an ***opportunity at the prior proceeding to develop the declarant's testimony*** (*i.e.,* by direct, cross, or redirect examination).

CMR **Exam Tip** Because grand jury proceedings do not provide an opportunity for cross-examination, the ***grand jury testimony*** of an unavailable declarant is not admissible against a defendant under the former testimony exception to the hearsay rule. Be careful not to confuse this with a prior inconsistent statement given under oath by a witness currently testifying. Grand jury testimony is admissible in that case, both as impeachment and substantive evidence.

3. Statements Against Interest

The statement of a person, now unavailable as a witness, against that person's pecuniary, proprietary, or penal interest ***when made***, as well as collateral facts contained in the statement, is admissible under the statement against interest exception to the hearsay rule. The declarant must also have had personal knowledge of the facts, and must have been aware that the statement was against her interest when she made it.

a. Risk of Criminal Liability

Note that when a criminal defendant wishes to show her innocence by introducing another's statements admitting the crime, ***corroborating circumstances*** indicating the trustworthiness of the statements are required.

b. "Statement" Means Single Remark

If a person makes a declaration containing statements that are against his interest (*e.g.,* "I sold the drugs") and statements that are not (*e.g.,* "X runs the drug ring"), the exception covers only those remarks that inculpate the declarant, not the entire extended declaration.

4. Dying Declarations—Statements Under Belief of Impending Death
In a ***homicide prosecution or a civil action***, a statement made by a now unavailable declarant is admissible if:

a. The declarant ***believed his death was imminent*** (he need not actually die); and

b. The statement concerned the ***cause or circumstances*** of what he believed to be his impending death.

CMR **Exam Tip** The bar exam will likely require you to distinguish the Federal Rule on dying declarations from the traditional rule. Beware of answer choices reflecting the traditional rule, which required that the declarant ultimately die of the injury and restricted the statement's use to homicide prosecutions.

5. Statements of Personal or Family History
Statements by a now unavailable declarant concerning births, marriages, divorces, relationship, genealogical status, etc., are admissible provided that:

a. The declarant is a ***member of the family*** in question or intimately associated with it; and

b. The statements are based on the declarant's ***personal knowledge*** of the facts or her knowledge of family reputation.

6. Statements Offered Against Party Procuring Declarant's Unavailability
The statement of a person (now unavailable as a witness) is admissible when offered against a party who has engaged or acquiesced in wrongdoing that ***intentionally procured the declarant's unavailability***.

D. HEARSAY EXCEPTIONS—DECLARANT'S AVAILABILITY IMMATERIAL
The following exceptions to the hearsay rule do not require that the declarant be unavailable.

1. Present State of Mind
A statement of a declarant's then-existing state of mind, emotion, sensation, or physical condition is admissible. It is usually offered to establish a person's intent or as circumstantial evidence that the intent was carried out. Except as to certain facts concerning the declarant's will, however, a statement of memory or belief is not admissible to prove the truth of the fact remembered or believed.

2. Excited Utterances
An out-of-court statement ***relating to a startling event***, made while under the stress of the excitement from the event (*i.e.*, ***before the declarant had time to reflect*** upon it), is admissible.

3. Present Sense Impressions
Comments made concurrently with the sense impression of an event that is not necessarily exciting may be admissible. There is little time for a calculated misstatement, and the contemporaneous nature of the statement makes it reliable.

4. Declarations of Physical Condition

a. Present Bodily Condition—Admissible

A spontaneous declaration of present bodily condition is admissible as an exception to the hearsay rule even though not made to a physician.

b. Past Bodily Condition—Admissible If to Assist Diagnosis or Treatment

Generally, declarations of past physical condition are inadmissible hearsay. Under the Federal Rules, however, these declarations are admissible if made to medical personnel to assist in diagnosing or treating the condition. Even declarations about the cause or source of the condition are admissible if pertinent to diagnosis or treatment.

Exam Tip Remember that, contrary to the majority state view, declarations of past physical condition made to a doctor employed to testify are ***admissible*** under the Federal Rules.

5. Business Records

Any writing or record made as a memorandum of any act or transaction is admissible in evidence as proof of that act or transaction. Under the Federal Rules and modern statutes, the main requirements for admissibility are as follows:

a. "Business"

"Business" includes every association, profession, occupation, or calling of any kind, whether or not conducted for profit.

b. Entry Made in Regular Course of Business

To be admissible, it must appear that the record was made in the course of a regularly conducted business activity, and that it was customary to make the type of entry involved (*i.e.,* the entrant had a duty to make the entry). Self-serving accident reports prepared primarily for litigation usually are inadmissible.

c. Personal Knowledge

The business record must consist of matters within the personal knowledge of the entrant or within the knowledge of someone with a ***duty*** to transmit such matters to the entrant.

CMR **Exam Tip** Watch for fact patterns involving police reports containing the statements of witnesses. While police reports may qualify as business records under some circumstances, remember that generally witnesses, or even parties, are not under a business duty to convey information to the police. Therefore, a report containing their statements cannot qualify as a business record, although it may be admissible under another exception (*see* 7., *infra*) or as an admission.

d. Entry Made Near Time of Event

The entry must be made at or near the time of the transaction.

e. Authentication

The authenticity of the record must be established. This can be accomplished by the custodian (i) ***testifying*** that the record is a business record, or (ii) ***certifying in writing*** that the record is a business record.

Exam Tip Business records may be used to prove the nonoccurrence or nonexistence of a matter if it was the regular practice of the business to record all such matters.

6. Past Recollection Recorded

If the witness's memory cannot be revived, a party may introduce a memorandum that the witness made at or near the time of the event. The writing itself is not admissible; it must be read to the jury.

7. Official Records and Other Official Writings

a. Public Records and Reports

The following are admissible: records setting forth the activities of the office or agency; recordings of matters observed pursuant to a duty imposed by law (except police observations in criminal cases); or in civil actions and ***against the government in criminal cases***, records of factual findings resulting from an investigation authorized by law. The writing must have been made by and within the scope of the duty of the public employee, and it must have been made at or near the time of the event.

CMR **Exam Tip** Police reports that do not qualify as business records may be admitted under the public records and reports exception. Even the officer's opinions and factual (not legal) conclusions would be admissible under this exception. Be careful, however, to test the statements of others contained in the report to make sure they are admissible under a hearsay exception; otherwise, those statements will be excluded even if the report is admitted.

CMR **Exam Tip** Remember that public records and reports generally are ***not admissible against the defendant in a criminal case***. This means that investigative reports by the police, FBI, and other agencies are inadmissible in this situation.

b. Records of Vital Statistics

Records of vital statistics are admissible if the report was made to a public officer pursuant to requirements of law.

c. Statement of Absence of Public Record

Evidence in the form of a certification or testimony from the custodian of public records that she has diligently searched and failed to find a record is admissible to prove that the matter was not recorded, or inferentially that the matter did not occur.

d. Judgments

A certified copy of a judgment is always admissible proof that such judgment has been entered.

1) Prior Criminal Conviction—Felony Conviction Admissible

Under the Federal Rules, judgments of felony convictions are admissible in criminal and civil actions to prove any fact essential to the judgment. In a criminal case, however, the government may use the judgment for this purpose only against the accused; it may be used only for impeachment purposes against others.

2) **Prior Criminal Acquittal—Excluded**
The exclusionary rule is still applied to records of prior acquittals.

3) **Judgment in Former Civil Case**
A civil judgment is clearly inadmissible in a subsequent criminal proceeding and generally inadmissible in subsequent civil proceedings.

8. Ancient Documents and Documents Affecting Property Interests

Under the Federal Rules, statements in any authenticated document ***20 years old or more*** are admissible, as are statements in ***any document affecting an interest in property***, regardless of age.

9. Learned Treatises

Treatises are admissible as substantive proof under the Federal Rules if:

a. Called to the attention of, or relied upon by, an expert witness; and

b. Established as reliable authority by the testimony of that witness, other expert testimony, or judicial notice.

10. Reputation

Reputation evidence is admissible, under several exceptions to the hearsay rule, as evidence of the following: (i) character; (ii) personal or family history; (iii) land boundaries; and (iv) a community's general history.

11. Family Records

Statements of fact concerning personal or family history contained in family Bibles, jewelry engravings, genealogies, tombstone engravings, etc., are admissible.

12. Market Reports

Market reports and other published compilations are admissible if generally used and relied upon by the public or by persons in a particular occupation.

E. RESIDUAL "CATCH-ALL" EXCEPTION OF FEDERAL RULES

For a hearsay statement that is not covered by a specific exception to be admitted, the Federal Rules provide a catch-all exception, which requires:

1. That the hearsay statement possess circumstantial guarantees of ***trustworthiness***;

2. That the statement be strictly ***necessary***; and

3. That ***notice*** be given to the adversary as to the nature of the statement.

F. CONSTITUTIONAL ISSUES

Because the use of hearsay evidence in a criminal case may violate the Confrontation Clause, prior testimonial evidence is inadmissible against a criminal defendant unless the hearsay declarant is

unavailable, and the defendant had an opportunity to cross-examine the hearsay declarant at the time the statement was made. However, the defendant forfeits his right of confrontation if he committed a wrongful act that was intended to keep the witness from testifying. In addition, hearsay rules and other exclusionary rules cannot be applied where such application would deprive the accused of her right to a fair trial or deny her right to compulsory process.

Evidence

Lecture Handout

Multistate Primer

EVIDENCE LECTURE HANDOUT

HEARSAY

A. Definition of Hearsay

1. **Hearsay** is an out-of-court statement offered *for the purpose of* establishing the truth of the matter asserted in the statement.

2. **Application of Definition**:

   Three questions:

   a. Is it an out-of-court statement?

   b. What precisely is the out-of-court statement?

   c. Is it being offered for the purpose of establishing its truth?

3. **Cast of Characters**

   a. One scenario

      1) Declarant (makes the out-of-court statement)

      2) Witness (reports the statement in court)

perception, memory, and sincerity are in issue.

5. **Specific Nonhearsay Situations** (*i.e.*, situations where the out-of-court statement is not being offered for its truth).

a. Verbal Acts or Legally Operative Facts—where the words spoken or written have relevant legal significance in the case by virtue of being spoken or written. (words of offer, acceptance, defamation, conspiracy, bribery, cancellation, misrepresentation, waiver, permission.)

HYPO 1A: Witness seeks to testify that Decla (the declarant) said "I accept your offer." Evidence is offered to prove an oral contract. Hearsay?

HYPO 1B: Witness seeks to testify that Decla said to insurance agent "Cancel my insurance" in order to prove policy cancellation. Hearsay?

HYPO 1C: Witness seeks to testify that Decla said "Take my car, go with it to Miami" in order to prove Decla gave permission to use his car. Hearsay?

HYPO 2B: Pl. sues for injuries caused by fall on stairs of store. Pl. calls witness who testifies that two days before Pl's fall, witness heard Decla tell store manager "Your stairs are defective, someone is bound to fall there." Offered to show notice to store. Hearsay?

HYPO 2C: Pl. sues for wrongful discharge by employer and claims that discharge was motivated by discrimination. Employer offers in evidence hundreds of letters written by customers complaining about Pl. Offered to show mental state of employer (*i.e.*, to show a non-discriminatory reason for the discharge). Hearsay?

c. Out-of-Court Statement offered not for its truth but as circumstantial evidence of declarant's relevant state of mind.

HYPO 3: Spano is charged with murder. Defense is insanity. Defense witness testifies that on the day before the killing, he heard Spano say "I am the Pope." Hearsay?

6. Prior Statements of the Witness

Can a witness's own prior statement be hearsay?

HYPO 4: Def. in a criminal case takes the stand to testify. Def's lawyer asks on direct examination "When you were arrested what did you tell the police?" Def. answers "I told them the truth—that I was innocent." Hearsay? Is it an admission?

other proceeding or deposition.

b. Prior Consistent Statements to rebut charge of recent fabrication or improper influence or motive.

c. Prior statement of identification made by a witness.

B. The Exceptions to the Rule Against Hearsay

1. Listing of Major Exceptions/Exclusions

a. admission of party

b. former testimony

c. statement against interest

d. dying declaration

e. spontaneous statements

1) Present state of mind in issue

2) Statement of existing intent to prove intended act

3) Excited utterance

4) Present sense impression

5) Declaration of present physical condition

6) Declaration of past physical condition

1) Need not be against interest at time of making statement. (Def. brags to neighbor that he made $2 million in 1999. Admissible in tax fraud prosecution.)

2) Need not be based on personal knowledge. (When informed that neighbor was bitten by a dog, Def. states "It must have been my dog that did it.")

3) Can be in form of legal conclusion. ("I was negligent.")

c. Party Admission is Considered Nonhearsay under Federal Rules of Evidence.

d. Vicarious Admission: A statement by the party's agent or servant concerning a matter within the scope of the agency or employment, made during existence of the relationship.

HYPO 5: Negligence action against Trucking Co. Truck Driver crashed through Pl's living room window and states "My brakes failed again; they failed three times last week. I told my boss about it but he does nothing. Now I am going to miss my last delivery for my employer." Does this statement come in against Trucking Co.?

b. **Requirements:** (1) meaningful opportunity for cross; and (2) unavailability of the declarant.

1) Meaningful opportunity to develop or cross-examine in the prior proceeding when the witness gave live testimony.****

a) same issue and motive

b) some identity of party. Party against whom offered must have been a party in first proceeding or, in civil case, at least in privity with party in first proceeding.

HYPO 6: In a one vehicle accident, a bus leaves the highway and crashes, injuring passengers A and B. In Action 1, A sues Bus Co. and W testifies live. In Action 2, B sues Bus Co. but W is no longer available.

May passenger B use W's former testimony against Bus Co.?

May Bus Co. use W's former testimony against passenger B?

2) Unavailability: Declarant is unavailable if court exempts declarant

4. Statement Against Interest

a. **Definition:** Declaration of a person, now unavailable as a witness, against that person's pecuniary, proprietary or penal interest (or statement which would expose declarant to civil liability or which would tend to defeat a civil claim by declarant) at the time the statement was made.

b. **Limitation**: A statement tending to expose the declarant to criminal liability and offered to exculpate the accused is not admissible unless "corroborating circumstances clearly indicate the trustworthiness of the statement."

HYPO 7: State v. Spano for murder of Victor Victim. W testifies for the defense that W heard Garibaldi say "I, not Spano, killed Victor." Is Garibaldi's out-of-court statement admissible as a statement against penal interest? (No, not unless there is also evidence of "corroborating circumstances" clearly indicating the trustworthiness of the content of the statement.)

c. Distinguish statement against interest from admission of party.

1) Statement against interest must be against interest at time statement made.

2) Statement against interest may be made by any person, not necessarily by a party.

HYPO 8: Harvey and Dan collide. Harvey confides to Neighbor that "It was all my fault." Harvey dies as a result of his injuries. Harvey's next of kin bring a wrongful death action against Dan. Dan calls Neighbor to testify that Harvey said "All my fault." Admissible? As an admission? As a statement against interest?

3) Statement against interest requires personal knowledge.

4) Statement against interest requires unavailability.

Is it accurate to say that a party admission always also qualifies as a statement against interest? No! Why not?

5. Dying Declaration—statement made under a sense of impending death.

a. **Definition:** In a prosecution for homicide or in a civil action or proceeding, a statement made by a declarant while believing that the declarant's death was imminent, concerning the cause or circumstances of the impending death.

b. **Requirements:**

1) State of Mind—made under a sense of impending death.

HYPO 9: Victor is stabbed and is lying in a gutter. Victor looks up at police officer and says "Spano did it." Victor promptly dies. A dying declaration?

2) Declarant need not die but must be unavailable at time of trial.

3) Kind of case in which admissible: homicide or civil case.

4) Content Limitation: Must concern cause or circumstances of impending death.

HYPO 10: Grutz is shot 12 times and is lying in the gutter. Grutz looks up at police officer and says "I'm dying, I know I'm dying. Too bad for me. By the way, my will was the product of undue influence. Don't let it be probated." Admissible as a dying declaration in the will probate proceeding?

6. Spontaneous Statements

A group of six exceptions for which unavailability is not required because the law regards prior statement as being at least as reliable as present in-court testimony.

a. Declaration of existing state of mind in issue

HYPO 11: Spano is on trial for murder. Defense: Insanity. Defense Witness testifies that on the eve of the killing, witness heard Spano say "I believe I am the Pope." Admissible?

b. Declaration of existing intent to do something in the future offered to infer that the intended future act was done

HYPO 12: Decla announces "On Monday of next week I am going to meet with Spano" offered to prove that Decla did meet Spano on Monday. Admissible?

c. Excited utterance

1) **Definition:** Statement relating to startling event or condition is admissible when made while declarant was still under stress of excitement caused by event or condition.

2) Requirements

- Startling event

- Made under stress of excitement

- Concerns the facts of the startling event

3) Considerations: Things to look for.

- Nature of event

- Time lapse and what is going on during time lapse

- Language of excitement

d. Present Sense Impression

1) **Definition:** A statement describing or explaining an event or condition made while declarant was perceiving the event or condition or immediately thereafter.

2) Distinguish from Excited Utterance

- Unnecessary to have startling event or excitement

- But must have almost precise contemporaneousness—no appreciable time lapse

HYPO 13: Victor is killed in his apartment on Sunday night. Spano is charged with his murder. Prosecution witness testifies that on Sunday night Witness called Victor and Victor said "Spano is here." Offered to show that Spano was present at about the time of the killing. Admissible? Dying declaration? Excited utterance? Present sense impression?

e. Declaration of *Present* Pain, Suffering or Physical Condition

Definition: A declaration of then-existing physical (or mental) condition is admissible to show the condition. ("It hurts!")

f. Declaration of Past Physical Condition

1) **Definition:** Statement made for purposes of diagnosis or treatment and describing medical history or past symptoms or the general character of the cause or external source of the symptoms insofar as reasonably pertinent to diagnosis or treatment.

2) **Requirements:**

- made to medical personnel
- pertinent to either diagnosis or treatment (even if diagnosis is only for the purpose of giving testimony)

HYPO 14: Pl. in personal injury case hires doctor to diagnose solely for the purpose of giving testimony. Doctor testifies and gives his opinion. Part of the basis of his opinion is the medical history given to him by Pl. May Doctor recite the medical history given him by Pl.? Is it admissible for its truth?

7. A Digression to Explore Recurring Test Issues and Hypos

a. Preliminary questions of fact upon which admissibility depends

Rule: Preliminary questions concerning the qualification of a person to be a witness, the existence of a privilege, or the admissibility of evidence shall be determined by the court. But in making its determination it is not bound by the rules of evidence.

HYPO 15: You offer the declarant's transcript into evidence as former testimony. Unavailability of the declarant is a fact question upon which admissibility depends. There is a dispute between you and your opponent over this fact question. You hand the judge a signed unauthenticated letter purporting to be from the declarant which states "I am unavailable." Who decides the question of unavailability, judge or jury? May whoever decides take account of the hearsay letter?

Answer: The judge decides and she may take account of the hearsay letter in making her decision.

HYPO 16: In a homicide case, officer attempts to testify to Victim's dying declaration. At issue is Victim declarant's state of mind. Was he speaking under a sense of impending death? The prosecutor offers a doctor's hearsay affidavit which states that, given Victim's medical condition, he must have known he was dying. Can the affidavit be used to determine Victim's state of mind? Used by whom? Judge or jury?

Answer: Same analysis as previous hypo. Yes, the affidavit, although it is hearsay, may be used by the judge, who is the one who determines the preliminary fact question of whether Victim was speaking under a sense of impending death.

b. <u>Impeaching the hearsay declarant</u>

Rule: When a hearsay statement has been admitted in evidence, the credibility of the declarant may be attacked by any evidence which would be admissible for that purpose if declarant had testified as a live witness.

HYPO 17: Victor is stabbed, goes to hospital and tells police officer "I am dying, Spano did it." Two days later, Victor is feeling much better and he tells Nurse "Bruno stabbed me. Now it looks like I will survive." Alas, Victor dies a week later. Spano is prosecuted for the murder of Victor. Officer is allowed to testify to Victor's dying declaration which implicates Spano. In rebuttal, the defense calls Nurse.

May she testify to Victor's statement to her that "Bruno stabbed me"?

Why or why not? If your answer is yes, what happens to the foundation requirement? Isn't the declarant, Victor, supposed to be given an opportunity to deny or explain the inconsistent statement?

> Answer: Victor's statement to the Nurse is not a dying declaration because Victor thought he would live when he made the statement. But it is admissible as a prior inconsistent statement to impeach Victor's credibility. Admissibility of the inconsistent statement is not subject to the usual foundation requirement.

c. Mixing hearsay and writings

HYPO 18: Victor is found shot dead in his business office with a dictaphone in his hand. He was apparently dictating business correspondence when an intruder entered and shot him. Police officer at the scene rewinds and plays back the dictaphone tape. Officer hears Victor dictating business letters but then hears Victor say "Spano, what are you doing here?" There is then the sound of a shot and the tape is silent. At Spano's trial, Officer is called by the prosecution. Officer seeks to testify to what he heard on the dictaphone tape.

Admissible? Why or why not? Is it hearsay? Is it admissible because it qualifies as a present sense impression? Any other problem beyond hearsay?

> Answer: The officer's testimony is hearsay but qualifies under the present sense impression exception to the rule against hearsay. So hearsay is not the problem. But the best evidence rule applies. The officer's testimony is not admissible unless the absence of the recording is explained.

8. Business Records

a. **Definition:** Records made at or near the time by, or from information transmitted by, a person with knowledge are admissible if kept in the regular course of business and if it was the regular course of that business to make the record unless the source of information or circumstances of preparation indicate a lack of trustworthiness.

b. **Rationale for Reliability:** Employees are under a business duty to be accurate in observing, reporting and recording business facts.

c. **Function of the Exception:** Allows the record to substitute for the in-court testimony of the employees.

d. **Typical Problem Areas:**

1) Does the exception apply?
Usually turns on whether entry is germane to the business.

HYPO 19: Grutz is involved in an automobile accident and is taken to the hospital emergency room where he tells Nurse "This accident was all my fault. I was grossly negligent." Nurse records Grutz's words in the hospital record. Plaintiff who was also injured sues Grutz for negligence.

At trial, can Nurse testify to Grutz's statements if called to the stand by Plaintiff?

May the hospital record be admitted if offered by Plaintiff to prove Grutz's statement?

2) The Multiple Hearsay Problem
Assume the entry is germane to the business so that the business records exception ordinarily applies. But suppose the record contains within it a statement made by someone outside the business. Reconsider the rationale and purpose of the exception.

HYPO 20: X, an outsider, not under a business duty to observe or report, perceives an event and reports it to the ABC Company. Company realizes that X's statement is germane to its business and includes X's statement in its record. Is the entry admissible under the business record exception to prove the truth of X's statement?

HYPO 21: Accident at a traffic light-controlled intersection. Investigating officer arrives at the scene 30 minutes later. He measures the skidmarks leading to Dan's car. He speaks to Schultz, an eyewitness, and also talks to Dan. He promptly prepares a police report which contains three entries as follows: (1) "Observations: 150' of skidmarks leading to Dan's car," (2) "Statement of witness: Schultz, an eyewitness, reports that Dan had the red light," (3) "Statement of Driver: Dan states that he, Dan, ran the red light." Plaintiff sues Dan for personal injuries resulting from the accident. At trial, Plaintiff offers the three entries as business records. Admissible?

Entry (1)

Entry (2)

Entry (3)

9. The Sixth Amendment Right of Confrontation

a. **Rule:** Even though an out-of-court statement qualifies as an exception to the rule against hearsay, the accused's Sixth Amendment right of confrontation may render the statement inadmissible when it is offered against the accused in a criminal case. The Supreme Court in *Crawford v. Washington* recently held that out-of-court statements, even if they fit a hearsay exception, will not be admitted if

1) the out-of court-statement is offered against the accused in a criminal case

-and-

2) the declarant is unavailable at the trial

-and-

3) the out-of-court statement was "testimonial"

-and-

4) the accused had no opportunity to cross-examine the declarant's "testimonial" statement when it was made;

-unless-

5) the prosecution demonstrates that the defendant has forfeited his Confrontation Clause objection by wrongdoing that prevented the declarant from testifying at trial.

b. **Definition of "Testimonial":** A hearsay statement is testimonial if declarant makes a statement that he or she anticipates will be used in the prosecution or investigation of the crime. (This would include witness statements made to police or other law enforcement officials in response to police questioning; any testimony given at a formal proceeding—preliminary hearing, grand jury, or motion to suppress; guilty plea allocutions of co-conspirators to prove that a conspiracy existed; forensic lab reports revealing drugs, fingerprints, firearms evidence, blood, DNA, etc.)

HYPO 22: Spano and Grutz are charged with the murder of Victor. Grutz tells the police "Spano and I did the murder." Grutz later pleads guilty but refuses to testify against Spano. In the prosecution of Spano, Cop seeks to testify that Grutz, the declarant, told Cop that "Spano and I did it." The out-of-court statement of Grutz is offered under the statement against interest exception to the rule against hearsay. The trial judge finds that the statement fits the exception and that it is reliable and has special guarantees of trustworthiness. Is it admissible?

Answer: No. It would violate the confrontation clause.

HYPO 23: Wife Madge makes a 911 call and tells the police responder that husband Harvey is jumping on her, threatening her and that Harvey is now driving off. In this call Madge identified Harvey as her attacker in response to questions from the responder. Madge did not show up and did not testify at Harvey's trial at which he was charged with domestic abuse and assault. Is the 911 call admissible?

Answer: Yes. It was held admissible as a present sense impression and excited utterance and on similar facts the U.S. Supreme Court held in 2006 that Madge's statements were not testimonial. *Davis v. Washington*

HYPO 24: Police were called to investigate a domestic disturbance. Wife Madge first told the police that everything was fine and invited them into the house. Husband Harvey was questioned separately by one officer and he reported that he and Madge had argued, but all was OK now. Under questioning by the other officer, Madge described how Harvey had assaulted her and she signed a police statement to that effect. At Harvey's trial for assault, Madge did not testify. May the officer testify to what Madge told him?

Answer: No. On similar facts, the U.S. Supreme Court held in 2006 that even if Madge's statements qualified as an exception to the rule against hearsay (unlikely), nevertheless the statements were testimonial and rendered inadmissible by the confrontation clause. *Hammon v. Indiana*

c. The difference between Hypo 23 and Hypo 24 was explained by the Supreme Court in these words:

1) Statements taken by police officers in the course of an investigation are "non-testimonial" and not subject to the confrontation clause when they are made under circumstances objectively indicating that the primary purpose of the interrogation is to enable police assistance to meet an ongoing emergency (*i.e.*, to secure the scene, to preserve the safety of the declarant, to answer the question "what is happening") (*e.g.*, Hypo 23).

2) Statements taken by police officers in the course of interrogation are testimonial and subject to the confrontation clause when the circumstances objectively indicate that there is no ongoing emergency and that the primary purpose of the interrogation is to establish or prove events potentially relevant to later criminal prosecution (*i.e.*, the emergency is over; the scene is secured; now we gather evidence; now we find out "what happened?") (*i.e.*, Hypo 24).

d. <u>Considerations in determining whether statements are testimonial</u>
The issue is very case specific but factors frequently considered are:

1) Likely motivation and intent of the *declarant* making the statement (to get help or provide evidence?).

2) Likely motivation and intent of *interrogator* (to safeguard the victim or secure the scene or to get evidence?).

3) The temporal element (ongoing emergency or description of past events?).

4) Identity of person eliciting the statement (law enforcement connected or acquaintance/relative of the declarant?).

5) Degree, amount, circumstances and location of police interrogation (preliminary on-scene questions or sustained, structured questioning?).

barbri®

Evidence

1. Ⓐ Ⓑ Ⓒ Ⓓ
2. Ⓐ Ⓑ Ⓒ Ⓓ
3. Ⓐ Ⓑ Ⓒ Ⓓ
4. Ⓐ Ⓑ Ⓒ Ⓓ
5. Ⓐ Ⓑ Ⓒ Ⓓ

6. Ⓐ Ⓑ Ⓒ Ⓓ
7. Ⓐ Ⓑ Ⓒ Ⓓ
8. Ⓐ Ⓑ Ⓒ Ⓓ
9. Ⓐ Ⓑ Ⓒ Ⓓ
10. Ⓐ Ⓑ Ⓒ Ⓓ

11. Ⓐ Ⓑ Ⓒ Ⓓ
12. Ⓐ Ⓑ Ⓒ Ⓓ
13. Ⓐ Ⓑ Ⓒ Ⓓ
14. Ⓐ Ⓑ Ⓒ Ⓓ
15. Ⓐ Ⓑ Ⓒ Ⓓ

16. Ⓐ Ⓑ Ⓒ Ⓓ
17. Ⓐ Ⓑ Ⓒ Ⓓ

EVIDENCE QUESTIONS

Question 1

An airline passenger was on trial for attempting to smuggle illegal drugs into the country. The prosecution is seeking to present evidence that when the passenger had passed the entry area carrying a small suitcase, a police dog had sniffed at the suitcase and started barking, prompting the passenger to run into a men's room, open his suitcase, and flush a bag down the toilet before anyone could apprehend him. The dog's handler is prepared to testify that the dog has been trained not to bark unless it detected illegal drugs, and that the dog started barking after sniffing the suitcase.

If the defense seeks to exclude the testimony by the dog handler describing the dog's reaction to the suitcase, the court should rule such testimony:

(A) Admissible, under a hearsay exception.

(B) Admissible, because the offered evidence shows that the dog would not have barked unless illegal drugs had been present.

(C) Inadmissible, because it is hearsay not within any recognized exception to the hearsay rule.

(D) Inadmissible, because it violates the Confrontation Clause of the United States Constitution.

Question 2

An engineer sued a business owner, claiming that they had entered into an oral agreement whereby the business owner agreed to hire the engineer as chief engineer of his business, that the engineer agreed to take the job at a specified salary, and that the business owner had subsequently breached their employment contract by refusing to hire the engineer. At the trial of the engineer's suit, the business owner took the stand and denied having any contract with the engineer for employment or otherwise. In response, the engineer offers into evidence an authenticated picture postcard that the business owner had mailed to his wife while on a business trip. One statement on the postcard clearly referring to the engineer reads, "Keep it under your hat for now, but I've offered him the chief engineer position and he's accepted." The business owner's attorney objects.

The postcard should be ruled:

(A) Admissible, because it is the statement of a party-opponent.

(B) Admissible, if it is a recent perception.

(C) Inadmissible, because it is a privileged communication between husband and wife.

(D) Inadmissible, because it is hearsay not within any recognized exception to the hearsay rule.

Question 3

The plaintiff slipped on a patch of ice at the defendant's home and is suing the defendant for negligence. The defendant denies that the plaintiff was injured in the fall. The defendant calls his neighbor to testify that right after the plaintiff fell, she said that she had a recurring hip injury and was experiencing a flare-up.

Should the court admit the neighbor's testimony?

(A) No, because it constitutes inadmissible hearsay.

(B) No, because it is irrelevant.

(C) Yes, because it qualifies as an excited utterance.

(D) Yes, because it is an admission of a party-opponent.

Question 4

At the defendant's arson trial, the prosecution offers to introduce the testimony of a police officer, who will testify that he showed a photographic lineup containing the defendant's picture to a witness who saw a man run from the building right before it burned down, and the witness selected the defendant's picture. The witness has moved out of state and cannot be persuaded or compelled to return to testify.

Should this evidence be admitted over the defendant's objection?

(A) Yes, it is a past recollection recorded.

(B) Yes, it is a prior identification.

(C) No, it is hearsay not within an exception.

(D) No, because the picture of the defendant is not properly authenticated.

Question 5

In a wrongful death action, the plaintiff claimed that the defendant intentionally caused the death of the plaintiff's husband, who was the defendant's co-worker. At trial, the plaintiff's attorney called another co-worker to the stand as a witness. The defendant's attorney did not object to the witness's testimony that there had been "bad blood" at work between the deceased and the defendant. However, the attorney objected to one line of questioning, but he was overruled by the judge. The line of questioning was as follows:

> Attorney: "Now, you've told us how the deceased came back to the shop after he had obviously been hit hard on the jaw. What did he say at that time?"
>
> Witness: "He said that the defendant did it, and just then I noticed that the defendant was in the shop too."
>
> Attorney: "What did the defendant do?"
>
> Witness: "He just smirked and started laughing."

Was the judge correct in overruling the objection to the admission of this portion of the witness's testimony?

(A) Yes, because it is a statement against interest by the defendant.

(B) Yes, because it is an adoptive admission by a party.

(C) No, because the introduction of the deceased's out-of-court statement would violate the defendant's right to confront witnesses.

(D) No, because the deceased's statement that the defendant did it is hearsay, and cannot qualify as a dying declaration.

Question 6

A pedestrian sued a driver, alleging that the driver's car ran a red light and struck the pedestrian in a crosswalk. At trial, the pedestrian's attorney wishes to call an emergency room nurse to testify that, when the pedestrian was brought in, she asked him how he was injured and he replied, "I was hit by a car that ran a red light."

If the driver's attorney objects to the nurse's testimony, the court is likely to rule that it is:

(A) Admissible hearsay.

(B) Admissible, because the statement was made to the nurse for purposes of medical treatment.

(C) Inadmissible hearsay not within any recognized exception to the hearsay rule.

(D) Inadmissible, because the pedestrian is available to testify.

Question 7

In an automobile collision case, the defendant's attorney called the defendant to the stand and asked, "Was the traffic light red, amber, or green when you entered the intersection?" The defendant replied, "It was green." Next, the defendant's attorney asked, "What did you tell the first police officer who arrived on the scene about the condition of the traffic light when you entered the intersection?" Before the defendant could reply with "I told him it was green," the plaintiff's attorney objected.

The objection should be:

(A) Sustained, because the statement is hearsay not within any recognized exception to the hearsay rule.

(B) Sustained, because the testimony is an irrelevant prior consistent statement.

(C) Overruled, because the statement is made from personal knowledge and, therefore, is nonhearsay.

(D) Overruled, because the defendant is in court and is subject to cross-examination by the plaintiff's attorney.

Question 8

At a homicide trial, the prosecution presented evidence that, on the day of the fatal shooting, the defendant and several members of his gang engaged in a running gun battle with the victim and members of his gang. The prosecution additionally presented evidence tending to prove that the defendant had been seen at the scene of the shooting around the time that the victim was killed. In his defense, the defendant proffered testimony of a witness that, one day before the victim's death, the defendant had said to him, "I'm flying to the state capital tonight for a two-day visit."

Should the witness's testimony be admitted over the objection of the prosecution?

(A) Yes, because it is not being offered for the truth of the matter asserted.

(B) Yes, because it tends to prove that the defendant was in the state capital at the time the charged crime was committed.

(C) No, because it is inadmissible hearsay.

(D) No, because it violates the propensity rule.

Question 9

The defendant is charged with burglary of a nearby jewelry store. The prosecution offers to introduce the testimony of a cabdriver who had picked up the defendant near the jewelry store shortly after the burglary occurred. The cabdriver saw some bracelets sticking out of a canvas bag that the defendant was carrying and asked, "Did you just bust into a jewelry store?" The defendant did not reply.

Is the court likely to admit this evidence over the defendant's objection?

(A) Yes, it is a present sense impression.

(B) Yes, his silence is an implied admission.

(C) No, it is inadmissible hearsay.

(D) No, because a reasonable person would not have denied the statement under the circumstances.

Question 10

During the defendant's trial for armed robbery, evidence was introduced establishing that a rifle was found in the trunk of the defendant's car when he was arrested. On cross-examination by the prosecutor, the defendant admitted that when he was arrested and the rifle was found, he stated, "That's my hunting rifle. I keep it with me for protection."

Should the court allow the testimony?

(A) Yes, because it is a statement against interest.

(B) Yes, because it is an excited utterance.

(C) No, because it is hearsay not within an exception.

(D) No, because it is a self-serving statement.

Question 11

A pedestrian sued a local bar for injuries he suffered when he was struck by a car driven by a bar patron that had run a red light. He claimed that the patron was permitted to drink too much liquor at the bar before leaving. At trial, the pedestrian called a witness to the stand. The witness testified that she and a friend had visited the bar on the night in question. The witness seeks to testify that she remarked about the patron to her friend, "Look at that guy. He's so drunk he can't even stand up."

The witness's testimony concerning her remark to her friend is:

(A) Admissible as a prior consistent statement.

(B) Admissible as a statement made by the witness regarding the condition she observed while she was observing it.

(C) Admissible as an excited utterance.

(D) Inadmissible as hearsay not within any exception.

Question 12

In a suit to recover injuries after a car accident at an intersection, the plaintiff testified that she had had the right-of-way at the intersection. The defendant's attorney did not cross-examine the plaintiff. The plaintiff then called a witness to testify that, shortly after the collision, as she pulled the plaintiff from the car, the witness heard the plaintiff say, "I think I'm dying! Didn't the other driver see I had the right-of-way?"

The witness's testimony should be:

(A) Admissible, because the plaintiff's statement was made under belief of impending death.

(B) Admissible, because the plaintiff's statement was an excited utterance.

(C) Inadmissible, because the plaintiff's credibility has not been attacked.

(D) Inadmissible, because the plaintiff's belief that she had the right-of-way has already been established without contradiction.

Question 13

The declarant collapsed at her wedding reception after drinking champagne during the wedding toast. A group of guests surrounded her after she collapsed. As she was struggling to maintain consciousness, she declared, "I knew my new husband was after my money. Make sure he is brought to justice for murdering me." The declarant lost consciousness and lapsed into a coma; she remains in a vegetative state. It was determined that she was poisoned and her husband was arrested and charged with attempted murder. At trial, the prosecution wishes to call one of the guests to testify to the declarant's statement after her collapse.

The court should find the testimony:

(A) Inadmissible, because it is hearsay not within any exception.

(B) Inadmissible, because dying declarations are not admissible unless the declarant is dead.

(C) Admissible, as evidence of the declarant's state of mind.

(D) Admissible, because it is a dying declaration.

Question 14

A passenger in a vehicle that was struck by another car sued the other car's driver, claiming that the collision severely injured his right leg. The defendant claimed that the plaintiff's leg injury resulted from an earlier, unrelated industrial accident. At trial, after having testified to his pain from the injury allegedly caused by the defendant, the plaintiff called as a witness the physician who treated him. The physician offers to testify that the plaintiff told him that his earlier leg problems had completely cleared up before the alleged injury caused by the defendant.

If the defendant objects to the admission of this testimony, the court will most likely hold the testimony to be:

(A) Admissible as a statement of a party.

(B) Admissible as a statement for purposes of diagnosis and treatment.

(C) Inadmissible, because of the physician-patient privilege.

(D) Inadmissible, because the statement related to a past physical condition.

Question 15

In a medical malpractice action, the plaintiff sought to have her neighbor testify that, the day after receiving treatment on her back from the defendant, the plaintiff told the neighbor that her back was getting worse.

On objection, this testimony will most likely be held to be:

(A) Admissible, because it is a statement of personal history.

(B) Admissible, because it is a statement of a then-existing physical condition.

(C) Inadmissible, because it is hearsay not within any exception.

(D) Inadmissible, because it was not made for the purpose of medical treatment.

Question 16

The issue in a civil case was whether the plaintiff was old enough to get married. The defendant sought to prove that the plaintiff was old enough by calling an employee of the county, who authenticated a photocopy of the plaintiff's birth certificate. The plaintiff objected to introduction of the photocopy.

Is the photocopy admissible?

(A) Yes, because it is a past recollection recorded.

(B) Yes, because it is a public record.

(C) No, because it is not the best evidence.

(D) No, because it is inadmissible hearsay.

Question 17

One of the issues in dispute at a civil trial was ownership of a particular building over a 50-year period. The plaintiff wishes to introduce into evidence a 25-year-old newspaper that will show that the defendant owned the building at that time. The defendant's attorney objects.

Should the newspaper be admitted?

(A) Yes, because it is an ancient document.

(B) Yes, because it is a self-authenticating document.

(C) Yes, because it is an ancient document and it is self-authenticating.

(D) No, because it is inadmissible hearsay.

EVIDENCE ANSWERS

Answer to Question 1

(B) The testimony is admissible with a proper foundation. Choice (B) essentially says that evidence of the dog's barking will be admissible because it is ***relevant***; it is relevant because it can be shown that, based on the dog's training, it would not have barked unless drugs had been present. (A) and (C) are incorrect because an animal cannot make a hearsay statement. For purposes of the hearsay rule, a "statement" is limited to an oral or written assertion (or nonverbal conduct intended to be an assertion) of a ***person.*** [Fed. R. Evid. 801(a)] Similarly, (D) is incorrect to conclude that such evidence is inadmissible because it violates the Confrontation Clause of the United States Constitution. For purposes of the Confrontation Clause, an animal would not be considered a "witness"; thus, a defendant has no right to "confront" the animal in court. The hearsay rule and the Confrontation Clause have a common rationale: human beings have a well-documented capacity for deception and lying. Cross-examination is an extremely useful way to test the veracity of a witness who might be lying. If the "witness" cannot be cross-examined, or can only be cross-examined months after making an out-of-court statement, the ability to test the truthfulness of the witness and the accuracy of his statements will be severely limited. However, unlike human beings, animals do not consciously lie. It thus makes little sense to say that evidence of a police dog's barking, under circumstances where the bark indicates the presence of drugs in a suitcase, should be inadmissible.

(A) The postcard is admissible because it is an admission by a party-opponent. Note that the admission can be in writing, and does not have to be against that party's interest at the time the statement is made. (D) is incorrect because, under the Federal Rules of Evidence, any admission by a party-opponent is not hearsay. (B) is wrong. There is no such basis for admission of evidence. (C) is also incorrect. Under the husband-wife privilege, confidential marital communications cannot be disclosed. However, since the means of communication was by a postcard, which could be read by anyone, there was no expectation of privacy, and the privilege is lost.

(D) The court should admit the testimony as an admission. An admission of a party-opponent is considered nonhearsay under the Federal Rules. An admission is a statement that amounts to a prior acknowledgment by one of the parties to an action of one of the relevant facts. If the party said or did something inconsistent with his contentions at trial, the law regards him as estopped from preventing its admission into evidence, and here the plaintiff's statement that her hip injury was a recurrence of an old injury may be inconsistent with her assertion that her hip was injured when she fell on the defendant's property. (A) is incorrect because, as discussed above, the plaintiff's statement is nonhearsay. (B) is incorrect because the statement is relevant—it relates to a time, event, or person in controversy. Here, the statement relates to whether the plaintiff's injury resulted from her fall on the defendant's property. As such, it is relevant. (C) is incorrect because an excited utterance must concern the immediate facts of a startling occurrence. Here, the plaintiff's statement does not refer to the accident itself but rather to the condition of her hip.

(C) The officer's testimony is being offered to prove the truth of the matter asserted: that the witness saw the defendant commit the arson and run from the scene. Thus, the testimony is hearsay and, not being within any exception, is inadmissible. Hearsay is a statement, other than one made by the declarant while testifying at the trial or hearing, offered in evidence to prove the truth of the matter asserted. [Fed. R. Evid. 801(c)] The officer is attempting to testify to the statement of the witness (an out-of-court declarant) that the defendant was the arsonist that the witness saw running from the scene. This statement is being offered to prove the truth of the matter asserted therein, namely, that the defendant committed the crime. Consequently, the testimony is hearsay. Because the testimony does not come within any of the hearsay exceptions, it should not be admitted. (A) is incorrect because past recollection recorded is an exception to the hearsay rule that allows the introduction into evidence of a writing made by or under the direction of a witness at or near the time of an event, where the witness is presently unable to remember the facts. [Fed. R. Evid. 803(5)] Here, there is no attempt to introduce into evidence a writing prepared by the officer, nor is the officer unable to remember the facts. Therefore, past recollection recorded is inapplicable. (B) is incorrect. A statement of prior identification of a person made after perceiving the person is not hearsay only if such prior statement was made by a testifying witness who is subject to cross-examination. [Fed. R. Evid. 801(d)(1)(C)] Here, the witness who made the prior identification is not testifying. Thus, the statement of identification remains hearsay. (D) is incorrect because the picture of the defendant is not even being offered into evidence. Generally, a photograph is admissible only if it is identified by a witness as a portrayal of certain relevant facts and verified by the witness as a correct representation of those facts. The evidence sought to be admitted is not the photograph, but rather a statement concerning the identification of the arsonist. Thus, the photograph need not be authenticated.

Answer to Question 5

(B) The judge was correct in overruling the objection because it was an adoptive admission. An adoptive admission, also referred to as an admission by silence, occurs when a party hears an accusation and fails to protest when a reasonable person would have protested if the accusation were untrue. Under those circumstances, both the accusation and the lack of protest can be introduced by the party opponent if relevant. Therefore, (B) is correct and (D) is wrong. (A) is wrong because the hearsay exception "statement against interest" can only be used when the declarant is unavailable to testify. (C) is wrong because the Confrontation Clause does not apply to civil cases.

Answer to Question 6

(C) The statement is inadmissible hearsay. This question involves interpretation of the hearsay exception for out-of-court statements made for purposes of medical diagnosis or treatment. Under the Federal Rules, statements about the cause or source of a medical condition are admissible if reasonably pertinent to diagnosis or treatment. [Fed. R. Evid. 803(4)] That a car struck the pedestrian is reasonably pertinent to medical diagnosis or treatment; a nurse or doctor would probably want to know what degree of force was absorbed by his body. This information would provide them with better insights as to the medical cause of the pedestrian's injuries. On the other hand, the color of the traffic light the car ran (red, yellow, or green) has no bearing on anything ***other than fault;*** that information would not help medical personnel diagnose or treat the pedestrian's injury. Hence, (A) and (B) are incorrect. (D) is incorrect because the fact that the out-of-court declarant (the pedestrian) is available to testify does not render his statement to the emergency room nurse inadmissible. This hearsay exception, like most, does not require that the declarant be unavailable to testify before evidence of his hearsay statement can be introduced.

Answer to Question 7

(A) The statement is hearsay not within any exception. This question involves the proposed testimony of a witness (the defendant) about his prior out-of-court statement (telling the officer that the light was green) that is ***consistent*** with his in-court testimony. It appears that the prior statement is being offered to prove the truth of the matter asserted in the statement, that the light was green, when the defendant entered the intersection. Thus, the proposed testimony is hearsay evidence and does not fall within any recognized exception to the hearsay rule. (B) is wrong because it states that the objection to the defendant's proposed testimony should be sustained because the prior consistent statement is irrelevant. Federal Rule 401 establishes a standard for relevance that is very easy to meet: relevant evidence is evidence having ***any*** tendency to make the existence of a consequential fact more probable or less probable than it would be without the evidence. The color of the traffic light at the time the defendant entered the intersection is clearly a consequential fact in the plaintiff's tort claim against the defendant. That the defendant immediately told the officer that the light was green would have ***some*** tendency to prove that the light was in fact green. The problem with the defendant's proposed testimony is not that it is ***substantively*** irrelevant, but rather that it is an unacceptable ***form*** of evidence, *i.e.,* hearsay. (C) is wrong because, if an item of evidence is hearsay and not within any hearsay exception, it does not become admissible simply because it was made from personal knowledge. Declarants typically make hearsay statements based on personal knowledge; that does not transform the statements into nonhearsay or somehow render them admissible. (D) is incorrect; the fact that the defendant is in court and subject to cross-examination does not change the nature of the statement. Federal Rule 801(d)(1)(B) defines when a witness's prior consistent statement is not considered hearsay evidence: when it is offered to rebut a charge against the witness of recent fabrication or improper influence or motive. This question in no way suggests that such a charge has been made against the defendant. (Note also that the absence of any facts indicating impeachment of the defendant may make the testimony inadmissible on the additional ground that it is improper bolstering of an unimpeached witness.)

Answer to Question 8

(B) The testimony should be admitted. When analyzing questions involving the admissibility of hearsay evidence, ask two things: (i) Is the proffered evidence hearsay (*i.e.,* an out-of-court statement by a declarant, being offered to prove the truth of the matter asserted in the statement)? (ii) If hearsay, is the proffered evidence nevertheless admissible because it fits within an exception to the hearsay rule? The witness's proffered testimony is hearsay because it matters whether the defendant's statement is true or false. If his statement is true (if the defendant actually intended to go to the state capital, as stated), then the likelihood that he actually went there is increased. (This is because people tend to act in a manner consistent with their previously stated intentions.) Since the witness's testimony would be used for the purpose of establishing the truth of the defendant's statement, it is hearsay evidence. However, the testimony fits within a hearsay exception. A declarant's statement of present intention to take an action in the future fits within the "state of mind" exception contained in Federal Rule of Evidence 803(3). One's intent is a part of one's state of mind. Thus, the testimony should be admitted. This two-step analysis of hearsay evidence also makes clear that (A) and (C) are incorrect. (A) states that the witness's testimony is not being offered for the truth of the matter asserted, but, as stated above, it is offered for its truth. (C) correctly characterizes the testimony as hearsay but incorrectly states that the evidence is inadmissible; it is admissible under the state-of-mind exception. (D) is a nonsensical answer. The witness's testimony does not pertain in any way to the defendant's character. Thus, the propensity rule, which states that evidence of a person's character trait is generally inadmissible to prove that the person acted in conformity with the trait on a particular occasion, is not implicated by this question.

Answer to Question 9

(B) The evidence should be admitted. The silence of a defendant in response to an accusatory statement may be considered an admission if a reasonable person would have denied the statement under the same circumstances, the defendant heard and understood the statement, and the defendant was capable of denying the statement. Here, the prosecution is offering the statement to show that the defendant impliedly admitted to the accusation by not replying to it. Under the given circumstances, a reasonable person would likely deny having committed the crime of burglary when questioned by someone seeing him carry jewelry in a bag. Thus, the court probably will admit the evidence as an implied admission. Therefore, (B) is correct and (D) is incorrect. (A) is incorrect because a present sense impression is in response to the declarant's having witnessed a particular event. Here, the cabdriver did not make the statement in response to having witnessed the defendant robbing a jewelry store. Therefore, the statement was not a present sense impression. (C) is not correct. To the extent that the evidence is being offered to prove the matter asserted, it would be admissible as an admission, which is not hearsay under the Federal Rules.

Answer to Question 10

(C) The defendant's testimony is being offered to prove the truth of the matter asserted (*i.e.*, that it is his hunting rifle and he keeps it for protection) and is hearsay. Hearsay is a statement, other than one made by the declarant while testifying at the trial or hearing, offered in evidence to prove the truth of the matter asserted. A hearsay problem can arise even if the out-of-court declarant and the in-court witness are the same person, as is the case here. Because the statement is not within any exception to the hearsay rule, it must be excluded. (A) is incorrect because a statement against interest is admissible, even if hearsay, only if the declarant is unavailable to testify. Here, the declarant is the defendant and he is clearly available and able to testify. Thus, the testimony is not admissible as a statement against interest. (B) is incorrect because an excited utterance applies only if made in response to a startling event. Although the conditions of the search might have been stressful to the defendant, it is not the type of situation that gives rise to an excited utterance. (D) is incorrect. The fact that a statement is self-serving is not grounds for its exclusion. All of a criminal defendant's evidence can be considered self-serving in the sense that it furthers his claim of innocence.

Answer to Question 11

(B) The witness's remark is admissible under the present sense impression exception to the hearsay rule. [Fed. R. Evid. 803(1)] Under this exception, a hearsay statement is admissible if it is made concurrently with the perception of an event. Here, the witness made the observation of the intoxicated patron while she was observing him. (A) is wrong. A prior consistent statement can be used to rebut evidence that the trial testimony is a recent fabrication or that a motive to falsify has arisen since the event. The facts do not indicate either claim was made. The statement is not an excited utterance; therefore, (C) is wrong. (D) is wrong because the statement comes within the present sense impression exception to the hearsay rule.

Answer to Question 12

(B) The witness's testimony should be admissible as an excited utterance. Statements made under the stress of some exciting event and relating to that event are admissible as exceptions to the hearsay rule. (A) is incorrect because the Federal Rules require the maker of a dying declaration to be unavailable for the declaration to be admissible. (C) is incorrect because the statement is not being offered for rehabilitation. (D) is incorrect because there is no rule limiting cumulative evidence to establish a point, so certainly testimony from a second witness tending to prove a key issue would be admissible. If this were the tenth person to testify on that point, then the testimony might not be relevant.

Answer to Question 13

(A) The statement is inadmissible hearsay. It is an out-of-court statement being offered to prove the truth of the matter asserted, *i.e.*, that the defendant tried to kill the declarant. The statement does not qualify as a dying declaration or as a declaration of the declarant's state of mind. (*See* below.) In addition, the statement does not constitute an excited utterance because it does not concern the immediate facts of the startling event. The fact that the declarant believes that the defendant tried to kill her does not concern what is happening to her at that moment except to give an opinion as to who tried to kill her. (B) is wrong because it is too broad. While the use of dying declarations in a criminal prosecution is limited to homicide cases, a dying declaration is admissible in a civil action even though the declarant did not die. (C) is incorrect because the state of mind exception covers statements of the declarant's then-existing state of mind, emotion, sensation, or physical condition, and is applicable only to show the declarant's state of mind when it is directly in issue or to show subsequent acts of the declarant. Neither of these situations is present here. Thus, this exception is inapplicable. (D) is wrong because the use of dying declarations is limited to civil actions and prosecutions for homicide. Here, the defendant is being tried for ***attempted*** murder. Thus, the statement does not qualify as a dying declaration.

Answer to Question 14

(B) The testimony will be admissible as a statement for purposes of diagnosis and treatment. Under the Federal Rules, statements regarding past symptoms and medical history made to assist in diagnosis or treatment are admissible if made to medical personnel, even if made to a doctor employed to testify. Here, the plaintiff visited the physician seeking treatment for his leg. Thus, (B) is correct and (D) is wrong. (A) is wrong because an admission is a statement of a ***party-opponent***; *i.e.*, a party's admission may be introduced by an opponent, and the party cannot keep the statement out of evidence, but the party cannot introduce his own out-of-court statement into evidence as an admission. (C) is wrong because the physician-patient privilege does not apply here. The plaintiff is offering his doctor's testimony as evidence; thus, the privilege has been waived.

Answer to Question 15

(B) The testimony will most likely be admissible as a statement of a then-existing physical condition. Declarations of existing physical condition are admissible as an exception to the hearsay rule. Under the Federal Rules, these declarations are admissible even though not made to medical personnel. (C) is incorrect. The statement would be hearsay but it would qualify under the exception for statements describing current physical condition. (D) is incorrect. Even though the statement does not qualify as a statement for purposes of medical treatment, the statement is admissible under the current physical condition exception. (A) is incorrect because statements of physical condition do not qualify as statements of personal history.

Answer to Question 16

(B) The birth certificate is admissible to prove the plaintiff's age as a self-authenticating public record. Although the birth certificate is being offered to prove the truth of the matter asserted therein (*i.e.*, the plaintiff's age), it is admissible hearsay because it falls within the public records exception to the hearsay rule. That exception provides that records of vital statistics are admissible if the report was made to a public office pursuant to requirements of law, and birth certificates meet this requirement. The certificate is self-authenticating because it is a certified copy of a public record. Thus, (D) is incorrect. (A) is incorrect. A past recollection recorded is admissible to prove the facts of a writing when a witness's memory cannot be revived, which is not the purpose of its admissibility under these facts. (C) is incorrect because the best evidence rule allows photocopies of official records to be admitted into evidence if the copy is certified as correct by the custodian of the document or other person authorized to do so. Here, the county employee is testifying as to the authenticity of the birth certificate; thus, the best evidence rule is satisfied.

Answer to Question 17

(C) The newspaper should be admitted because it is an ancient document and it is self-authenticating. Under the Federal Rules, a statement in any authenticated document 20 years old or more is admissible as a hearsay exception. Newspapers are self-authenticating documents, *i.e.,* they "prove themselves." The newspaper at issue here is more than 20 years old and is self-authenticating. (A) and (B) are incorrect because each answer alone is not a complete reason why the newspaper will be admitted. (D) is incorrect because, as stated, authenticated "ancient" documents are admissible under an exception to the hearsay rule.

Real Property

Landlord-Tenant

Servitudes

REAL PROPERTY

I. LANDLORD AND TENANT

A. LEASES

A lease is a contract that governs the landlord-tenant relationship. Covenants in the lease are generally ***independent***; *i.e.,* if one party breaches a covenant, the other party can recover damages but must still perform his promises and cannot terminate the landlord-tenant relationship. The doctrines of actual and constructive eviction and the implied warranty of habitability are exceptions to this rule. Also, many states have created a statutory exception allowing the landlord to terminate the lease for the nonpayment of rent.

B. TENANT DUTIES AND LANDLORD REMEDIES

1. Tenant's Duty to Repair (Doctrine of Waste)

A tenant cannot damage (*i.e.,* commit waste on) the leased premises. The rules governing waste in the leasehold context are much like those governing waste in the life estate context.

a. Types of Waste

There are three types of waste:

1) ***Voluntary (affirmative) waste*** results when the tenant intentionally or negligently damages the premises or exploits minerals on the property.

2) ***Permissive waste*** occurs when the tenant fails to take reasonable steps to protect the premises from damage from the elements. The tenant is liable for all ***ordinary*** repairs, excluding ordinary wear and tear. If the duty is shifted to the landlord (by lease or statute), the tenant has a duty to report deficiencies promptly.

3) ***Ameliorative waste*** occurs when the tenant alters the leased property, thereby increasing its value. Generally, the tenant is liable for the cost of restoration. There is a modern exception to this rule, however, which permits a tenant to make this type of change if he is a long-term tenant and the change reflects changes in the neighborhood.

b. Destruction of Premises Without Fault

If the leased premises are destroyed without the fault of either the landlord or the tenant, no waste is involved. In the absence of lease language or a statute to the contrary, neither party has a duty to restore the premises, but the tenant has a duty to continue paying rent. In most states, statutes or case law now give the tenant the option to terminate the lease in this situation, even in the presence of an explicit covenant to repair.

c. Tenant's Liability for Covenants to Repair

If a ***residential*** tenant covenants to repair, the landlord usually remains obligated to repair (except for damages caused by the tenant) under the nonwaivable "implied warranty of habitability" (*see* C.3., *infra*). However, a ***nonresidential*** tenant's covenant to repair is enforceable, and a landlord may be awarded damages for breach based on the property's condition when the lease terminates compared with its condition when the lease commenced. A tenant who covenants to repair is ***not*** usually liable to rebuild after structural damage or casualty destruction, unless the covenant ***expressly includes*** these types of repairs. In the absence of a specific reference to ordinary wear and tear, a covenant to repair usually ***includes*** such repairs. However, repair covenants frequently ***exclude*** ordinary wear and tear.

2. Duty to Not Use Premises for Illegal Purpose

If the tenant uses the premises for an illegal purpose, the landlord may terminate the lease or obtain damages and injunctive relief. Occasional unlawful conduct by the tenant does not breach this duty.

3. Duty to Pay Rent

At common law, rent was due at the end of the leasehold term. However, leases usually contain a provision making rent payable at some other time (*e.g.*, "monthly in advance"). Most states today have statutes providing that if the leasehold terminates before the time originally agreed upon, the tenant must pay a ***proportionate amount*** of the agreed rent.

a. Rent Deposits

The landlord is not permitted to retain a ***security deposit*** beyond the damages actually suffered. If a rent deposit is denominated a ***"bonus,"*** the landlord can retain it after the tenant is evicted.

b. Termination of Rent Liability—Surrender

If a tenant effectively conveys (surrenders) his leasehold interest back to the landlord, his duty to pay rent ends.

4. Landlord Remedies

a. Tenant on Premises But Fails to Pay Rent—Evict or Sue for Rent

At common law, a breach of the lease, such as failure to pay rent, resulted only in a cause of action for money damages; a breach did not give rise to a right to terminate the lease. Most modern leases, however, give the nonbreaching party the right to terminate. Thus, if a tenant is on the premises and fails to pay rent, the landlord may bring suit for rent due or may evict the tenant under the state's ***unlawful detainer*** statute. The ***only*** issue in an unlawful detainer proceeding is whether the tenant has the right to possession; the tenant cannot raise counterclaims.

b. Tenant Abandons—Do Nothing or Repossess

If the tenant ***unjustifiably*** abandons the property, the majority view is that the landlord has a duty to mitigate damages by seeking to relet the premises. If the landlord repossesses and/or relets, the tenant's liability depends on whether the landlord has ***accepted the surrender***. If surrender is not found, the tenant is liable for the difference between the promised rent and the fair rental value of the property (in cases of reletting, between the promised rent and the rent received from the reletting). If surrender is found, the tenant is free from any rent liability accruing after abandonment. Note that the landlord's resumption of possession for himself constitutes acceptance of surrender.

C. LANDLORD DUTIES AND TENANT REMEDIES

Subject to modification by the lease, a statute, or the implied warranty of habitability, the general rule is that a landlord has ***no duty to repair or maintain*** the premises.

1. **Duty to Deliver Possession of Premises**
   Statutes in most states require the landlord to put the tenant in ***actual*** possession of the premises at the beginning of the leasehold term; *i.e.,* the landlord is in breach if he has not evicted a hold-over tenant by the beginning of the lease term.

2. **Quiet Enjoyment**
   Every lease has an implied covenant that neither the landlord nor a paramount title holder (*e.g.*, a prior mortgagee who forecloses) will interfere with the tenant's quiet enjoyment and possession of the premises. This covenant may be breached in the following ways:

   a. **Actual Eviction**
      Actual eviction occurs when the landlord or paramount title holder, or a hold-over tenant, excludes the tenant from the ***entire*** leased premises. Actual eviction terminates the tenant's obligation to pay rent.

   b. **Partial Eviction**
      Partial actual eviction occurs when the tenant is physically excluded from only part of the leased premises. Partial eviction ***by the landlord*** relieves the tenant of the obligation to pay rent for the ***entire*** premises, even though the tenant continues in possession of the remainder. Partial eviction ***by a third person*** with paramount title results in an ***apportionment*** of rent; *i.e.,* the tenant is liable for the reasonable rental value of the portion she continues to possess.

   c. **Constructive Eviction**
      If the landlord does something (or, more often, fails to provide a service he has a legal duty to provide) that renders the property ***uninhabitable***, the tenant may terminate the lease and seek damages. The conditions must be the result of the ***landlord's actions*** (not a neighbor's or other third party's), and the tenant ***must vacate*** the premises within a reasonable time.

3. **Implied Warranty of Habitability**
   Most jurisdictions imply a covenant of habitability into ***residential leases***. This warranty is ***nonwaivable***. The landlord's duty is tied to standards of local housing codes. In the event of a breach, the tenant may: (i) ***terminate*** the lease; (ii) ***make repairs and offset*** the cost against future rent; (iii) ***abate the rent*** to an amount equal to the fair rental value in view of the defects; or (iv) remain in possession, pay full rent, and ***sue for damages.***

CMR **Exam Tip** Keep in mind that the implied warranty of habitability does ***not*** apply to commercial tenants—only to residential tenants.

4. **Retaliatory Eviction**
   In many states, a landlord may not terminate a lease or otherwise penalize a tenant in retaliation for the tenant's exercise of her legal rights, including reporting housing or building code violations. Many statutes presume a retaliatory motive if the landlord acts within, *e.g.,* 90 to 180 days after the tenant exercises her rights. To overcome the presumption, the landlord must show a valid, nonretaliatory reason for his actions.

5. **Discrimination**
   Tenants and potential tenants are protected by the ***Civil Rights Act*** of 1866, which bars

racial or ethnic discrimination, and the ***Fair Housing Act***, which bars discrimination based on ethnicity, religion, national origin, gender, and disability, as well as discrimination against families with children (except in senior housing).

D. ASSIGNMENTS AND SUBLEASES

Absent an express restriction in the lease, a tenant may freely transfer her leasehold interest, in whole or in part. A ***complete*** transfer of the entire remaining term is an ***assignment***. If the tenant retains any part of the remaining term (other than a right to reenter upon breach), the transfer is a ***sublease***.

CMR **Exam Tip** For bar exam purposes, a transfer will be considered a sublease, rather than an assignment, only when the original tenant reserves time for herself (*e.g.,* the last month of the lease).

1. Consequences of Assignment

An assignee stands in the shoes of the original tenant in a direct relationship with the landlord; *i.e.,* the assignee and the landlord are in ***"privity of estate,"*** and each is liable to the other on all covenants in the lease that "run with the land."

a. Covenants that Run with the Land

A covenant runs with the land if the original parties to the lease so intend and if the covenant ***"touches and concerns"*** the land (*i.e.,* benefits the landlord and burdens the tenant (or vice versa) with respect to their interests in the property).

b. Rent Covenants

Because a covenant to pay rent runs with the land, the assignee owes rent ***directly*** to the landlord. After assignment, the original tenant is no longer in privity of estate with the landlord but remains liable on the ***original contractual obligation*** to pay rent (***privity of contract***). If the assignee reassigns the leasehold interest, his privity of estate with the landlord ends, and he has no liability for the subsequent assignee's failure to pay rent.

2. Consequences of Sublease—Sublessee Not in Privity with Landlord

A sublessee is the tenant of the original lessee and usually pays rent to the original lessee, who then pays the landlord. A sublessee is not personally liable to the landlord for rent or for the performance of any of the covenants in the main lease unless the sublessee ***expressly assumes*** the covenants.

a. Landlord's Remedies

The landlord may terminate the main lease for nonpayment of rent or breach of other covenants if the lease so states or the power is given by statute. The sublease automatically terminates with the main lease. Also, many states allow a landlord who does not receive rent to assert a lien on personal property found on the premises; this applies to a sublessee's property as well as that of the original tenant.

b. Rights of Sublessee

A sublessee cannot enforce any covenants made by the landlord in the main lease, except a residential sublessee may be able to enforce the implied warranty of habitability against the landlord.

3. **Covenants Against Assignment or Sublease**
Lease covenants restricting assignment and sublease are strictly ***construed against the landlord***. (Thus, a covenant prohibiting assignment does not prohibit subleasing and vice versa.)

a. **Waiver**
A valid covenant against assignment is considered waived if the landlord was aware of the assignment and did not object (*e.g.,* by knowingly accepting rent from the assignee). Once the landlord consents to one transfer, he waives the covenant as to future transfers unless he expressly reserves it.

b. **Transfer in Violation of Lease**
If a tenant assigns or sublets in violation of a lease provision, the transfer is not void. The landlord, however, usually may terminate the lease or sue for damages.

4. **Assignments by Landlords**
A landlord may assign the rents and reversion interest he owns. This is usually done by deed when the landlord conveys a building to a new owner. The tenants' consent is ***not*** required.

a. **Rights of Assignee Against Tenants—Attornment**
Once tenants are given reasonable notice of the assignment, they must recognize and pay rent to the new owner as their landlord. The benefit of all tenant covenants that touch and concern the land runs with the landlord's estate to the new owner.

b. **Liabilities of Assignee to Tenants**
The burden of the landlord's covenants that touch and concern the land runs with the landlord's estate to the assignee; thus, the assignee is liable for the performance of those covenants. ***The original landlord also remains liable on all of the covenants he made in the lease.***

E. CONDEMNATION OF LEASEHOLDS
If the ***entire leasehold*** is taken by eminent domain, the tenant's liability for rent is extinguished because both the leasehold and reversion have merged in the condemnor and there is no longer a leasehold estate. The lessee is entitled to compensation. However, if the taking is ***temporary*** or ***partial***, the tenant is ***not*** discharged from the rent obligation, but is entitled to compensation (*i.e.,* a share of the condemnation award) for the taking.

II. FIXTURES

A. IN GENERAL
A fixture is a chattel that has been so affixed to land that it has ceased being personal property and has become part of the realty. A fixture passes with the ownership of the land.

B. CHATTELS INCORPORATED INTO STRUCTURE
When items are incorporated into the realty so that they lose their identity (*e.g.,* bricks, concrete), they are fixtures, as are items that are identifiable but whose removal would cause considerable damage (*e.g.,* plumbing, heating ducts).

C. COMMON OWNERSHIP CASES
A common ownership case is one in which the person who brings the chattel to the land owns

both the chattel and the land (*e.g.*, X installs a furnace in his home). An item is a "fixture" if the ***objective intention*** of the party who made the "annexation" was to make the item part of the realty. This intention is determined by: the ***nature of the article***; the ***manner of attachment***; the ***amount of damage*** that would be caused by its removal; and the ***adaptation*** of the item to the use of the realty.

1. Constructive Annexation

An article of personal property that is so uniquely adapted to the real estate that it makes no sense to separate it (*e.g.*, keys to doors, custom curtain rods) may be considered a fixture even if it is not physically annexed to the property.

D. DIVIDED OWNERSHIP CASES

In divided ownership cases, the chattel is owned and brought to the realty by someone other than the landowner (*e.g.*, tenant, licensee, or trespasser).

1. Landlord-Tenant

An ***agreement*** between the landlord and tenant is controlling on whether an annexed chattel is a fixture. Absent an agreement, a tenant is deemed to lack the intent to permanently improve the property, and thus may remove his annexed chattels if removal would not damage the premises or destroy the chattel. Annexed chattels must be removed ***by the end of the lease term*** (or within a reasonable time after the termination of an indefinite tenancy), and the tenant is responsible for repairing any damage caused by the removal.

2. Life Tenant and Remainderman

The same rules apply in the life tenant-remainderman context as in landlord-tenant situations, except that the life tenant must remove annexations ***before the end of his tenancy***.

3. Licensee or Trespasser and Landowner

Licensees are treated much like tenants, whereas trespassers normally lose their annexations. Thus, absent a statute, an adverse possessor or good faith trespasser cannot remove fixtures (*e.g.*, house erroneously constructed on a parcel that possessor believed she owned). Some courts, however, allow a good faith trespasser recovery measured by the value added to the land (not construction costs).

E. THIRD-PARTY CASES

1. Third-Party Lien on Land to Which Chattel Affixed

Generally, the mortgagee has no greater rights than the mortgagor. Thus, chattels annexed by the mortgagor's tenant are generally not within the lien of the mortgagee ***except*** where the mortgage is made after the lease and the mortgagee is without notice of the tenant's rights.

2. Third-Party Lien on Chattel Affixed to Land

Suppose a landowner affixes a chattel to the land. The seller of the chattel retains a security interest in the chattel, and the landowner mortgages the land. If the landowner then defaults on both chattel and mortgage payments, as between the seller and the mortgagee, the general rule is that the first to record his interest wins. However, under the U.C.C., a seller wins if the "fixture filing" is recorded within 20 days after the chattel is affixed to the land. The seller must compensate the mortgagee for damage or repair caused by removal.

III. RIGHTS IN THE LAND OF ANOTHER—EASEMENTS, PROFITS, COVENANTS, AND SERVITUDES

A. IN GENERAL

Easements, profits, covenants, and servitudes are ***nonpossessory*** interests in land, creating a right to ***use land possessed by someone else***.

B. EASEMENTS

1. Introduction

An easement holder has the right to use another's tract of land for a special purpose (*e.g.,* to lay pipe, to access a road or lake), but has no right to possess or enjoy that land. An easement is presumed to be of ***perpetual duration*** unless the grant specifically limits the interest.

a. Types of Easements

Most easements are ***affirmative***, which means the holder is entitled to make affirmative use of the servient tenement. ***Negative*** easements, which entitle the holder to compel the possessor of the servient tenement to refrain from engaging in an activity on the servient estate (*e.g.,* building a structure in excess of three stories), are generally confined to only four types of easements: (i) for ***light***, (ii) for ***air***, (iii) for lateral and subjacent ***support***, and (iv) for ***flow*** of an artificial stream.

CMR **Exam Tip** Negative easements are really restrictive covenants. Thus, for exam purposes, a restriction relating to light, air, support, or flow of an artificial stream can be either a negative easement or a restrictive covenant. Restrictions relating to anything else, however, are considered restrictive covenants.

b. Easement Appurtenant

An easement is appurtenant when it benefits the holder in his physical use or enjoyment of another tract of land. Thus, for an easement to be appurtenant, there must be ***two tracts***: the ***dominant*** tenement (the estate benefited by the easement), and the ***servient*** tenement (the estate subject to the easement right). An easement appurtenant passes with the transfer of the benefited land, regardless of whether it is mentioned in the conveyance. The burden of the easement also passes automatically with the servient estate unless the new owner is a bona fide purchaser with no actual or constructive notice of the easement.

CMR **Exam Tip** It is important to remember that the easement appurtenant ***passes with the benefited land***. Don't be fooled by questions that make you think it must be specifically mentioned in the deed. Similarly, recall that an easement appurtenant cannot be conveyed apart from the dominant tenement (unless it is conveyed to the owner of the servient tenement to ***extinguish*** the easement).

c. Easement in Gross

The holder of an easement in gross acquires a right to use the servient tenement independent of his possession of another tract of land; *i.e.,* the easement benefits the holder rather than another parcel. An easement in gross for the holder's personal pleasure (*e.g.,* right to swim in the pond on Blackacre) is not transferable, but one that serves an economic or commercial interest (*e.g.,* right to erect billboards on Blackacre) is transferable.

2. Creation of Easements

The basic methods of creating an easement are: express grant or reservation, implication, and prescription.

a. Express Grant

Any easement must be in writing and signed by the holder of the servient tenement unless its duration is brief enough (commonly one year or less) to be outside a particular state's Statute of Frauds coverage. A grant of easement must comply with all the formal requisites of a deed.

b. Express Reservation

An easement by reservation arises when a grantor conveys title to land, but reserves the right to continue to use the tract for a special purpose.

Exam Tip Watch for fact patterns in which a grantor reserves an easement for someone else. Under the majority view, an easement can be reserved only for the ***grantor***. An attempt to reserve an easement for anyone else is ***void***.

c. Implication

An easement by implication is created by operation of law; it is an exception to the Statute of Frauds. There are three types of easements by implication:

1) Easement Implied from Existing Use ("Quasi-Easement")

An easement may be implied if:

(i) ***Prior to the division*** of a single tract;

(ii) An ***apparent and continuous*** use exists on the "servient" part;

(iii) That is ***reasonably necessary*** for the enjoyment of the "dominant" part; and

(iv) The court determines that the parties ***intended*** the use to continue after division of the land.

2) Easement Implied Without Any Existing Use

In two limited situations, easements may be implied without preexisting use.

a) Subdivision Plat

When lots are sold in a subdivision with reference to a recorded plat or map that also shows streets leading to the lots, buyers of the lots have implied easements to use the streets to access their lots.

b) Profit a Prendre

The holder of the profit a prendre (*see* C., *infra*) has an implied easement to pass over the surface of the land and to use it as reasonably necessary to extract the product.

3) Easement by Necessity

An easement by necessity arises when a landowner sells a portion of his tract and by this division deprives one lot of access to a public road or utility line. The owner of the servient parcel has the right to locate the easement.

d. Prescription
Acquiring an easement by prescription is analogous to acquiring property by adverse possession. To acquire a prescriptive easement, the use must be:

(i) ***Open and notorious*** (*i.e.,* discoverable upon inspection);

(ii) ***Adverse*** (*i.e.,* without the owner's permission); and

(iii) ***Continuous and uninterrupted***;

(iv) For the ***statutory period***.

Generally, prescriptive easements cannot be acquired in public land.

3. Scope
In the absence of specific limitations in the grant, courts assume that the easement was intended to meet both present and future needs of the dominant tenement (*e.g.,* easement may widen to accommodate new, wider cars). If, however, the dominant parcel is subdivided, the lot owners will not succeed to the easement if to do so would unreasonably overburden the servient estate.

Exam Tip When confronted with an exam question involving overuse or misuse of an easement, remember that such use ***does not terminate*** the easement. The appropriate remedy for the servient owner is an injunction against the misuse.

a. Use of Servient Estate—Repairs
The servient owner generally may use her land in any way she wishes so long as her conduct does not interfere with performance of the easement. The easement holder has the duty to make repairs to the easement if he is the sole user; but if both parties are using the easement, the court will apportion the repair costs.

4. Termination of Easements
An easement can be terminated in the following ways:

a. Stated Conditions
The original easement grant may specify when or under what conditions the easement will terminate.

b. Unity of Ownership (Merger)
If the same person acquires ownership of both the easement and the servient estate, the dominant and servient estates merge and the easement is destroyed. Even though there may be later separation, the easement will not be automatically revived. The unity must be complete (*e.g.,* the holder of the easement must acquire an interest in the servient tenement of ***equal or greater duration*** than the duration of the easement privilege).

c. Release
An easement (including an easement in gross, which is otherwise inalienable) can be terminated by a deed of release from the owner of the easement to the owner of the servient tenement.

d. **Abandonment**
An easement is extinguished when its holder demonstrates by physical action (*e.g.*, building a structure that blocks access to easement on adjoining lot) an intent to permanently abandon the easement. Merely expressing a wish to abandon does not extinguish the easement; neither does mere nonuse.

e. **Estoppel**
Oral expressions of an intent to abandon do not terminate an easement unless committed to writing (release) or accompanied by action (abandonment). But if the owner of the servient estate changes his position in reasonable reliance on the representations made or conduct by the owner of the easement, the easement terminates through estoppel.

f. **Prescription**
To terminate an easement by prescription, there must be an adverse, continuous interruption of the use for the prescriptive period (typically 20 years).

g. **Necessity**
Easements created by necessity expire as soon as the necessity ends.

h. **Condemnation and Destruction**
Condemnation of the servient estate extinguishes all easements. Courts are split as to whether easement holders are entitled to compensation. Involuntary destruction of a structure in which there is an easement extinguishes the easement; voluntary destruction of such a structure does not.

5. **Compare—Licenses**
Licenses privilege their holders to go upon the land of another. But unlike an easement, a license is not an interest in land; it is merely a privilege, ***revocable*** at the will of the licensor. A license is personal to the licensee and, thus, inalienable. Any attempt to transfer a license results in revocation by operation of law.

CMR **Exam Tip** A failed attempt to create an easement results in a license. Thus, if a grantor orally grants an easement for more than one year, it is unenforceable because it is not in writing. The grantee does not have a valid easement but does have a license.

a. **Irrevocable Licenses**
A license becomes irrevocable in the following circumstances:

1) **Estoppel**
If a licensee invests substantial amounts of money or labor in reliance on the license, the licensor is estopped to revoke. The license becomes an easement by estoppel, which lasts until the holder receives sufficient benefit to reimburse him for his expenditures.

2) **License Coupled with an Interest**
A license coupled with an interest is irrevocable as long as the interest lasts. For example, the vendee of a chattel may enter the seller's land to remove the chattel, and a future interest holder may enter and inspect the land for waste.

C. PROFITS

Profits entitle the holder of the benefit to take some resources (*e.g.,* soil, timber, materials, fish) from the servient estate. Implied in every profit is an easement entitling the benefit holder to enter the servient estate to remove the resources. All of the rules governing creation, alienation, and termination of easements are applicable to profits. In addition, a profit may be extinguished through ***surcharge*** (misuse that overly burdens the servient estate).

D. COVENANTS RUNNING WITH THE LAND AT LAW (REAL COVENANTS)

A real covenant, normally found in a deed, is a ***written promise*** to do something on the land (*e.g.,* maintain a fence) or a promise not to do something on the land (*e.g.,* not build a multi-family dwelling). Real covenants run with the land at law, which means that subsequent owners may enforce or be burdened by the covenants.

1. Requirements for Burden to Run

If the following requirements are met, any successor in interest to the burdened estate will be bound by the covenant as if she had herself expressly agreed to it:

a. Intent

The covenanting parties must have ***intended*** that successors in interest to the covenantor be bound by the terms of the covenant. This intent may be inferred from circumstances surrounding the creation of the covenant, but is usually found in the language of the conveyance itself.

b. Notice

Under modern recording acts, to be bound by a covenant, a subsequent purchaser for value must have had actual, inquiry, or record notice of the arrangement at the time of purchase.

CMR **Exam Tip** Because the notice requirement arises under the recording acts, remember that it will protect ***only purchasers for value***. Someone who does not give value may be bound by a covenant at law (not equity) even if he has no actual or constructive notice of the covenant.

c. Horizontal Privity

At the time the promisor entered into the covenant with the promisee, the two must have shared ***some interest*** in the land independent of the covenant (*e.g.,* grantor-grantee, landlord-tenant, mortgagee-mortgagor).

CMR **Exam Tip** Horizontal privity concerns only the ***original*** parties. Even if successors in interest are trying to enforce the covenant, you must look only to the original covenanting parties to determine horizontal privity.

d. Vertical Privity

To be bound, the successor in interest to the covenanting party must hold the ***entire durational interest*** held by the covenantor at the time he made the covenant.

e. Touch and Concern

Negative covenants touch and concern the land if they restrict the holder of the servient estate in his ***use of that parcel*** of land. Affirmative covenants touch and concern the land if they require the holder of the servient estate to ***do something***, which increases his obligations in connection with his enjoyment of the land.

2. **Requirements for Benefit to Run**
If the following three requirements are met, the promisee's successor in interest may enforce the covenant:

a. **Intent**
The covenanting parties must have ***intended*** that the successors in interest to the covenantee be able to enforce the covenant.

b. **Vertical Privity**
The benefits of a covenant run to the assignees of the ***original estate or any lesser estate***; *i.e.*, ***any*** succeeding possessory estate may enforce the benefit.

CMR **Exam Tip** Horizontal privity is not required for the benefit to run. Thus, where horizontal privity is lacking, the promisee's successors can enforce the covenant against the promisor, but not against the promisor's successors.

c. **Touch and Concern**
The benefit of a covenant touches and concerns the land if the promised performance benefits the covenantee and her successors in their use and enjoyment of the benefited land.

3. **Specific Situations Involving Real Covenants**
Generally, promises to ***pay money*** to be used in connection with the land (*e.g.*, homeowners' association fees) and covenants ***not to compete*** run with the land. Racially restrictive covenants are unenforceable.

4. **Remedy—Damages Only**
A breach of a real covenant is remedied by an award of money damages, collectible from the defendant's general assets. If an injunction is sought, the promise must be enforced as an equitable servitude (*see* below) rather than a real covenant.

5. **Termination**
As with all other nonpossessory interests, a covenant may be terminated by: (i) a written ***release***, (ii) the ***merger*** of the benefited and burdened estates, or (iii) the ***condemnation*** of the burdened property. (*See* B.4., *supra.*)

E. EQUITABLE SERVITUDES

An equitable servitude is a covenant that, regardless of whether it runs with the land at law, equity will enforce against the assignees of the burdened land who have ***notice*** of the covenant. The usual remedy is an injunction.

CMR **Exam Tip** The crucial difference between real covenants and equitable servitudes is the ***remedy sought***. If money damages are sought, you must use the real covenant analysis. If a party seeks an injunction, you must consider whether the requirements for enforcement as an equitable servitude have been met. A single promise can create both a real covenant and an equitable servitude.

1. **Creation**
Generally, as with real covenants, equitable servitudes are created by ***covenants*** contained in a ***writing*** that satisfies the Statute of Frauds. There is ***one exception***: Negative equitable servitudes may be implied from a common scheme for development of a residential subdivision. Thus, if a developer subdivides land, and some deeds contain negative covenants while others do not, the negative covenants will be binding on all parcels provided there was a common scheme of development and notice of the covenants.

 a. **Common Scheme**
 Reciprocal negative servitudes will be implied only if, at the time that sales in the subdivision began, the developer had a plan that all parcels would be subject to the restriction. The scheme may be evidenced by: (i) a ***recorded plat***, (ii) a ***general pattern*** of restrictions, or (iii) ***oral representations*** to early buyers.

CMR **Exam Tip** If the scheme arises after some lots are sold, no implied servitude can arise with respect to the lots already sold without express covenants. So remember, if Lots 1 through 5 are sold without a restrictive covenant and the deeds to Lots 6 through 50 contain one, the covenant cannot be enforced as a servitude against the owners of Lots 1 through 5.

 b. **Notice**
 To be bound by a covenant not in her deed, a grantee must have had notice of the covenants in the deeds of others in the subdivision. Notice may be ***actual*** (direct knowledge of covenants), ***inquiry*** (neighborhood appears to conform to common restrictions), or ***record*** (prior deed with covenant in grantee's chain of title).

2. **Requirements for Burden to Run**
A successor of the promisor is bound if:

 a. The covenanting parties ***intended*** that the servitude be enforceable by and against assignees;

 b. The successor of the promisor has ***actual***, ***inquiry***, ***or record*** notice of the servitude; and

 c. The covenant ***touches and concerns*** the land (*i.e.,* it restricts the holder of the servient estate in his use of that parcel).

3. **Requirements for Benefit to Run**
The benefit of an equitable servitude runs with the land, and thus is enforceable by the promisee's successors, if: (i) the original parties so ***intended***, and (ii) the servitude ***touches and concerns*** the benefited property.

CMR **Exam Tip** In contrast to real covenants, which require vertical and horizontal privity of estate for burdens to run, and vertical privity for benefits to run, ***no privity of estate is required*** for an equitable servitude to be enforceable by and against assignees.

4. **Equitable Defenses to Enforcement**
A court will not enforce an equitable servitude if:

a. The person seeking enforcement is violating a similar restriction on his own land (***unclean hands***);

b. A benefited party ***acquiesced*** in a violation of the servitude by one burdened party;

c. A benefited party acted in such a way that a reasonable person would believe the covenant was abandoned (***estoppel***);

d. The benefited party fails to bring suit against the violator within a reasonable time (***laches***); or

e. The ***neighborhood has changed*** so significantly that enforcement would be inequitable.

5. Termination

Like other nonpossessory interests, an equitable servitude may be extinguished by: (i) ***written release*** from the benefit holders, (ii) ***merger*** of the benefited and burdened estates, or (iii) ***condemnation*** of the burdened property. (*See* B.4., *supra.*)

F. PARTY WALLS AND COMMON DRIVEWAYS

Courts will treat a wall erected partly on the property of each of two adjoining landowners as belonging to each owner to the extent it rests upon her land. Courts will also imply mutual cross-easements of support, with the result that each party can use the wall or driveway and neither party can unilaterally destroy it.

1. Creation

A ***written agreement*** is required by the Statute of Frauds for the express creation of a party wall or common driveway agreement, but an "irrevocable license" can arise from detrimental reliance on a parol agreement. Party walls and common driveways can also result from ***implication*** or ***prescription***.

2. Running of Covenants

If party wall or common driveway owners agree to be mutually responsible for maintaining the wall or driveway, the burdens and benefits of these covenants run to the successive owners of each parcel.

Real Property

Lecture Handout

Multistate Early Bar Prep

REAL PROPERTY LECTURE HANDOUT

LANDLORD-TENANT LAW
The Landlord-Tenant Relationship

I. Tenant's Duties:

1) T's liability to third parties;
2) T's duty to repair;
3) T's duty to pay rent.

1) T's liability to third parties:

T is responsible for keeping the premises:

T is liable for injuries sustained by ____________________, even where ____
____.

Example 1: L leases a building to T, expressly promising to maintain the premises in a state of good repair. T's invitee trips over a loose floorboard and sues T. If invitee sues T, what result?

(It does not matter that T may seek indemnification from L. Vis-a-vis the plaintiff, who is a guest, ____________.)

2) T's duty to repair:

a) T's duty to repair when the lease is silent:

i. The standard:

ii. T must not commit waste:

Remember the three species of waste:

1) Voluntary waste:

2) Permissive waste:

3) Ameliorative waste:

iii. The law of fixtures:

When a tenant removes a fixture: ______________________________.

A fixture is a once-movable chattel that, by virtue of its annexation to realty:

____

____.

Common examples:

T MUST NOT _________________________, NO MATTER THAT ____.

FIXTURES PASS WITH OWNERSHIP OF THE LAND.

Example 2: Janet Jackson, a tenant, installs a beautiful heirloom chandelier in the dining room. At the conclusion of the leasehold, as she is about to remove it, Landlord demands that the chandelier stay put. If the chandelier qualifies as a fixture,

____.

How to tell when a tenant installation qualifies as a fixture:

1) Express agreement controls:

2) In the absence of agreement, T may remove a chattel that she has installed so long as: ______________________
____.

If removal will cause substantial damage, then in **objective judgment** T has shown:
____
____

b) T's duty to repair when T has expressly covenanted in the lease to maintain the property in good condition for the duration of the lease:

At common law, historically: ______________________________
____
____

Today, the majority view: ________________________________
____

3) T's duty to pay rent:

a) T breaches this duty and is in possession of the premises:

The landlord's only options are to ______________________ or ____. If the landlord moves to evict, she is nonetheless entitled ___________

from the tenant until the tenant, who is now ________________
________________, vacates.

LANDLORD MUST NOT: ____________________, such as:
____
____.

Self-help is flatly outlawed, and is punishable ______________ and
____.

b) T breaches this duty but is out of possession:

For example, T wrongfully vacates with time left on a term of years lease.

Remember S I R:

i. **S**urrender:

L could choose to treat T's abandonment as ____________
____.

What is surrender?

If the unexpired term is greater than one year: ___________
____.

ii. **I**gnore the abandonment and hold T responsible for ________
________________, just as if T ____________________.
This option is available only in a ______________ of states.

iii. **R**e-let the premises on the wrongdoer tenant's behalf, and hold him or her ________________________________.

Majority rule:

L must at least ___________________________________.

This is a ______________________________________.

II. Landlord's Duties

1) Duty to deliver possession:

The majority rule requires that L put T ________________________ of the premises. Thus, if at the start of T's lease a prior holdover T is still in possession, L ______________________________ and the new T ____.

2) The implied covenant of quiet enjoyment:

Applies to <u>both</u> ___________________ and ___________________ leases.

T has a right to ____, without interference from L.

a) Breach by actual wrongful eviction:

This occurs when ____________________________________ ____.

b) Breach by **constructive eviction:**

For example, every time it rains, Dido's apartment floods. She has a claim for constructive eviction if three elements are met.

To recall the elements of constructive eviction, remember **S I N G:**

i. **S**ubstantial **I**nterference:

ii. Notice:

iii. Goodbye:

Is landlord liable for acts of other tenants?

General rule:

Two exceptions:

1)

2)

3) The implied warranty of habitability:

Applies only to ______________________ leases.

The implied warranty of habitability is non-waivable.

i. The standard:

The appropriate standard may be supplied by ________________ or ____.

The sorts of problems to trigger breach of the implied warranty of habitability include:

ii. T's entitlements when the implied warranty of habitability is breached:

Remember **M R[3]: Move, Repair, Reduce, Remain.**

M: ____.

R: ____________________________, allowable by statute in a growing number of jurisdictions. T may make the reasonable repairs and deduct their cost from future rent.

R: ____________________________ or withhold all rent until the court determines fair rental value. Typically, T must place withheld rent ____________________________ to show her good faith.

R: ____________________________, pay rent and affirmatively seek money damages.

4) **Retaliatory eviction: If T lawfully reports L for housing code violations,** L is barred from penalizing T, by, for example, ____ ____.

SERVITUDES

A SUMMARY OF SERVITUDES

Form of Servitude	Method of Creation	Parties Bound	Remedy
Affirmative Easements.	P - I - N - G **P** - Prescription (use that is continuous, open and notorious, actual under a claim of right that is hostile for request statutory period). **I** - Implication (implied from prior use; at time land is severed, a use of one part existed from which it can be inferred that an easement permitting its continuation was intended). **N** - Necessity (division of a tract deprives one lot of means of access out). **G** - Grant (writing signed by grantor).	Easement appurtenant is transferred automatically with dominant tenement. Easement in gross for commercial purposes is assignable.	Injunction or Damages
Negative Easements (L-A-S-S: Light, Air, Support, and Streamwater).	Can be created only by writing signed by grantor.		Injunction or Damages

Form of Servitude	Method of Creation	Parties Bound	Remedy
Real Covenants.	Writing signed by grantor.	Burden of promise will run to successor of burdened lot if WITHN requirements are satisfied: Writing, Intent, Touch & concern, Horizontal and vertical privity and Notice. Benefit of promise will run to successor of benefited lot if WITV: Writing, Intent, Touch and concern and Vertical privity.	Damages.
Equitable Servitudes.	Writing signed by grantor (unless implied by General Scheme Doctrine).	Successors bound if WITNes: Writing, Intent, Touch and concern, Notice (privity not required).	Injunction.
Reciprocal Negative Servitudes (General Scheme Doctrine).	According to majority, in a subdivision, residential restriction contained in prior deeds conveyed by common grantor will bind subsequent grantees whose deeds contain no such restriction if: At start of subdividing, (i) grantor had common scheme and (ii) unrestricted lot holders had notice. (Note: Minority rule will not bind subsequent grantees unless their lots are expressly restricted in writing.)	Where common scheme exists, subsequent purchasers with notice are bound.	Injunction.

I. Easements

1) Defined: the ________________ of a nonpossessory property interest that entitles its holder to some form of use or enjoyment of another's land, called ____.

   Common examples: the privilege to lay utility lines on another's land; the easement giving its holder the right of access across a tract of land.

2) Easements can be affirmative or negative.

   a) Most easements are affirmative:

   b) Negative easements: The negative easement entitles its holder to prevent the servient landowner from doing something that would otherwise be permissible. Negative easements are generally recognized in only four categories:

Remember L A S S :

L:

A:

S:

S:

NEGATIVE EASEMENTS CAN ONLY BE CREATED EXPRESSLY, BY WRITING SIGNED BY THE GRANTOR. THERE IS NO NATURAL OR AUTOMATIC RIGHT TO A NEGATIVE EASEMENT.

3) An easement is either appurtenant to land or it is held in gross.

a) The easement is appurtenant when it benefits its holder in his physical use or enjoyment of his property. How will you know when you've got an easement appurtenant?

Example 3: A grants B a right of way across A's land, so that B can more easily reach his land. B's land is benefited by the easement. In easement parlance, it is the dominant tenement. A's land is serving B's easement. It is the servient tenement. Notice that two parcels are involved.

B has:

b) The easement is in gross if it confers upon its holder only some personal or pecuniary advantage that is not related to his use or enjoyment of his land. Here, servient land is burdened. However, there is no benefited or dominant tenement.

Common examples:

4) The easement and transferability:

a) The appurtenant easement passes automatically with the dominant tenement, regardless of whether it is even mentioned in the conveyance.

Example 4: A has an easement entitling her to cut across B's lawn to get more easily to her land.

This is: ____________________.

A's land is: ____________________.

B's land is: ____________________.

Now A sells her parcel to Mr. X, with no mention of the easement. Does Mr. X enjoy the easement?

____

____

Note that the burden of the easement appurtenant also passes automatically with the servient estate, unless the new owner is:

____

____

b) An easement in gross is not transferable unless it is for commercial purposes.

Example 5: A has an easement entitling her to swim in B's lake.

This is: ____________________.

Is it transferable? ____________________.

Example 6: Starkist has an easement to use B's lake to fish for bait for Starkist's tuna company.

This is: ____________________.

Is it transferable? ____________________.

5) Creation of an affirmative easement:

Remember **P I N G:**

P:

I:

N:

G:

a) By grant:

An easement to endure for more than one year ______________ ________________________ that complies with the formal elements of a deed.

This is because of ______________________________. The writing to evidence the easement is called ________________________.

b) By implication (also known as the easement implied from existing use):

Example 7: A owns two lots. Lot 1 is hooked up to a sewer drain located on lot 2. A sells lot 1 to B, with no mention of B's right to continue to use the drain on A's remaining lot 2. The court may nonetheless imply an easement on B's behalf if:

1) the previous use ______________________ ______________________________ and

2) the parties expected ___________________ __________________________ because it is reasonably necessary to ________________ ___________________________________.

c) By necessity: The landlocked setting. An easement of right of way will be implied by necessity if grantor conveys a portion of his land:

____

____.

d) By prescription: An easement may be acquired by satisfying the elements of ____________________.

Remember **C O A H:**

C:

O:

A:

H:

Note: Permission defeats the acquisition of an easement by prescription. An easement by prescription requires that the use be hostile.

6) The scope of an easement is determined by:

Example 8: A grants B an easement to use A's private road to get to and from B's parcel, Blackacre.

B has: ________________________________.

A's parcel is: ____________________________.

Subsequently, B purchases the adjacent Greenacre, with its small marina. May B unilaterally expand the use of the easement to benefit Greenacre?

____

_______________________________________.

7) Termination of an easement:

Remember **END CRAMP:**

a) **E**stoppel: Here, the servient owner materially changes his or her position in reasonable reliance on the easement holder's assurances that the easement ______________________________________.

Example 9: A tells B that A will no longer be using her right of way across B's parcel. In reasonable reliance, B builds a swimming pool on B's parcel, thereby depriving A of the easement. In equity:

b) **N**ecessity: Easements created by necessity expire as soon as:_____ ____________________________________. However, if the easement, attributable to necessity, was nonetheless created by express grant:

Example 10: O conveys a portion of his 10-acre tract to A, with no means of access out except over a portion of O's remaining land. The parties reduce their understanding to express writing. Thereafter, the city builds a public roadway affording A access out. The easement:

c) **D**estruction of the servient land, other than through the willful conduct of the servient owner:

d) **C**ondemnation of the servient estate:

e) **R**elease: A written release, given by ______________________ to the __________________________.

f) **A**bandonment: The easement holder must demonstrate by physical action:

____.

Note: Abandonment requires physical action by the easement holder.

Example 11: A has a right of way across B's parcel. A erects a structure on A's parcel that precludes her from ever again reaching B's parcel. That is the sort of action to signify abandonment. By contrast, mere nonuse, or mere words, are insufficient to terminate by abandonment.

g) **M**erger doctrine (also known as unity of ownership):

The easement is extinguished when title to __________________ and title to ________________________ become vested in the same person.

Example 12: A has a right of way across B's parcel, to enable A to better reach her parcel. A's land is: _____________ ________________________. A is: ___________ ____.

B's land is: ___________________________________.

Later, A buys B's parcel. The result: ____.

Note: If complete unity of title is achieved, the easement is extinguished. Even though there may be later separation of title:

____

____

For example, assume now that A later sells the parcel over which she once enjoyed the right of way. The easement:

____

____

h) **Prescription**: The servient owner may extinguish the easement by interfering with it in accordance with the elements of __________ ____.

Remember COAH:

C:

O:

A:

H:

Example 13: A has an easement of right of way across B's parcel. B erects a chain link fence on B's parcel, thereby precluding A from reaching it. Over time, B may succeed in extinguishing the easement through: ____.

II. The License

1) Defined:

2) Licenses are not subject to: ________________. Thus, you do not need a ________________ to create a license.

3) Licenses are ______________________________, at the will of the licensor, unless ________________________ to bar revocation.

4) The classic license cases:

a) The ticket cases:

Tickets create ______________________________.

b) Neighbors talking by the fence:

Example 14: Neighbor A, talking by the fence with neighbor B, says, "B, you can have that right of way across my land." This oral easement:

____

____.

An oral easement creates instead ____________

____.

c) Estoppel will apply to bar revocation only when the licensee has invested ____ in reasonable reliance on the license's continuation.

III. The Profit

1. The profit entitles its holder to enter the servient land and take from it: ______________________________ ______________________________.

2. The profit shares: ______________________________.

IV. The Covenant

1) Defined: The covenant is a promise to do or not do something related to land. It is UNLIKE the easement because it is not the grant of a property interest, but rather ______________________ or promise regarding land.

2) Covenants can be negative (known as restrictive covenants): The restrictive covenant is a promise to refrain from doing something related to land. For example: ______________________________ ______________________________.

   Covenants can be affirmative: The affirmative covenant is a promise to do something related to land. For example: ______________________________ ______________________________.

3) How to know whether to construe the given promise as a covenant or as an equitable servitude: ______________________________ ______________________________ ______________________________.

4) In covenant parlance, one tract is burdened by the promise and another is benefited.

When will the covenant run with the land? When it is capable of binding successors.

Example 15: Neighbor A promises neighbor B that A will not build for commercial purposes on A's property. A's parcel is burdened by the promise. B's parcel is benefited. Later, A sells her burdened parcel to A-1. B sells his benefited parcel to B-1. Now, A-1 has commenced manufacture of a steak sauce plant on the premises. B-1 wishes to proceed against A-1 for money damages. Will B-1 succeed?
It depends on whether the facts support the conclusion that the burden and benefit run.

(burdened parcel) A ⇦- - - - - - - - - - - - ⇨ B (benefited parcel)

horizontal privity

vertical privity (A ⇩ A-1)

vertical privity (B ⇩ B-1)

A-1 B-1

In answering, two separate contests must be resolved:

First, does the burden of A's promise to B run from A to A-1?

Remember W I T H N :

The elements necessary for the burden to run:

i) **W**riting:

ii) **I**ntent:

Note: Courts are generous in finding the requisite intent.

iii) **T**ouch and concern the land:

The promise must affect the parties' legal relations as __________, and not simply as members of ________________________________.

Note: Covenants to pay money to be used in connection with the land (such as homeowners' association fees) and covenants not to compete do touch and concern the land.

iv) **H**orizontal and vertical privity:

Horizontal privity refers to the nexus between:

It requires that they be in ________________________________, meaning that they were in a ________________________________ or ____________________________ or ____________________________ relationship.

Vertical privity refers to the nexus between ___________________.
It simply requires some ___________________________, such as:

The only time that vertical privity will be absent is if A-1 acquired her interest through:

v) Notice:

Second, does the benefit of A's promise to B run from B to B-1?

Remember W I T V :

i) Writing

ii) Intent

iii) Touch and Concern

iv) Vertical Privity

Note: Horizontal privity is not required for the benefit to run.

V. Equitable Servitudes

1) Defined: The equitable servitude is a promise that equity will enforce against successors. It is accompanied by ______________________.

2) To create an equitable servitude that will bind successors:

Remember W I T N E S :

i) **W**riting

ii) **I**ntent

iii) **T**ouch and Concern

iv) **N**otice

NOTE: PRIVITY IS NOT REQUIRED TO BIND SUCCESSORS.

3) The implied equitable servitude—the general or common scheme doctrine:

Example 16: A subdivides her land into 50 lots. She sells lots 1 through 45 through deeds that contain covenants restricting use to residential purposes. A then sells one of the remaining lots to a commercial entity, B, by deed containing no such covenant. B now seeks to build a convenience store on his lot. Can he be enjoined from doing so?

Yes, if the two elements of the general or common scheme doctrine apply. Under the common scheme doctrine, the court will imply a reciprocal negative servitude to hold the unrestricted lot holder to the restrictive covenant.

The two elements of the general or common scheme doctrine:

i) When the sales began, the subdivider (A): ____________________
____
____.

ii) The defendant lotholder (B):
____
____.

There are three forms of notice potentially imputed to defendant:

Remember A I R:

A: Actual notice, meaning: ______________________________
____.

I: Inquiry notice, meaning: ______________________________
____.

R: Record notice, meaning the form of notice sometimes imputed to buyers on the basis of: ______________________________.

Note: With respect to record notice, the courts are split. Some take the view that a subsequent buyer is on record notice of the contents of prior deeds transferred to others by a common grantor. The better view, taken by other courts, is that the subsequent buyer does NOT have record notice of the contents of those prior deeds transferred to others by the common grantor.

4) Equitable defenses to enforcement of an equitable servitude:

a) Changed conditions:

The changed circumstances alleged by the party seeking release from the terms of an equitable servitude must be: ____________________
____.

What is never good enough?
____.

barbri®

Real Property

1. Ⓐ Ⓑ Ⓒ Ⓓ
2. Ⓐ Ⓑ Ⓒ Ⓓ
3. Ⓐ Ⓑ Ⓒ Ⓓ
4. Ⓐ Ⓑ Ⓒ Ⓓ
5. Ⓐ Ⓑ Ⓒ Ⓓ

6. Ⓐ Ⓑ Ⓒ Ⓓ
7. Ⓐ Ⓑ Ⓒ Ⓓ
8. Ⓐ Ⓑ Ⓒ Ⓓ
9. Ⓐ Ⓑ Ⓒ Ⓓ
10. Ⓐ Ⓑ Ⓒ Ⓓ

11. Ⓐ Ⓑ Ⓒ Ⓓ
12. Ⓐ Ⓑ Ⓒ Ⓓ
13. Ⓐ Ⓑ Ⓒ Ⓓ
14. Ⓐ Ⓑ Ⓒ Ⓓ
15. Ⓐ Ⓑ Ⓒ Ⓓ

16. Ⓐ Ⓑ Ⓒ Ⓓ
17. Ⓐ Ⓑ Ⓒ Ⓓ

REAL PROPERTY QUESTIONS

Question 1

On December 1, a landlord rented an apartment to a tenant for one year, commencing January 1. The tenant paid the first and last months' rent. Both the landlord and the tenant were aware that, at the time of the making of the lease, the apartment in question was occupied by a student, who had a lease on the premises until December 31. The student refused to leave the apartment on December 31, and the landlord served the appropriate legal notices to vacate the premises. The student still did not vacate the apartment, and the landlord instituted an unlawful detainer action against the student. She succeeded in getting the marshal to enforce the judgment and take possession of the apartment, and the tenant received possession of the apartment on February 1. The lease between the landlord and the tenant contained the following statement: "The tenant, on payment of the monthly rent and compliance with all of the covenants and conditions stated herein, shall have the quiet enjoyment of the premises."

If the tenant now sues the landlord for damages resulting from the delay in the tenant's possession of the premises, the landlord's best defense is that:

(A) The landlord did not breach any specific promise to deliver the premises on January 1.

(B) The jurisdiction follows the majority rule regarding the landlord's duty to deliver possession, and the landlord did everything within her power to eject the student in a timely manner.

(C) The landlord's obligation to the tenant ended with the signing of the lease.

(D) The jurisdiction follows the minority rule regarding the landlord's duty to deliver possession, and because the terms of the lease gave the tenant the right to possession rather than the landlord, it was up to the tenant to bring an action against the student.

Question 2

A tenant moved out of the dormitory at a state college and rented a one-bedroom apartment not far from campus. She signed a one-year lease and moved in on September 1, two weeks before classes began. Rent was specified in the lease to be $750 per month. When classes began, she started walking from her apartment building to the college, and quickly found that the walk, much of which was on a busy street with no sidewalks, was much more difficult than she had thought it would be. After a month, the tenant moved out when she found another apartment. She sent the landlord the keys, together with a note apologizing for the sudden departure.

The landlord immediately cleaned up the apartment and placed an ad in the paper. Since school had already started, it was difficult to find someone to take the apartment, and when the landlord found someone, the rent had to be lowered to $620.

Which of the following is the most accurate statement concerning the landlord's rights?

(A) The landlord was obligated to attempt to re-rent the property to help lower the tenant's damages, but will be able to recover his costs of the re-rental, any unpaid rent until he re-rented the apartment, and $130 per month for the balance of the lease.

(B) The landlord was not obligated to attempt to re-rent the property to help lower the tenant's damages, but since he did he will be able to recover the costs of re-rental, any unpaid rent until he re-rented the apartment, and $130 per month for the balance of the lease.

(C) The landlord was obligated to attempt to re-rent the property to help lower the tenant's damages, but will be unable to recover the costs of the re-rental since it was mandatory; however, he will be able to recover the difference in rent between what the tenant promised to pay and the amount secured on the re-rental.

(D) The landlord was not obligated to attempt to re-rent the property to help lower the tenant's damages, and under these facts the tenant is only liable for the unpaid rent up to the time the landlord retook the apartment, and is not liable for any unpaid rent up to the re-renting, nor for any deficiency in rent.

Question 3

A landlord owns a six-unit strip mall. He offered to lease one of the units to a barista, who planned to open a gourmet coffee shop. Because the mall is located on a busy street, the barista insisted that the landlord install a metal fence around the outdoor seating area that would protect her customers. The landlord agreed to do so and the barista signed a 10-year lease. A term in the lease stated, "The landlord agrees to maintain all structures on the property in good repair." Eight years later, the landlord sold the strip mall to a buyer. The buyer did not agree to perform any obligations under the leases. As instructed, the barista began paying rent to the buyer. The following year, the metal fence was in desperate need of repairs. Citing the lease terms, the barista asked the buyer to repair the fence, but the buyer continually refused to do so. The barista finally repaired the fence herself at a cost of $3,000 and then brought an appropriate lawsuit to recover the money.

Absent any other facts, the barista is likely to recover:

(A) $3,000 from either the landlord or the buyer, because they are both in privity with the barista.

(B) $2,700 from the landlord and $300 from the buyer, because that represents their pro rata shares.

(C) $3,000 from the landlord only, because the buyer did not assume the lease obligations.

(D) $3,000 from the buyer only, because a covenant to repair runs with the land.

Question 4

A landlord leased an office building suite to an accounting firm for 10 years. The written lease contained a provision that utilities for the suite would be paid by "the lessee, his successors, and assigns." The accounting firm occupied the suite and paid the rent and utilities for four years. At that time, the accounting firm assigned the balance of the lease to a publishing company and vacated the premises. The assignment was in writing but contained no provision concerning the publishing company's assumption of the duties under the lease. The publishing company now occupies the suite and has paid the rent but not the utilities.

If the landlord sues the publishing company for failure to pay the utilities, which of the following would be the publishing company's best defense?

(A) The covenant to pay utilities does not run with the land.

(B) The publishing company did not assume the covenant to pay utilities.

(C) The accounting firm is solely liable for the utilities.

(D) The publishing company and the landlord are not in privity of estate.

Question 5

A landlord leased a portion of the lobby of his office building to a vendor under a written lease for a term of 10 years at $500 per month. The lease provided that the shop was to be used as a candy and cigarette counter, which would be the "exclusive" vending facility in the building. The lease was silent as to the vendor's right to transfer the leasehold interest.

Later, the vendor transferred his interest to a retailer by a writing providing that the vendor could reenter if the retailer failed to make rental payments to the landlord. The landlord subsequently sold the building to an investor, who installed several automatic candy and cigarette vending machines throughout the building. As a result, the retailer's sales declined and she refused to pay any rent.

If the investor files suit against the retailer for the rent due, a court following common law principles should rule that:

(A) The investor has no direct claim against the retailer personally; his only remedy is to terminate the lease and sue the vendor for the rent.

(B) The investor can recover $500 per month rent from the retailer.

(C) The investor can recover nothing from the retailer because his installation of the vending machines allowed the retailer to immediately terminate her duties under the lease.

(D) The investor can recover $500 per month rent from the retailer but only if the vending machines are removed.

Question 6

A property owner owned a large farm that was bisected by a state highway. The westernmost boundary of the owner's land was formed by a large river. On the easternmost boundary of the land was a large state park. The owner leased the eastern portion to a farmer, who used it to grow cotton. The owner leased the western portion to a rancher. The rancher had not yet started using the land, but he planned to bring some cattle onto it once spring arrived.

Under state law, the state could purchase land to expand the state park system and save land threatened by commercial development. After an extensive process of evaluation, the state decided to use its powers of eminent domain to take roughly two-thirds of the owner's land. The state took all of the easterly portion—the part leased to the farmer—and part of the westerly portion adjacent to the river. The owner was left with only about one-third of his original farm, all of it lying just west of the highway and all of it part of the property leased to the rancher.

Which of the following statements is correct concerning the rights of the farmer and the rancher?

(A) The rancher and the farmer may continue to occupy their leased land, as eminent domain proceedings concern only the fee simple interest and do not affect those who hold valid leaseholds.

(B) Neither the rancher nor the farmer may continue to occupy the land taken by the state, although the rancher may continue to occupy the portion not taken, and the rancher remains liable to the owner for rent for the portion not taken by the state, but neither the rancher nor the farmer are liable to the owner for rent for the land taken.

(C) Neither the rancher nor the farmer may continue to occupy the land taken by the state, and the farmer is not liable for any further rent to the owner, but the rancher must continue to pay full rent to the owner for all the land under his lease, even that portion taken by the state.

(D) In the condemnation award, the rancher and the farmer are each entitled to share in the award based on the value of the remaining term of the lease on the property taken, less rent that would have been paid during that period.

Question 7

A landlord leased a vacant commercial building to a tenant for a 10-year term. On taking possession, the tenant installed a bar, booths, special lighting, and a raised dance floor. The bar and booths were simply placed on the floor and were not secured to it. The lights were installed by a qualified electrician and were directly wired into the building's electrical system. The special dance floor was bolted to the building's cement floor by installation crews from the company that made the dance floor. After installation of the above, the tenant then operated her business for almost 10 years. At that time, she decided that business was so good that she would move to a larger space down the street. She told the landlord that she would not be renewing her lease and that she would be removing the lights, booths, bar, and dance floor. The landlord told her that none of the installations could be removed because they are now part of the building.

If a court were called upon to resolve this dispute, it would likely rule that:

(A) The tenant may remove the dance floor, bar, and lights, but not the booths.

(B) The tenant may remove the bar and the booths, but not the dance floor and the lights.

(C) The tenant may remove the bar, booths, dance floor, and lights because they were all used for the purpose of her business.

(D) The tenant may not remove either the bar, booths, dance floor, or lights because they are all affixed to the building and are deemed fixtures.

Question 8

An investor entered into an installment land contract with a seller for the purchase of a townhouse. The seller promptly and properly recorded the contract. A few years later, the investor leased the townhouse to an architect for a five-year term. The lease did not contain any provisions regarding improvements to the townhouse. The architect began making improvements to the townhouse, including an entertainment wall unit that she purchased and bolted to the wall. To purchase the wall unit, the architect signed a security agreement granting the vendor a security interest in the wall unit in exchange for financing. The vendor did not file or record the security interest. By the end of the lease term, the investor had defaulted on his installment payments to the seller, and the architect had defaulted on her loan payments to the vendor. In preparing forfeiture proceedings against the investor, the seller learned that the architect was planning to remove the wall unit and take it with her when she moved out within the next few weeks. The seller filed an action against the architect, claiming ownership of the wall unit, and joined the investor and the vendor in the proceedings.

Which party has a superior claim to the wall unit?

(A) The seller, because its security interest attaches to all fixtures on the real estate and it has priority over the vendor.

(B) The investor, because the wall unit was annexed to the real estate after execution of the installment land contract.

(C) The architect, because removal of the wall unit will not cause substantial damage to the real estate.

(D) The vendor, because it has a valid security interest in the wall unit even though it was not recorded.

Question 9

A developer purchased an 18-hole golf course located across the street from a college. She plans to subdivide the land and build luxury townhouses, but anticipates that it will take her another year to obtain the necessary permits and funds. Until then, she wishes to allow the college to use the land for intramural athletics.

Which of the following would best accomplish the developer's goals?

(A) Lease the land to the college for one year.

(B) Convey the land "to the college for one year."

(C) Grant the college an easement for intramural athletics use for one year.

(D) Covenant that the college may use the land for intramural athletics for one year.

Question 10

An owner of a large parcel of land divided the parcel into two halves. The front parcel abutted a public highway. The shortest route from the back parcel to the highway was over a small private road that crossed the front parcel. There was another route from the back parcel to the highway that did not involve crossing the front parcel, but it wound through the woods for over four miles. The owner sold the back parcel to a purchaser who planned to open an inn on the property, and included an express easement in the deed permitting her to access the highway via the private road across the front parcel. The purchaser never properly recorded her deed to the back parcel. Although the purchaser built the inn, she never opened it to the public because of financial circumstances and only rarely used the road across the front parcel.

Fifteen years after that transaction, the purchaser sold the land to a buyer who planned to open the inn to the public. The buyer promptly recorded her deed to the property from the purchaser, but the buyer's deed made no mention of the right to cross the front parcel via the private road. Shortly after the buyer took possession of the back parcel, she learned of the provision in the original deed. The buyer told the owner, who still owned the front parcel, that she planned to use the road across his property when she opened the inn, but the owner refused to grant permission to do so.

Does the buyer have a right to cross the front parcel?

(A) No, because the easement is not mentioned in the buyer's deed, and the purchaser's deed containing the easement was not recorded.

(B) No, because the buyer's opening of the inn would increase the use of the easement.

(C) Yes, because the purchaser exercised her right to use the easement when she owned the back parcel.

(D) Yes, because the easement was not extinguished.

Question 11

A landowner granted an easement over his front yard to a railway several decades ago for the purpose of operating a cable car system, which the railway then built. The railway used the system for many years, but ceased its operations when the system became rundown and unprofitable. Over 10 years ago, the railway removed the cables and tracks because they had become an eyesore. Three years ago, the landowner planted the area with grass.

The applicable statute provides for a prescriptive period of 10 years. Last year, the railway received a state subsidy to reopen its system and is now planning to lay new tracks and cables over its right-of-way. The landowner has brought an action to quiet title and to restrain the railway from building on the landowner's land.

If the landowner wins, it will be because:

(A) The railway's removal of its cable and tracks combined with many years of nonuse indicates an intent to abandon the easement.

(B) The railway's plan to build the new system will unreasonably interfere with the landowner's use of his fee simple.

(C) The railway's easement terminated when it was no longer practical to utilize the easement for the purpose for which it was granted.

(D) The railway's nonuse of the easement for a period beyond the prescription period terminated the easement.

Question 12

The owner of 50 acres of unimproved property prepared and recorded a subdivision plan calling for 80 home sites on one-half acre each. Purchasers were required to build their homes using one of five different approved plans. Each deed, which referred to the recorded plan, stated that "no residence shall be erected on any lot that has not been approved by the homeowners' association." An investor who bought one of the lots but did not build on it resold it to a purchaser a few years later. The deed from the investor to the purchaser did not contain any reference to the recorded plan nor the obligation regarding approval by the homeowners' association. The purchaser began to build a very modernistic house on her one-half acre. A neighbor who had built a house using one of the approved plans brought an action to enjoin the construction.

The probable result of this action will be in favor of:

(A) The purchaser, because her deed contained no restrictive covenants.

(B) The purchaser, because any restrictive covenant can only be enforced by the opposite party to the covenant or that person's successor in title.

(C) The neighbor, because the recorded subdivision plan, taken with the fact that all lots were similarly restricted and the purchaser had notice of this, gave him the right to enforce the covenant on the purchaser's property.

(D) The neighbor, because his deed contained the restrictive covenant.

Question 13

A developer divided his tract of land into four standard lots, which he conveyed to a doctor, a pilot, a carpenter, and an athlete, respectively. Each deed granted by the developer contained a covenant requiring that the property be used only for single-family housing. All deeds were duly recorded in the office of the county recorder of deeds. The doctor and the pilot proceeded to build single-family houses on their lots. The carpenter and the athlete did not develop their properties immediately.

The doctor later sold her property to a nurse and included the covenant limiting use to single-family dwellings in the deed. The pilot sold his property to a flight attendant, but did not include the covenant in the deed. The carpenter sold her property to an electrician, and the deed contained the restriction. The athlete sold his property to a physical therapist, and the deed did not contain the restriction. All but the electrician's deed were duly recorded.

Subsequently, the nurse died and her property passed by will to her daughter. The flight attendant gave her land to her son "for life." The electrician sold his property for value to a plumber. All three transfers of title were recorded, but none of the deeds mentioned the covenant.

Which of the current owners below is not bound by the covenant?

(A) The nurse's daughter, who received the property by will.

(B) The flight attendant's son, who received the property for life.

(C) The plumber, who purchased the property from the electrician.

(D) The physical therapist, who purchased the property from the athlete.

Question 14

A recorded subdivision plan contained a provision for 20 one-half acre open spaces designated as "dedicated public parks." One year later, the city in which the subdivision was located decided to put picnic benches and other recreational facilities on the 20 open areas and to establish these areas for public use for the first time. Homeowners in the subdivision and the homeowners' association filed suit to prevent the city from proceeding with this plan, claiming that the resulting congestion and health and safety problems would drive down the value of their property.

The probable result will be:

(A) The plan will be blocked, because the city is guilty of laches in not accepting the dedication when it was first offered.

(B) The plan will be blocked, unless the city pays damages to the homeowners because of the decrease in value to their property due to this inverse condemnation.

(C) The suit will be dismissed, because many of the homeowners had notice of the proposed use of these areas.

(D) The suit will be dismissed, because the dedication of the parkland was appropriate and required no acceptance by the city at the time.

Question 15

An investor purchased a parcel of land and subdivided it into 25 one-acre lots. He prepared and filed a subdivision map, obtained all the necessary approvals, and began selling the lots. Each of the deeds conveying the lots contained language specifying that the property shall be used for residential purposes only and binding all buyers, their heirs and assigns, and their successors. Three years later, all but two of the lots had been developed as single-family residences. A developer whose commercial land abutted these remaining two lots purchased them from the investor, and received a deed that did not contain any language restricting the use of the property. The developer then sold the lots to a fast food chain, which intended to erect a franchise on the property. An accountant, who had purchased a lot from the investor and earned her living preparing tax forms out of her home for her neighbors, brings suit against the fast food chain, seeking to enforce the restrictions in the original deeds and enjoin construction of the restaurant.

Which of the following is the fast food chain's best defense?

(A) The fast food chain was not aware of the restrictions when it purchased the property.

(B) The neighborhood has significantly changed and allowing commercial use of the two lots will not affect the enforceability of the deed restrictions of the other 23 lots.

(C) The accountant is violating the restriction contained in her deed.

(D) The deed by which the developer took the property from the investor did not contain any restrictions on use.

Question 16

A landowner who owned five acres on the shore of a lake gave verbal permission to a neighbor to cross over her land to get to the lake so he could fish. About three years later, a trespasser built a boat dock on the far west end of the landowner's land without her permission. The land was heavily wooded, and the dock could not be seen from the landowner's house, although if she had taken a walk along the shore she would have found it. The neighbor and the trespasser would see each other frequently while they were fishing, and when the neighbor bought a boat, the trespasser gave him permission to tie up the boat to the dock at any time. Soon thereafter, the trespasser died and left all of his property to his son, who lived in another state. Although the neighbor never contacted the trespasser's son, he kept his boat at the dock. About two years later, the landowner discovered the dock on her land and told the neighbor to remove his boat because she was going to have the dock torn down.

The neighbor filed for an injunction to prevent the landowner from tearing down the dock and to establish his right to continue to use it. Although the trespasser had died before he had sufficient time to gain title by adverse possession to the land on which his dock was built, the neighbor had been crossing over the landowner's land for about five and one-half years. The jurisdiction has a five-year requirement to establish title to land by adverse possession or to acquire prescriptive easements.

The court should rule that:

(A) The landowner cannot tear down the dock because the neighbor had been using the dock for a sufficient amount of time to gain an easement by prescription.

(B) The landowner can tear down the dock because, although the neighbor has an easement by prescription, he did not build the dock himself and, therefore, had no right to gain title to the land by adverse possession.

(C) The landowner can tear down the dock, and the neighbor does not have an easement by prescription.

(D) The landowner can tear down the dock because once the trespasser died, the neighbor no longer had permission to use the dock and he did not have time to gain an adverse interest as to the neighbor's son.

Question 17

A landowner and her neighbor owned adjoining rural tracts of land. Twenty years ago, the landowner installed an above-ground propane tank on land she thought she owned, but which was in fact owned by the neighbor. The copper pipes running from the tank to the house crossed only the landowner's land. Six years ago, the landowner died intestate, leaving her mentally incapacitated son as her only heir. The son and his conservator continued to live on the landowner's property. The neighbor now files suit to eject the son and quiet title. The statute of limitations for ejectment is 15 years.

Who is most likely to prevail in the lawsuit?

(A) The neighbor, because the son's possession was not continuous.

(B) The neighbor, because the statute of limitations was tolled during the son's incapacity.

(C) The son, because he has acquired title by adverse possession.

(D) The son, because he has an implied easement.

REAL PROPERTY ANSWERS

Answer to Question 1

(D) The landlord's best defense is that the jurisdiction follows the minority approach regarding the landlord's duty to deliver possession. In most states, statutes require the landlord to put the tenant in actual possession at the beginning of the lease term. In a minority of states, the landlord's obligation is merely to give the tenant the legal right to possession; it is up to the new tenant to bring eviction proceedings against a hold-over tenant. Here, if the jurisdiction follows the minority rule, the landlord will have a complete defense because she has no liability for the student's refusing to vacate the apartment when his lease ended. (A) is incorrect because there need not be a specific promise to deliver the premises at the start of the lease period; that duty will be implied in the lease. (B) is incorrect because, under the majority rule, it is not enough that the landlord did everything in her power to eject the student in a timely manner. She had a duty to deliver actual possession to the tenant, and she is liable under the majority rule for any damages the tenant suffered from the delay in delivering possession. (C) is incorrect because the scope of the landlord's obligation depends on whether the jurisdiction follows the majority rule or the minority rule.

Answer to Question 2

(A) The landlord was obligated to attempt to re-rent the property but may recover all of his damages. When a tenant wrongfully abandons the leasehold, the landlord has two choices: (i) treat the abandonment as an offer of surrender and accept by retaking the property, thus ending the leasehold and terminating the tenant's obligations from that moment; or (ii) attempt to relet the property on the tenant's account and hold the tenant liable for any difference between what the lease specified and what the landlord can now get on the reletting. For the landlord to choose option (ii), the mitigation of the tenant's damages and holding the tenant liable for the difference, the landlord's retaking and reletting must be done to mitigate the tenant's damages. (B) and (D) are incorrect, since the landlord is under an obligation to mitigate the tenant's damages. (C) is incorrect. Since a reletting was being attempted, the landlord could recover all losses, including the costs of reletting, the unpaid rent, and the difference in rent.

Answer to Question 3

(A) The barista may recover the cost of the repairs from either the landlord or the buyer. A landlord's promise in a lease to maintain the property does not terminate because the property is sold. Although no longer in privity of estate, the original landlord and tenant remain in privity of contract, and the original landlord remains liable on the covenant unless there is a novation. A novation substitutes a new party for an original party to the contract. It requires the assent of all parties, and completely releases the original party. Because neither the barista nor the buyer has agreed to a novation, the landlord remains liable for the covenant because he and the barista remain in privity of contract even after the sale. Thus, the promise to repair can be enforced against the landlord. When leased property is sold, the purchaser is liable to the tenants for performance of all covenants made by the original landlord in the lease, provided that those covenants run with the land. A covenant runs with the land if the parties to the lease so intend and the covenant touches and concerns the land. Generally, promises to do a physical act, such as maintain or repair the property, are considered to run with the land. Thus, the buyer is liable because he is in privity of estate with the barista and the covenant to repair runs with the land. Consequently, both the landlord and the buyer are potentially liable to the barista for the repairs. (B) is incorrect because the barista may recover the ***full amount*** from either the landlord or the buyer. (C) is incorrect because the burdens of covenants that touch and concern the land run with the landlord's estate and become the burdens of the new landlord, regardless of whether the new landlord assumes the lease obligations. (D) is incorrect because, although it is true that a covenant to repair touches and concerns the land and runs with it upon assignment, the landlord as well as the buyer can be held liable.

Answer to Question 4

(A) The publishing company's best defense would be that the covenant to pay utilities does not run with the land. The best way to get the correct answer is to use a process of elimination. (B) is incorrect because after an assignment, the assignee stands in the shoes of the original tenant in a direct relationship with the landlord. The assignee and the landlord are in ***privity of estate***, and each is liable to the other on all covenants in the lease that run with the land, regardless of whether the assignee assumed the lease obligations. An assignment arises when a tenant makes a complete transfer of the entire remaining lease term, retaining no interest in the assigned premises. Here, the accounting firm transferred the remaining six years of the lease to the publishing company and retained no other interest. Accordingly, this was an assignment and the publishing company would be liable under privity of estate if the covenant to pay utilities runs with the land. Thus, not assuming the covenant is not a valid defense. (C) is incorrect because, although the original tenant is no longer in privity of estate with the landlord after an assignment, a tenant may still be held liable on its original contractual obligations to the landlord on ***privity of contract*** grounds. However, the publishing company also would be liable on privity of estate grounds, so the accounting firm is not ***solely*** liable. (D) is incorrect because, as explained above, the publishing company and the landlord ***are*** in privity of estate. Thus, the publishing company's best defense would be that the covenant to pay utilities does not run with the land, as choice (A) states. If it does not run with the land, the publishing company would not be bound to pay the utilities unless it assumed the covenant, which it did not.

Answer to Question 5

(B) The investor can recover $500 per month rent from the retailer. The retailer is liable to the investor for the rent because of her status as an assignee, and because at common law the rent and anti-competition covenants are independent. Absent an express restriction in the lease, a tenant may freely transfer his leasehold interest. To be an assignment, a transfer must be on the same terms as the original leasehold ***except*** that the transferring tenant may reserve a right of termination (reentry) for breach of the terms of the original lease that has been assigned. Because the vendor transferred all of his interest to the retailer, this transfer will be given effect as an assignment rather than a sublease despite the vendor's reservation of a right of reentry. An assignee takes the place of the original tenant in a direct relationship with the landlord. The assignee and landlord are in privity of estate, so that each is liable to the other on all lease covenants that run with the land. Covenants held to run with the land include covenants to pay money. Because a covenant to pay rent runs with the land, an assignee owes the rent directly to the landlord, for the time that they are in privity of estate. The investor and the retailer are in privity of estate. Thus, the burden of the vendor's original covenant to pay rent runs with the land and binds the retailer. (A) incorrectly states that the investor has no direct claim against the retailer personally for payment of the rent. (C) and (D) are wrong because, at common law, a tenant's duty to pay rent is considered an obligation independent of the landlord's performance of his obligations. The landlord's original agreement that the space leased to the vendor would be the exclusive vending facility in the building ran with the land. The provision would certainly have been intended to run with the land (it is highly doubtful that the vendor would have intended that a successor in interest to the landlord could lease space for competing vending facilities). Also, this agreement touched and concerned the leased premises because it benefited the tenant and burdened the landlord with respect to their interests in the property. The investor has breached this covenant by installing the vending machines. This breach by the investor will not, however, allow the retailer to terminate the lease or her obligation to pay rent under the lease—*i.e.*, the retailer's duty to pay rent is independent of the investor's performance of his agreement that there would be no other vending facilities in the building. Thus, the investor can recover the rent payments regardless of whether the vending machines are removed, and the retailer's remedy for the investor's breach is to bring an action against the investor for any damages resulting from his installation of the vending machines.

Answer to Question 6

(C) Neither the rancher nor the farmer may continue to occupy the land taken by the state, but the rancher remains liable for the full rent. To handle this question you must notice that ***all*** of the farmer's leasehold is taken, while only ***part*** of the rancher's is taken, and the rules are different. In both cases, however, when the state takes land by eminent domain, tenants lose the right of possession. If there is an entire taking, the leasehold terminates and the tenant has no obligation to pay further rent to the landlord. So the farmer is off the hook. If the taking is partial, the tenant must continue to pay full rent to the landlord. In the condemnation award, the tenant will get an amount equal to the rent to be paid over the remainder of the lease for the portion of the property taken. Thus, the rancher will get, from the state, the rent that the rancher will pay to the owner over the rest of the lease for the part taken, but the rancher remains obligated for the full rent to the owner. (A) is incorrect because when the state takes by eminent domain, possessory rights of tenants end. (B) is incorrect because the rancher continues to be liable for full rent, even for the property taken by the state. (D) is incorrect. While the measure of recovery is correct for the farmer since his entire leasehold was taken, it is incorrect for the rancher. Because the rancher will remain liable to the owner for the full rent on all of the land the rancher leased, the rancher's measure of recovery from the state is the full amount of the rent under the lease for the property taken.

Answer to Question 7

(C) All of the items listed may be removed because they were used in the tenant's business and may properly be termed trade fixtures. As long as the tenant can remove trade fixtures with little damage to the real property, the tenant may always take them when the tenant moves. (A) is incorrect. The booths, along with the bar, were not even attached to the realty; thus, they cannot, under any circumstances, be considered fixtures and the tenant may always take them, whether they are deemed trade fixtures or not. For a chattel to be deemed a fixture (and thus remain as a part of the realty) it must be affixed to the real property. (B) is incorrect. If these were not trade fixtures, an argument could be made that the tenant could take the items not affixed (bar and booths) but not the ones affixed (lights and dance floor). But even items strongly attached to the realty may be detached by the tenants who installed them if they are tools of the trade. (D) is incorrect. The booths and bar were not affixed, and even though the lights and dance floor were attached, they can be removed as trade fixtures.

Answer to Question 8

(D) The vendor has a superior claim to the wall unit because it has a valid security interest in the wall unit even though the security agreement was not recorded. In a fixture case involving divided ownership, the majority rule is that, absent an agreement to the contrary, a tenant may remove a chattel that she has attached to the demised premises as long as the removal does not cause substantial damage to the demised premises or the virtual destruction of the chattel. Furthermore, if the buyer under an installment land contract leases to a tenant who annexes a chattel to the premises, the seller has no greater rights in the chattel than the buyer, provided that the original sufficiency of the security is not impaired (*e.g.,* removal would not cause substantial damage to the premises). Finally, as between the tenant-purchaser of the chattel (the architect here) and the holder of a properly created security interest, the holder of the security interest can reclaim possession of the chattel upon the purchaser's default according to the terms of the security agreement, which is effective between the parties signing it even though it was not recorded. Therefore, the vendor has a claim to the wall unit that is superior to the other listed parties. (A) is incorrect because it states the rule applicable to common ownership cases, *i.e.,* cases in which the person who brings the chattel onto the land owns both the chattel and the real estate. As with mortgagees, the seller's interest under a land sale contract attaches to all fixtures on the land in the absence of an agreement to the contrary. In that case, the vendor's failure to make a fixture filing for its purchase money security interest would have caused it to lose priority. However, as discussed above, this rule does not apply in divided ownership cases where the tenant brings the chattel onto the premises. (B) is incorrect because the landlord would not prevail against a tenant who brought the chattel onto the leased premises, as long as the chattel could be removed without substantial damage to the premises. Here, absent the security agreement with the vendor, the architect would have been free to remove the wall unit that she purchased and retain possession of it because its removal would not substantially damage the leased premises. Thus, (C) is also incorrect. The architect's rights are superior to those of the investor, but not the vendor.

Answer to Question 9

(C) The best way for the developer to accomplish her goals is to grant the college an easement for intramural athletics use for one year. The holder of an easement has the right to use a tract of land (called the servient tenement) for a specific purpose, but has no right to possess and enjoy the tract of land. The owner of the servient tenement continues to have the right of full possession and enjoyment subject only to the limitation that she cannot interfere with the right of special use created in the easement holder. Here, an easement would allow the college to use the land only for the purposes provided for in the easement, and the developer could limit the purposes to intramural athletics. (A) would not be a good choice because a lease would give the college more control over the land than an easement. A lease grants the tenant the exclusive right to possess the premises and broad rights to use them in any manner, unless specifically restricted. Moreover, a landlord owes certain duties to her tenants, and can be held liable for breach of those duties and for certain defects in the leased premises. Thus, if the developer leases the land to the college, she would not have access to her land, and if she wanted it used only for intramural athletics purposes, she would have to specifically restrict any undesired uses. Any restriction not included in the lease would be unenforceable. An easement, on the other hand, grants only a limited interest in the land—to use it only for those purposes stated in the easement; thus, it would be a better choice than a lease. (B) would not be a good choice because, although the land would revert to the developer after one year, she would be giving title to the land to the college during that time and the college would have broader rights than the developer wants. (D) would not be a good choice because covenants usually are made in conjunction with a lease, deed, or other instrument; they promise some act or forbearance with respect to property and are generally not used to grant rights for access to property.

Answer to Question 10

(D) The buyer has an easement to cross the front parcel because the easement was never extinguished. The original easement granted to the purchaser was an easement appurtenant, the benefit of which passes with a transfer of the benefited land. An easement is deemed appurtenant when the right of special use benefits the easement holder in her physical use or enjoyment of another tract of land. The land subject to the easement is the servient tenement, while the land having the benefit of the easement is the dominant tenement. The benefit of an easement appurtenant passes with transfers of the benefited land, regardless of whether the easement is mentioned in the conveyance. All who possess or subsequently succeed to title to the dominant tenement are entitled to the benefit of the easement. The easement granted to the purchaser was an easement appurtenant because the right to use the private road across the front parcel (the servient tenement) benefited the purchaser in her use and enjoyment of the back parcel (the dominant tenement) by providing her with the most convenient access to the public highway. Thus, when the purchaser sold the benefited land to the buyer, the benefit of the easement also passed to the buyer as an incident of possession of the back parcel. (A) is wrong because, as explained above, this benefit passed to the buyer despite the fact that the deed to the buyer made no mention of the easement. The failure to record does not affect the validity of the easement. Recordation is not essential to the validity of a deed, but only serves to protect the interests of a grantee against subsequent purchasers. Here, the dispute is between the original grantor and the successor of the original easement holder. (B) is incorrect because the buyer's use of the easement would not be a change in its use. This choice goes to the scope of the easement. The key for determining the scope is the reasonable intent of the original parties, including the reasonable present and future needs of the dominant tenement. Here, because the owner knew of the purchaser's plans to open an inn, he knew that she and her guests would use the road across the front parcel. The buyer's use of the easement would be the same—her use and that of her guests. This is not a change in intended use sufficient to allow the owner to legally prevent the buyer's use of the easement. (C) is incorrect because nonuse does not extinguish an easement. Abandonment, which does terminate an easement, requires a physical act by the easement holder that manifests an intent to permanently abandon the easement (*e.g.*, erecting a building that blocks access to an easement of way). Since there is no indication of such an act by the purchaser, the easement would have continued to benefit the back parcel even if the purchaser had never used it.

Answer to Question 11

(A) If the landowner wins it will be because the railway intended to abandon its easement. An easement can be abandoned provided two things are satisfied: nonuse of the easement together with some affirmative act taken on the property which would indicate an intent to abandon the easement. Mere nonuse would not be enough, no matter how long the easement was not used. It is the act taken on the property that shows the intent to abandon that is crucial. Here, the railway's acts in removing the cables and tracks can show the necessary intent. (B) is incorrect. The landowner had granted the easement to the railway, and if the easement has not been terminated, any interference claimed by the landowner is irrelevant. There is no indication that the railway is planning to use the easement in any way different from the use contemplated in the original grant. (C) is incorrect because easements are not terminated simply because the purpose is no longer "practical." (D) is incorrect. Nonuse of an easement will not terminate the easement unless there is also some physical act taken on the property itself that would show an intent to abandon the easement.

Answer to Question 12

(C) The neighbor will likely prevail because the purchaser had inquiry and constructive notice of the restriction. When a subdivision is created with similar covenants in all deeds, there is a mutual right of enforcement (each lot owner can enforce against every other lot owner) if two things are satisfied: (i) a common scheme for development existed at the time that sales of parcels in the subdivision began; and (ii) there was notice of the existence of the covenant to the party sued. Here, there was a common scheme evidenced by the recorded plan, and the fact that the covenant was in the purchaser's chain of title gave her constructive notice of the restriction. Therefore, not only does the covenant apply to the purchaser's land, but the neighbor (or any other lot owner) can enforce it as a reciprocal negative servitude. (A) is incorrect. While it is true that the purchaser's deed had no restrictions, those restrictions are binding if they are in her chain of title so as to give her notice of them. The restriction was in the deed from the owner to the investor, so the fact that it was omitted in the deed from the investor to the purchaser is of no significance. (B) is incorrect. While a covenant is normally only enforceable by the party receiving the promise (here, the owner), this is a situation of mutual rights of enforcement within a geographically defined area, which gives every lot owner in the area the right of enforcement, even though they did not directly receive the benefit of the promise. (D) is incorrect. The fact that gives the neighbor the right of enforcement is not just that his deed contains the covenant, but that the same covenant was in all of the deeds from the owner, including the one to the purchaser's predecessor in title.

Answer to Question 13

(B) The covenant may not be enforced at law against the son. If all requirements are met for the burden of a covenant to run, the successors in interest to the burdened estates will be bound by the arrangement entered into by their predecessors as effectively as if they had expressly agreed to be bound. The requirements are: (i) The covenanting parties must have intended that successors in interest to the covenantor be bound by the terms of the covenant. The requisite intent may be inferred from circumstances surrounding creation of the covenant. This requirement is satisfied because the developer's deed to each of the grantees contained a covenant requiring that the property be used only for single-family housing. (ii) By virtue of the recording statutes, a subsequent purchaser of the promisor's land must have actual, inquiry, or constructive (record) notice of the arrangement at the time she purchased the land; otherwise, she is not bound. Here, the daughter, the son, and the physical therapist have at least constructive notice of the restriction because it is in their chain of title. Because the electrician's deed was never recorded, the plumber had a duty to inquire of the electrician where he obtained the property. Thus, the notice requirement is met. (iii) The covenant must "touch and concern" the land; *i.e.*, the performance of the burden must diminish the landowner's rights, privileges, and powers in connection with her enjoyment of the land. The current owners' rights as landowners are diminished because they cannot use their land to construct multifamily dwellings. (iv) Finally, there must be horizontal and vertical privity. Horizontal privity requires that, at the time the promisor entered into the covenant with the promisee, the two shared some interest in the land independent of the covenant. The developer and each of the four original owners, as grantor and grantees, shared an interest in the land independent of the covenant. Vertical privity exists when the successor in interest to the covenanting party holds the entire interest that was held by the covenantor at the time she made the covenant. Here, the daughter, the plumber, and the physical therapist took the entire interest (fee simple absolute) from their predecessors. However, the son possesses only a life estate in the property, which is less than the fee simple absolute held by the flight attendant. Thus, vertical privity is lacking and the son cannot be bound by the covenant. (A) is incorrect because the daughter is bound by the covenant as discussed above. The fact that she took the property by will is irrelevant. In fact, taking in this manner increases the chance that the daughter will be bound because it means she is not a bona fide purchaser for value and thus not protected by the notice requirement of the recording act. (C) is incorrect because the plumber also is bound because he is charged with inquiry notice of the electrician's unrecorded deed, which contained the single-family restriction. (D) is incorrect because even though the physical therapist's deed did not contain the restriction, she will be charged with constructive notice of it. The restriction appears in the developer's deed to the athlete and thus is in the physical therapist's chain of title. Hence, she also is bound by the covenant.

Answer to Question 14

(D) The suit will be dismissed because the city's creation of the parkland is appropriate. Even if the city did not expressly accept the dedication of the parkland at the time the plat was filed, the announcement of the construction of the recreational facilities could be taken as acceptance. (A) is incorrect. Laches is a defense, not an affirmative cause of action, and it additionally does not appear that the failure of the city to immediately affirmatively accept the parkland prejudiced the homeowners' rights. (B) is incorrect. There is no inverse condemnation here, because the city has in no way regulated or otherwise interfered with the homeowners' use of their land. (C) is incorrect. It is not the homeowners' notice of the proposed use that binds them but the notice of the dedication of the land for park use that is contained in the recorded plat.

Answer to Question 15

(B) The fast food chain's best defense is that the neighborhood has significantly changed and that allowing commercial use of the two lots will not affect the enforceability of the deed restrictions of the other 23 lots. An injunction against breaching a covenant may be obtained by enforcing the covenant as an equitable servitude. An equitable servitude can be created by a writing complying with the Statute of Frauds concerning a promise that touches and concerns the land and indicates that the servitude exists, as long as notice is given to the future owners of the burdened land. Here, there was a promise that touched and concerned the land and indicated that a servitude existed (the deed restrictions), but the promise was not contained in the fast food chain's deed. Nevertheless, the court will imply a covenant—known as a reciprocal negative servitude—where evidence shows that the developer had a scheme for development when sales began and the grantee in question had notice of the plan. The covenant protects the parties who purchased in reliance on the scheme. Evidence of the scheme can be obtained from the general pattern of other restrictions, and notice can be from actual notice, record notice, or inquiry notice. Here, the recorded subdivision map evidences the investor's common scheme, and the fast food chain has inquiry notice of the restriction regarding nonresidential use because of the uniform residential character of the other lots in the subdivision. Thus, the covenant would be implied. However, a court may withhold injunctive relief if the neighborhood has changed significantly since the time the servitude was created such that it would be inequitable to enforce the restriction. But under the concept of the "entering wedge," if removing the restriction on an outer parcel will produce changed conditions for surrounding parcels, requiring that their restrictions also be lifted, the injunction will probably be allowed. Here, if the fast food chain can show that removing the restriction and allowing commercial development of the two lots would ***not*** produce changed conditions for the neighboring, similarly restricted lots, an injunction probably will not issue and the restriction will be terminated as to the two lots. (A) is incorrect because actual awareness of the restriction on the part of the fast food chain is not essential. Because it has inquiry notice (*see* above), the restriction could be enforced against the two lots absent a defense. (C) is incorrect because, although unclean hands ***is*** a valid defense to the enforcement of an equitable servitude, (B) is a ***better*** defense because it may result in ***termination*** of the restriction, whereas unclean hands only protects the fast food chain as against the accountant (but not as against other owners in the subdivision). (D) is incorrect because an implied negative servitude would bind subsequent purchasers with notice whether or not the restriction appeared in their deeds.

Answer to Question 16

(C) The landowner can tear down the dock and the neighbor has no easement right. The neighbor's original right to cross the landowner's land was with her oral permission and, therefore, he had a license only. Regardless of how the neighbor's use of the dock is viewed with regard to the landowner's interest, there was not a sufficient amount of time for the neighbor to have gained a prescriptive easement because at least the first three years of his use were not adverse. Hence, (A) and (B) are wrong. (D) is wrong because it would only be relevant that the neighbor had gained an adverse interest against the trespasser's son if the son had gained an adverse interest against the landowner, and the facts indicate that he had not. Although tacking is permitted where the subsequent possessor takes by descent, devise, or deed purporting to convey title, the trespasser's son never possessed the property. Thus, the trespasser's son had not gained title to the property by adverse possession and the landowner could tear down the dock.

Answer to Question 17

(C) The son is most likely to prevail in the lawsuit because he has acquired title to the land on which the propane tank was installed by adverse possession. To establish title by adverse possession, the possession must be (i) actual and exclusive, (ii) open and notorious, (iii) adverse (hostile), and (iv) continuous throughout the statutory period. Exclusive possession generally means not sharing possession with the true owner or the general public. Possession is open and notorious when it is such as the usual owner would make of the land and is sufficient to put the true owner on notice of the fact of possession. Possession is hostile when it is without the owner's consent; it does not matter whether the possessor believes she is on her own land or knows she is trespassing on someone else's land. Continuous possession is possession that the average owner would make of the property under the circumstances. There need not be continuous possession by the same person. Separate periods of adverse possession may be "tacked" together to make up the full statutory period, provided there is privity between the successive adverse holders. Privity is satisfied if the subsequent purchaser takes by descent, devise, or deed purporting to convey title. Here, the landowner's possession of the neighbor's land was clearly actual and exclusive, because she did not share possession with the neighbor or the general public. Her possession was open and notorious, because the installation and maintenance of a propane tank to supply fuel to a rural house is a use that the usual owner would make of the land. Moreover, the tank was above ground and thus visible to the neighbor. Although the landowner believed she was on her own land, her state of mind is irrelevant. Because she did not enter with the neighbor's permission, the landowner's possession was hostile. Finally, the landowner possessed the property for 14 years, one year short of the limitations period. However, title to the landowner's land descended to her son on her death, and he continued to possess the land on which the propane tank was installed for six years, for a total of five years beyond that required by the statute of limitations. Thus, (A) is incorrect. (B) is incorrect because the statute of limitations may be tolled by the ***true owner's***, not the adverse possessor's, disability. (D) is incorrect because an implied easement, like easements generally, is a nonexclusive right to use the land rather than an exclusive right to possess and enjoy the land. The typical easement gives its holder the right of access across a tract of land (*e.g.*, a utility line or road) without precluding the owner of the land from also using it. Here, the landowner's installation of the propane tank amounted to a permanent and exclusive possession of the neighbor's land.

Torts

Selected Topics in Negligence

TORTS

I. NEGLIGENCE

A. PRIMA FACIE CASE

Elements of the prima facie case:

(i) A ***duty*** on the part of defendant ***to conform to a specific standard of conduct*** for protection of plaintiff against an unreasonable risk of injury;

(ii) A ***breach*** of that duty by defendant;

(iii) The breach is the ***actual and proximate cause*** of plaintiff's injury; and

(iv) ***Damage***.

B. DUTY OF CARE

A duty of care is owed to all foreseeable plaintiffs. The extent of the duty is determined by the applicable standard of care. Therefore, when confronted with a negligence question, always ask:

(i) Was the plaintiff foreseeable?

(ii) If so, what is the applicable standard of care?

1. Foreseeable/Unforeseeable Plaintiffs

A duty of care is owed only to foreseeable plaintiffs. However, a problem arises where defendant breaches a duty to one plaintiff ("P1") and also causes injury to another (possibly unforeseeable) plaintiff ("P2"). There are two possible outcomes:

a. Cardozo View (Majority)—Foreseeable Zone of Danger

P2 can recover only if she can establish that a reasonable person would have foreseen a risk of injury to her under the circumstances; *i.e.,* she was located in the foreseeable zone of danger.

b. Andrews View (Minority)—Everyone Is Foreseeable

P2 may establish the existence of a duty extending from defendant to her by a showing that defendant has breached a duty owed to P1.

2. Specific Situations

a. Rescuers

A rescuer is a foreseeable plaintiff where defendant negligently put himself or a third person in peril (*i.e.,* danger invites rescue). However, firefighters and police officers may be barred by the "firefighter's rule" from recovering for injuries caused by the risks of a rescue.

b. Intended Beneficiaries of Economic Transactions

A third party for whose economic benefit a legal or business transaction was made (*e.g.,* a beneficiary of a will) may be a foreseeable plaintiff.

3. Standards of Care

a. **Basic Standard—The Reasonable Person**
The reasonable person standard is an ***objective*** standard, *i.e.,* one's conduct measured against what the average person would do. A defendant's ***mental*** deficiencies and inexperience are not taken into account (*i.e.,* stupidity is no excuse). However, the "reasonable person" is considered to have the same ***physical*** characteristics as defendant (but remember, one is expected to know one's physical handicaps and to exercise the care of a person with such knowledge—*e.g.,* a blind person should not fly a plane).

b. **Particular Standards of Conduct**

1) **Professionals**
A professional or someone with special occupational skills is required to possess the knowledge and skill of a member of the profession or occupation in good standing in similar communities. Medical specialists will be held to a national standard of care.

a) **Duty to Disclose Risks of Treatment**
A doctor has a duty to disclose the risks of treatment to enable a patient to give an informed consent. A doctor breaches this duty if an undisclosed risk was serious enough that a reasonable person in the patient's position would have withheld consent on learning of the risk.

2) **Children**
Children are held to the standard of a child of ***like age***, ***education***, ***intelligence***, ***and experience***. This is a ***subjective*** test. A child under four is usually without the capacity to be negligent. Children engaged in adult activities may be required to conform to an "adult" standard of care.

3) **Emergency Situations**
A defendant must act as a reasonable person would under the same emergency conditions. The emergency is not to be considered, however, if it is of defendant's own making.

c. **Statutory Standards of Care**
A statute's specific duty may replace the more general common law duty of due care if: (i) the statute provides for a ***criminal penalty***, (ii) the statute ***clearly defines the standard*** of conduct, (iii) plaintiff is ***within the protected class***, and (iv) the statute was ***designed to prevent the type of harm suffered*** by plaintiff.

1) **Excuse for Violation**
Violation of some statutes may be excused where compliance would cause more danger than violation or where compliance would be beyond defendant's control.

2) **Effect of Violation or Compliance**
Under the majority view, an unexcused statutory violation is negligence per se; *i.e.,* it establishes the first two requirements in the prima facie case—a ***conclusive*** presumption of duty and breach of duty. In contrast, even though violation of the applicable statute may be negligence, compliance with the statute will not necessarily establish due care.

4. **Affirmative Duties to Act**
Generally, one does not have a legal duty to act. Exceptions to this rule exist, however:

a. **Assumption of Duty by Acting**
One may assume a duty to act by acting (*e.g.,* once defendant undertakes to aid someone, he must do so with reasonable care).

Exception: Many states have enacted Good Samaritan statutes, which exempt doctors, nurses, etc., from liability for ordinary, but not gross, negligence.

b. **Peril Due to Defendant's Conduct**
One has a duty to assist someone he has negligently or innocently placed in peril.

c. **Special Relationship Between Parties**
A special relationship between the parties (*e.g.,* parent-child) may create a duty to act. Similarly, ***common carriers***, ***innkeepers***, ***shopkeepers***, and others that gather the public for profit owe duties of reasonable care to aid or assist their patrons. In addition, places of public accommodation have a duty to prevent injury to guests by third persons.

d. **Duty to Control Third Persons**
Generally, there is no duty to prevent a third person from injuring another. An affirmative duty may be imposed, however, if one has the actual ability and authority to control a person's actions, and knows or should know the person is likely to commit acts that would require exercise of this control.

C. **BREACH OF DUTY**
Where defendant's conduct falls short of that level required by the applicable standard of care owed to the plaintiff, she has breached her duty. Whether the duty of care is breached in an individual case is a question for the trier of fact. The main problem relates to proof of the breach. Plaintiff may use one of the following theories:

1. **Custom or Usage**
Custom or usage may be used to establish standard of care, but does not control the question of whether certain conduct amounted to negligence. For example, although certain behavior is custom in an industry, a court may find that the entire industry is acting negligently.

2. **Violation of Statute**
Existence of a duty owed to plaintiff and breach thereof may be established as a matter of law by proof that defendant violated an applicable statute ("negligence per se"). Causation and damages must still be established by plaintiff.

3. **Res Ipsa Loquitur**
In some cases, the very occurrence of an event may tend to establish a breach of duty. The doctrine of res ipsa loquitur requires plaintiff to show that (i) the accident causing the injury is a type that would not normally occur unless someone was negligent, and (ii) the negligence is attributable to defendant (*i.e.,* this type of accident ordinarily happens because of the negligence of someone in defendant's position). This can often be shown by evidence that the instrumentality causing the injury was in the exclusive control of defendant. (Plaintiff must also establish freedom from fault on his part.)

a. **Effect of Res Ipsa Loquitur**
Where res ipsa loquitur is established, plaintiff has ***made a prima facie case*** and no directed verdict may be given for defendant. Plaintiff can still lose, however, if the inference of negligence is rejected by the trier of fact.

CMR **Exam Tip** Questions testing on res ipsa loquitur often have the defendant making a ***motion for a directed verdict***. These questions don't require you to memorize rules of civil procedure—all you need to remember is the following:

(i) ***Deny*** defendant's motion for directed verdict if plaintiff has established res ipsa loquitur or presented some other evidence of breach of duty (such as defendant's violation of a statute);

(ii) ***Grant*** defendant's motion if plaintiff has failed to establish res ipsa loquitur and failed to present some other evidence of breach of duty.

Occasionally, plaintiff may also move for a directed verdict. Plaintiff's motion should always be ***denied*** except in the rare case where plaintiff has established negligence per se through violation of an applicable statute ***and*** there are no issues of proximate cause.

D. CAUSATION

Once negligent conduct is shown (a breach of the standard of care owed a foreseeable plaintiff), plaintiff must show that the conduct was the cause of his injury. For liability to attach, plaintiff must show ***both*** actual cause and proximate cause.

1. **Actual Cause (Causation in Fact)**
Before defendant's conduct can be considered a proximate cause of plaintiff's injury, it must first be a cause in fact of the injury. Several tests exist:

a. **"But For" Test**
Act or omission is the cause in fact of an injury when the injury would not have occurred but for the act. This test applies where several acts (each insufficient to cause the injury alone) combine to cause the injury.

b. **Joint Causes—Substantial Factor Test**
Where several causes bring about injury, and any one alone would have been sufficient to cause the injury, defendant's conduct is the cause in fact if it was a substantial factor in causing the injury.

c. **Alternative Causes Approach**
This test applies when there are two acts, only one of which causes injury, but it is not known which one. The burden of proof shifts to defendants, and each must show that his negligence is not the actual cause. [Summers v. Tice]

Exam Tip Distinguish these last two tests: Under the joint causes approach, both parties caused the harm. Under the alternative causes approach, although both parties acted negligently, only one caused the harm.

2. **Proximate Cause (Legal Causation)**
In addition to being a cause in fact, the defendant's conduct must also be the proximate

cause of the injury. Even though the conduct actually caused plaintiff's injury, it might not be deemed to be the proximate cause. Thus, the doctrine of proximate causation is a ***limitation of liability*** and deals with liability or nonliability for unforeseeable or unusual consequences of one's acts.

a. General Rule—Scope of Foreseeable Risk

A defendant generally is liable for all harmful results that are the normal incidents of and within the increased risk caused by his acts. This is a ***foreseeability*** test.

CMR **Exam Tip** Questions raising proximate cause issues will not require you to make a judgment call on foreseeability in a close case. Often the call of the question will be whether one or both parties are entitled to summary judgment—which should be denied if there is ***any issue of foreseeability for the jury***. In other cases, the facts in the question will be so clear-cut that ***common sense*** will tell you immediately whether the harm that occurred was foreseeable.

b. Liability in Direct Cause Cases

In a direct cause case, where there is an uninterrupted chain of events from the negligent act to plaintiff's injury, defendant is liable for all ***foreseeable harmful results***, regardless of unusual manner or timing. Defendant is not liable for ***unforeseeable harmful results*** not within the risk created by defendant's negligence. Most harmful results will be deemed foreseeable in direct cause cases.

c. Liability in Indirect Cause Cases

In an indirect cause case, an affirmative intervening force (*e.g.,* an act by a third person, an act of God) comes into motion after defendant's negligent act and combines with it to cause plaintiff's injury.

1) Foreseeable Results Caused by Foreseeable Intervening Forces—Defendant Liable

Defendant is liable where his negligence caused a foreseeable harmful response or reaction from a dependent intervening force or created a foreseeable risk that an independent intervening force would harm plaintiff.

a) Common Dependent Intervening Forces

The following dependent intervening forces are ***almost always foreseeable:*** (i) subsequent medical malpractice, (ii) negligence of rescuers, (iii) efforts to protect the person or property of oneself or another, (iv) injuries caused by another "reacting" to defendant's actions, (v) subsequent diseases caused by a weakened condition, and (vi) subsequent accident substantially caused by the original injury.

b) Independent Intervening Forces

Independent intervening forces that are not a natural response or reaction to the situation created by the defendant's conduct may be foreseeable if defendant's negligence increased the risk of harm from these forces. Independent intervening forces include (i) negligent acts of third persons, (ii) crimes and intentional torts of third persons, and (iii) acts of God.

2) **Foreseeable Results Caused by Unforeseeable Intervening Forces—Defendant Usually Liable**
Defendant is liable where his negligence increased the risk of a foreseeable harmful result and that result is ultimately produced by an unforeseeable intervening force. This rule does not apply where the unforeseeable intervening force was a crime or intentional tort of a third person.

3) **Unforeseeable Results Caused by Foreseeable Intervening Forces—Defendant Not Liable**
In the rare case where a totally unforeseeable result was caused by a foreseeable intervening force, most courts hold defendant not liable.

4) **Unforeseeable Results Caused by Unforeseeable Intervening Forces—Defendant Not Liable**
Intervening forces that produce unforeseeable results (results not within the increased risk created by defendant's negligence) are generally deemed unforeseeable and ***superseding***. Superseding forces break the causal connection between defendant's initial negligent act and plaintiff's ultimate injury, thus relieving defendant of liability.

d. **Unforeseeable Extent or Severity of Harm—Defendant Liable**
In all cases, defendant takes his plaintiff as he finds him; *i.e.,* defendant is liable for all damages, including aggravation of an existing condition, even if the extent or severity of the damages was unforeseeable. This is also known as the "eggshell-skull plaintiff" rule.

E. DAMAGES

Damage is an essential element of negligence; thus, damage will not be presumed (and nominal damages are not available).

1. **Personal Injury**
Plaintiff is to be compensated for all his damages (past, present, and prospective), both ***economic*** damages (such as medical expenses) and ***noneconomic*** damages (such as pain and suffering). Foreseeability of the extent of harm is generally irrelevant; *i.e.*, one takes one's plaintiff as one finds him. A plaintiff suffering physical injury also may recover damages for any resulting emotional distress.

2. **Property Damage**
The measure of damage is the reasonable cost of repair or, if the property is nearly destroyed, the fair market value at the time of the accident.

3. **Punitive Damages**
Plaintiff may recover punitive damages if defendant's conduct is "wanton and willful," reckless, or malicious.

4. **Nonrecoverable Items**
Nonrecoverable items include: (i) interest from the date of damage in a personal injury action, and (ii) attorneys' fees.

5. **Duty to Mitigate**
As in all cases, plaintiff has a duty to take reasonable steps to mitigate damages (*e.g.*, seek appropriate treatment).

6. **Collateral Source Rule**
Damages are not reduced just because plaintiff received benefits from other sources (*e.g.*, health insurance).

barbri®

Torts

1. Ⓐ Ⓑ Ⓒ Ⓓ
2. Ⓐ Ⓑ Ⓒ Ⓓ
3. Ⓐ Ⓑ Ⓒ Ⓓ
4. Ⓐ Ⓑ Ⓒ Ⓓ
5. Ⓐ Ⓑ Ⓒ Ⓓ

6. Ⓐ Ⓑ Ⓒ Ⓓ
7. Ⓐ Ⓑ Ⓒ Ⓓ
8. Ⓐ Ⓑ Ⓒ Ⓓ
9. Ⓐ Ⓑ Ⓒ Ⓓ
10. Ⓐ Ⓑ Ⓒ Ⓓ

11. Ⓐ Ⓑ Ⓒ Ⓓ
12. Ⓐ Ⓑ Ⓒ Ⓓ
13. Ⓐ Ⓑ Ⓒ Ⓓ
14. Ⓐ Ⓑ Ⓒ Ⓓ
15. Ⓐ Ⓑ Ⓒ Ⓓ

16. Ⓐ Ⓑ Ⓒ Ⓓ
17. Ⓐ Ⓑ Ⓒ Ⓓ

TORTS QUESTIONS

Question 1

The owner of a self-propelled riding mower started the engine to mow his front lawn when the clutch of the mower suddenly engaged, causing it to lurch forward rapidly and throw him off. By the time the owner caught up with the mower, it had started into the street. A motorist swerved to avoid the mower and struck a tree on the opposite side of the street. Investigation revealed that the sudden shift of the clutch was caused by a defective gear in the transmission.

If the motorist brings a negligence action for personal injuries and property damage against the owner, she will:

(A) Not prevail, because the owner was so startled by the mower's sudden movement that he was unable to react swiftly enough to prevent the harm.

(B) Not prevail, because the sudden movement was caused by a defective gear in the mower.

(C) Prevail, because her damages were caused by the owner's operation of a dangerously defective piece of machinery.

(D) Prevail, because a landowner owes a duty to passersby to exercise reasonable care in activities on his land.

Question 2

A depressed man intending to commit suicide parked his car outside of town, attached a hose to the tailpipe of his car and pushed it through a small opening in a rear window. With all the other windows rolled up, he sat in the driver's seat and started the engine. About 10 minutes later, a jogger went past the man's car and immediately realized what was happening. Finding the doors locked, she smashed open a window with her bare fist, badly cutting her hand. She got the car door open and dragged the unconscious man from the vehicle. He was hospitalized but recovered. The jogger's hand required surgery and she has suffered some permanent disability. Attempted suicide is not a crime in this jurisdiction.

If the jogger sues the man for her injuries, what is the most likely result?

(A) The jogger wins, because she successfully saved the man's life.

(B) The jogger wins, because the man intentionally put himself in a position of peril.

(C) The jogger loses, because the man did not intend to harm another person.

(D) The jogger loses, because attempted suicide is not a crime in the jurisdiction.

Question 3

A landlord employed his friend as the on-site manager of one of his apartment buildings despite being aware that he had previously been arrested for criminal battery, disorderly conduct, and driving while intoxicated. The manager did a good job dealing with the general maintenance of the apartment building, although the landlord was aware that he continued to drink heavily.

One night the manager, who was extremely intoxicated, attempted to swat an insect on the ceiling of his apartment and could not do so after several attempts. Enraged, he took a pistol from his drawer and shot at the insect. The bullet missed the insect and passed through the ceiling of his apartment into the apartment above, lodging in the leg of a tenant's social guest.

Does the guest have a viable cause of action against the landlord?

(A) Yes, because the guest was a licensee of the tenant.

(B) Yes, because the landlord was aware of the manager's habitual drunkenness and propensity for violence.

(C) No, because the landlord cannot be held liable for the manager's intentional torts.

(D) No, because shooting an insect was outside the scope of the manager's employment.

Question 4

On New Year's Eve, some of the guests of a popular downtown hotel began throwing ice cubes out the hotel's windows. When the hotel manager discovered this fact, he instructed hotel employees to patrol the hallways, telling guests to refrain from such conduct. Later that evening, as a pedestrian was walking past the hotel on the sidewalk, he was hit and injured by an ice cube thrown out of an upper story window.

The pedestrian sued the hotel owner, who was out of town when the incident occurred, and the above facts are established at trial. At the close of evidence, the pedestrian moves for a directed verdict.

Should the court grant the motion?

(A) Yes, because a landowner is strictly liable for injuries to persons off the premises caused by an object from the landowner's premises.

(B) Yes, because an ice cube thrown from that height becomes a dangerous instrumentality.

(C) No, because the trier of fact could determine that the hotel owner had no personal knowledge of the conduct of the hotel guests.

(D) No, because the trier of fact could determine that the hotel employees had taken reasonable precautions to prevent such an injury.

Question 5

An 18-year-old had been refused a driver's license due to a seizure disorder not controlled by medication. Nevertheless, he borrowed a friend's car for a short drive. While he was driving, he suffered a seizure and struck a bicyclist with the car, causing him serious bodily injury.

If the bicyclist sues the driver for negligence and prevails, it will be because:

(A) The driver failed to exercise ordinary and reasonable care under the circumstances.

(B) The driver failed to exercise the amount of care that an 18-year-old of like education, intelligence, and experience would have exercised.

(C) The driver failed to exercise the ordinary and reasonable care that a person with his disability would have exercised.

(D) The driver violated the law when he drove without a license.

Question 6

A 12-year-old snowboarder at a ski resort lost control while he was going down a slope and collided with a middle-aged skier who was ahead of him. The collision caused the skier to fall hard and sustain multiple fractures of her leg. The injuries required surgery and several months of rehabilitation before the skier could walk again.

If the skier prevails in a personal injury action against the snowboarder, it will be because:

(A) The skier had not signed a ski resort waiver assuming the risk of any injuries suffered while skiing.

(B) The severity of the skier's injuries dictated that an adult standard of care be applied to the snowboarder's activity.

(C) A snowboarder of like age, education, intelligence, and experience would have avoided the accident in the exercise of reasonable care.

(D) The snowboarder had used a fake pass to gain entrance to the ski resort.

Question 7

A 15-year-old took the keys to the family car, which was parked on the street in front of the house, and began driving. He turned right at the first intersection, swinging a little bit wide as he turned. A motorist coming down the street from the opposite direction swerved his auto to the right because he feared a collision. He lost control of the auto and struck a tree in a landowner's front yard. As the motorist staggered out of his auto, dazed but otherwise unhurt, he tripped over some decorative boulders that the landowner had placed in his yard and fell, breaking his wrist as he landed.

The motorist brought an action against the 15-year-old for personal injuries and established the above facts. At the close of the motorist's case, the attorney for the 15-year-old moves for a directed verdict.

The court is likely to:

(A) Grant the motion, because the motorist has failed to establish a prima facie case.

(B) Deny the motion, because the motorist's fear of an imminent harmful contact with the 15-year-old's car was unreasonable.

(C) Deny the motion, because the jury could find that the 15-year-old has not acted as a reasonably prudent person would have acted in similar circumstances.

(D) Deny the motion, because the jury could find that the 15-year-old has not acted as a reasonably prudent child of similar age and experience would have acted in similar circumstances.

Question 8

A patient with a degenerative eye disease visited a well-known eye surgeon, who told him that there were two ways to treat his eye: a more traditional surgical method or a recently developed injection method. Although the injection method had the advantage of a higher success rate, it also carried a 25% risk that vision would be lost completely, whereas such a risk was only 10% by the surgical method. The surgeon described both methods to the patient but did not tell the patient of the risk factors involved. The surgeon asked the patient which method he would like to use, but the patient told the surgeon to choose whichever method he preferred because he was the expert. The surgeon selected the injection method and carefully injected the patient's eye with the amount of medicine recommended by the medical literature and known to the surgeon from past experience.

Unfortunately for the patient, the attempt to restore his vision to normal failed, and, in fact, he suffered a complete loss of vision as a result of the injection. Afterward, the patient learned of the different risk factors of the two methods.

The patient sued the surgeon for his loss of vision. At trial, the above facts were established. The patient testified that he would have chosen the surgery had he known of the varying risk factors. At the close of the patient's case, the surgeon moved for a directed verdict.

The court should:

(A) Deny the motion, because the jury could find that a reasonable person would not have consented to the injection procedure if informed of the risks.

(B) Deny the motion, because the patient would not have undergone the injection procedure had he known of the risks.

(C) Grant the motion, because the facts establish that the patient consented to the surgeon's selection of the procedure to use.

(D) Grant the motion, because there are no facts to indicate that the surgeon performed the procedure negligently.

Question 9

A patient visited a physician because of a painful foot. The physician told the patient that he could choose several weeks of physical therapy or undergo elective surgery to correct the problem. The physician did not tell the patient that there was a risk of nerve damage if he underwent the surgery. The patient chose the surgery and the physician performed the surgery successfully. However, the patient was upset when he learned afterward about the risk of nerve damage, because, had he known of the risks of the surgery, he would have chosen the therapy instead. The jurisdiction applies a national standard to determine a physician's duty of care.

In an action against the physician for failing to inform the patient of the risks of the surgery, the patient most likely will:

(A) Prevail, because he would have refused the operation had he known of the risks.

(B) Prevail, because the jurisdiction uses a higher national standard to determine a physician's duty of care.

(C) Not prevail, unless the jury concludes that a reasonable person would have withheld consent to the operation if informed of the risks.

(D) Not prevail, because the surgery was successful.

Question 10

A state barred the use of studded snow tires on its roads because of the damage they caused to the road surface. Although he knew of the state law, a motorist did not remove his studded tires from his vehicle because he enjoyed the extra traction they gave him driving on snow and ice. As he was driving over some rough roads, a metal stud broke off his tire and struck a pedestrian in the eye, causing permanent loss of vision in that eye.

The pedestrian sued the motorist for damages. At trial, the pedestrian introduced the statute and presented evidence that the motorist operated a vehicle equipped with studded tires in violation of the statute. The pedestrian testified as to his injuries and presented evidence of his damages, and then rested his case. The defense immediately moved for a directed verdict.

The court is most likely to rule:

(A) In favor of the motion, because the statute was designed to protect roads, not people.

(B) In favor of the motion, because violation of motor vehicle statutes is not sufficient evidence of negligence.

(C) Against the motion, because violation of a statute is generally negligence per se.

(D) Against the motion, because the statute has a rational basis and is designed for the good of all citizens.

Question 11

A state child safety statute required children under eight years of age to be in a government-approved car seat when riding in a motor vehicle. A father was driving to a ballgame with his seven-year-old child, who was buckled in the back seat with a regular seat belt. The father did not notice when the child unbuckled himself and started climbing into the front seat. The child grabbed the steering wheel "to help daddy steer," causing the car to swerve into the other lane and collide with another motorist's car. The motorist was seriously injured from the collision; the father and his child were unhurt.

The motorist sued the father to recover damages for her injuries. At trial, the motorist presented evidence of the statute, her injuries, and the facts stated above. At the conclusion of the proofs, both parties moved for a directed verdict.

How should the trial judge proceed?

(A) Grant the motorist's motion, because the father's violation of the statute constituted negligence per se.

(B) Grant the father's motion, because the motorist offered no evidence that the statute was intended to prevent the harm that occurred.

(C) Deny both motions and submit the case to the jury, because the jury could find that the father is liable for his child's negligent conduct.

(D) Deny both motions and submit the case to the jury, because the jury could find that the father breached his duty of care owed to the motorist.

Question 12

A motorist driving home one night on a desolate two-lane road stopped when he saw a person lying on the road next to a bicycle. The cyclist had slipped and fell off his bicycle, and was knocked unconscious when he hit his head on the pavement. Not wishing to get involved and seeing that no one else was around, the motorist got back into his car and drove away without making any effort to help the cyclist, even though he had a cell phone with which he could have summoned aid. The cyclist remained lying in the same place and was later struck by another car.

If the cyclist brings suit against the motorist for injuries suffered when he was struck by the other car, will the cyclist prevail?

(A) Yes, because a reasonable person under the same circumstances would have come to the cyclist's aid.

(B) Yes, because by stopping and examining the cyclist, the motorist, as a matter of law, assumed a duty to aid him.

(C) No, because the motorist was not responsible for causing the cyclist to be lying by the side of the road.

(D) No, because the motorist did not in any way make the cyclist's situation worse.

Question 13

In a state that imposed a maximum speed limit of 65 m.p.h. by statute, a truck driver was going 75 m.p.h. on a stretch of highway when a car pulled in front of her. The truck driver was unable to stop in time and hit the car, seriously injuring the driver.

In an action against the truck driver for negligence, evidence was introduced that the truck driver would not have been able to stop in time if she had been going 65 m.p.h.

The injured driver most likely will:

(A) Prevail, because the truck driver's breach of the speed limit statute was negligence per se.

(B) Prevail, because the truck driver's conduct was criminal as well as tortious.

(C) Prevail, but the injured driver's recovery will be reduced by the percentage of his fault for pulling in front of the truck driver.

(D) Not prevail, because the violation of the speed law was not the cause in fact of the harm.

Question 14

When a jogger came to a bike path that passed under a road, he used the path to save some time, despite a sign reciting a city ordinance that permitted only bicycles to use the path and prohibited pedestrians. After he reached the road on the other side, he had gone about 30 feet when a motorist pulled out of an alley and hit him with her car, injuring him. There was a stop sign at the end of the alley, but the motorist had failed to see it and stop. Had the jogger not ignored the sign and not used the bicycle path, he would not have been near the alley when the motorist drove out.

If the jogger is deemed to have violated the ordinance, the violation can be characterized as:

(A) The actual cause of his injury.

(B) A concurring actual cause of his injury.

(C) An intervening cause of his injury.

(D) An existing condition having no factual relationship to his injury.

Question 15

A state statute required that anyone performing construction work for another in exchange for value must either have a contractor's license or work for someone who is licensed. A homeowner wishing to remodel his kitchen and living room knew that a friend had previously worked for a licensed contractor for many years and was extremely knowledgeable about her trade, so he offered her money to assist in the project. When the friend explained that she would not be able to get a contractor's license in time to do the work, the homeowner responded that he did not care about her lack of a license. The friend began working in the homeowner's house, and parked her truck containing all her tools and materials in his driveway. Late in the day, a meteoroid fell from the sky and struck a can of solvent lying in the bed of her pickup. The solvent exploded from the force of the impact, setting the truck afire, which itself exploded when the gas tank caught fire, in turn igniting the homeowner's house.

Is the friend liable for the damage to the house?

(A) No, because the homeowner assumed the risk of any property damage when he knowingly solicited her to work without a contractor's license.

(B) No, because no carelessness on her part was a legal cause of the property damage to the homeowner.

(C) Yes, because her lack of a contractor's license is negligence per se.

(D) Yes, because there would have been no damage to the homeowner's house but for the friend's decision to park her truck in his driveway.

Question 16

Two neighbors who worked in a large city nearby alternated days driving. Because the commute took them through a crime-ridden area, one commuter was vigilant about keeping her car well-maintained, but the other failed to maintain her car or bring it in for servicing, despite the first commuter's complaints and dashboard warning lights indicating that it needed servicing. One evening after dark when the latter was driving them both home from work, her car died just as they were passing through a dangerous neighborhood. The passenger, who was calling for assistance on her cell phone, protested when the driver opened her door to look at the engine. Two assailants appeared and beat and robbed the driver and passenger.

If the passenger brings an action against the driver for her injuries, she will probably:

(A) Recover, because the driver owed her the same increased level of care that a common carrier owed its passenger.

(B) Recover, because the driver's negligence increased the risk that the passenger would be the victim of criminal activity.

(C) Not recover, because the criminal acts of the assailants were independent, intervening causes of the passenger's injuries, which supersede any negligence by the driver.

(D) Not recover, because the driver had no duty to prevent criminal attacks upon the passenger.

Question 17

A motorist was driving his car down the street when he struck a 10-year-old boy who had darted into the road to retrieve a bouncing ball. After the accident, the boy's mother refused to take the boy for treatment on religious grounds. As a result, the boy's injuries were more severe than they would otherwise have been.

The boy's best chance to recover for all of his injuries is to argue that:

(A) The doctrine of avoidable consequences at most bars recovery for the aggravation of his injuries, but not for the original injuries themselves.

(B) Any negligence on the mother's part is not to be imputed to her child.

(C) Victims have no duty to take steps for their own safety after the accident.

(D) Defendants must take their victims as they find them, including their mothers' attitudes toward medical treatment.

TORTS ANSWERS

Answer to Question 1

(A) The motorist will not prevail under these facts because the owner does not appear to have breached his duty of care to her. A prima facie case for negligence consists of: (i) a duty on the part of the defendant to conform to a specific standard of conduct for the protection of the plaintiff against an unreasonable risk of injury; (ii) breach of that duty by the defendant; (iii) such breach was the actual and proximate cause of the plaintiff's injury; and (iv) damage to the plaintiff's person or property. While the owner owed a duty of care to the motorist because she was passing by his property while he was operating his riding mower, the facts do not suggest a breach of duty. He was thrown off by the sudden forward movement of the mower and could not catch up to it before it entered the street. Absent the owner's breach of duty, the motorist cannot recover. (B) is incorrect because the owner may be found liable for negligence in his operation of the mower regardless of what caused the sudden movement. Here, however, nothing suggests that he was negligent in starting the mower or failing to discover or guard against the defect. (C) is incorrect because the motorist must prove that the owner knew or should have known of the defect and was therefore negligent in operating the mower while it was in such a defective condition. Merely showing the defective condition of the mower, without more, will not suffice to impose liability on the owner, and nothing in the facts indicates that the owner knew of the defect. (D) is incorrect even though a landowner does owe a duty of reasonable care to passersby, such as the motorist. As discussed above, nothing in the facts indicates that the owner breached that duty.

Answer to Question 2

(B) The man will be liable to the jogger for her injuries. When a person intentionally or negligently places himself in a position of peril, it is foreseeable that someone might try to rescue him (*i.e.*, danger invites rescue) and the rescuer may recover for any injuries suffered from the person's placing himself in peril. Because the man intentionally placed himself in the position of peril, it was foreseeable that someone might rescue him, so he owed a duty to the jogger. (A) is incorrect because the jogger's cause of action is not dependent on whether she succeeded. (C) is incorrect because even though the man has no liability for an intentional tort, he is liable in a negligence action for breach of his duty to the jogger. (D) is incorrect because the jogger will prevail regardless of the fact that the man committed no crime.

Answer to Question 3

(B) Because the landlord knew about the manager's continued heavy drinking and tendencies toward violence, the guest has a cause of action for negligence in his hiring of the manager. An employer owes a duty to all those who may foreseeably come into contact with his employee to exercise due care in the hiring, supervision, and retention of the employee, and the landlord's retention of the manager under these circumstances may be a breach of that duty. (A) is incorrect because the landlord's liability here is based on negligent hiring rather than the guest's status on the property. (C) is also incorrect. An employer can be held directly liable for the intentional tort of an employee if it was foreseeable and the employer was negligent in hiring or retaining the employee. (D) is a true statement that would be relevant for vicarious liability purposes. However, it does not preclude the landlord from being liable for his own negligence based on the foreseeability of his employee acting violently.

Answer to Question 4

(D) The pedestrian's motion will not be granted because the trier of fact could determine that the hotel employees exercised reasonable care. The owner of the hotel owed a duty of care to passersby such as the pedestrian. Once his employees knew of the conduct of the hotel's guests, a duty arose to try to prevent it. It is the function of the trier of fact to determine whether the precautions they took satisfied that duty. (A) is an incorrect statement of the law—strict liability does not apply. (B) is incorrect because it is not the determining factor as to the hotel owner's liability. (C) would be no defense because the hotel owner would be vicariously liable for the conduct of his employees. Because his employees were aware of the conduct of the guests, they had a duty to take precautions to prevent it.

Answer to Question 5

(C) If the bicyclist prevails it will be because the driver failed to exercise ordinary care, given his physical disability. In a lawsuit based on negligence, the usual standard of care is ordinary and reasonable care under the circumstances. The standard changes when the defendant has a major physical disability such as a seizure disorder. In that situation, the standard becomes ordinary and reasonable care for a person with that disability, which in this case would have been to refrain from driving. Therefore, (C) is a more accurate answer than (A). (B) is wrong. It correctly states the standard to be applied to children, but that standard would not be applied to an 18-year-old car driver. (D) is a true statement. However, the statutory violation of failure to obtain a license was not the cause of the accident.

Answer to Question 6

(C) The skier will prevail if a 12-year-old snowboarder acting reasonably would have been able to avoid the accident. A child is required to conform to the standard of care of a child of like age, education, intelligence, and experience in the usual case. This permits a subjective evaluation of whether that particular defendant acted reasonably under the circumstances. If the snowboarder acted unreasonably under this standard, the skier will recover. (A) is incorrect because even if a waiver had been signed by the skier, it would allow only the ski resort to raise the defense of express assumption of risk if sued; the snowboarder could not rely on a waiver to which he was not a party. Thus, the skier's failure to sign a waiver is irrelevant. (B) is wrong because the severity of the skier's injuries do not dictate whether an adult standard of care applies. Courts will require children to conform to an adult standard of care when they are engaged in activities that normally only adults engage in, such as driving an automobile. Snowboarding would not be considered that type of activity, so an adult standard of care would not apply regardless of the severity of the skier's injuries. (D) is incorrect because the fact that the snowboarder had used a fake pass to gain entrance to the resort does not indicate whether he was complying with the applicable standard of care when he struck the skier, which is the critical question here.

Answer to Question 7

(C) The court will deny the motion because the trier of fact could find that the 15-year-old acted negligently under the circumstances. The general rule is that the actions of a child are measured by the standard of a reasonably prudent child of similar age, intelligence, and experience. This rule does not apply where the child engages in an adult activity. The driving of an automobile is an adult activity, and so the 15-year-old will be held to an adult standard of care. It is up to the trier of fact to determine whether the 15-year-old has satisfied the standard of the reasonably prudent adult. (C) is therefore correct and (D) is incorrect. (A) is incorrect because the facts establish all elements of the prima facie case sufficient to submit the case to the jury. (B) is incorrect because the motorist's fear may have been reasonable and his actions foreseeable in an attempt to avoid an accident. It will be up to the jury to make that determination.

Answer to Question 8

(A) The motion should be denied because the jury could find that a reasonable person would not have undergone the procedure had he been informed of the risks. A doctor has a duty to disclose the risks of treatment to enable a patient to make an informed consent. To establish breach of this duty, an undisclosed risk must have been serious enough that a reasonable person in the patient's position would have withheld consent. In other words, the patient will recover only if he can establish that the failure to disclose was the proximate cause of his injury. This will be a determination of fact for the jury to make. (B) is wrong because it does not address the reason why the case should be sent to the jury. While it establishes the element of actual cause, it does not establish the preliminary element of breach of duty, which the jury must decide based on its factual determination of whether a reasonable person would have consented. The jury must determine whether proximate cause exists. (C) is wrong because the patient's consent to the procedure protects the doctor from a battery action, but the patient can still recover for negligence if his consent was uninformed. (D) is wrong because the crux of informed consent is not that the procedure was not performed with due care but that the doctor has breached the duty of disclosure.

Answer to Question 9

(D) The patient most likely will not prevail because the surgery was successful. Physicians owe a duty to patients to provide them with enough information about the risks of a proposed course of treatment or surgical procedure to enable them to give "informed consent" to the treatment. If an undisclosed risk was serious enough that a reasonable person in the patient's position would have withheld consent to the treatment, the physician has breached this duty. However, breach of duty is only one element of a cause of action for negligence. The plaintiff must also establish actual and proximate cause and some damage to the plaintiff's person or property. Damage means actual harm or injury. Unlike for some intentional torts, damage will not be presumed in a negligence action, and nominal damages are not available. While a complete absence of consent to a medical or surgical procedure may in some cases constitute battery, which does not require damage as an element, a nondisclosure of the ***risks*** of the procedure is characterized instead as a breach of the duty of care. Here, the patient's surgery was successful and no other injury is apparent from the facts. The patient's distress at not being informed of the risk is not, standing alone, a compensable injury. [Restatement (Second) of Torts §436A] Hence, the patient is not likely to prevail. (A) is incorrect. While a showing that he would have refused consent had he known of the risks would establish causation for any injury, the patient still needs to establish damages. (B) is wrong because, even though the jurisdiction uses a higher national standard of care that may require disclosure of more information than under a community standard of care, the damage element must be shown as part of the prima facie case. (C) is incorrect even though that fact would establish breach of duty by the physician. As discussed above, the patient will not prevail absent evidence of damages.

Answer to Question 10

(A) The court is most likely to grant the motorist's motion. This statute was designed to protect roads from being damaged by studded snow tires. The pedestrian does not have a case for negligence based on violation of the statute, because the pedestrian is not a member of the class the statute was designed to protect. The statute was designed to protect roads from damage to the metal studs, not people. The pedestrian may have had a cause of action based on a breach of ordinary care, but the facts tell us that the pedestrian only presented evidence of violation of the statute. So the court will grant the defense's motion. (B) is incorrect. If a motor vehicle statute is applicable, its violation will be sufficient evidence of negligence. (C) is wrong because the statute must be applicable before violation of the statute can be considered negligence per se. (D) states a rationale applicable to constitutional law rather than torts. The statute may be constitutionally valid, but it does not establish liability here.

Answer to Question 11

(D) The court should deny both motions and submit the case to the jury, because the jury could find that the father was negligent in not preventing his child from grabbing the steering wheel. Under ordinary negligence principles, the father owed a duty to other motorists to maintain control of his vehicle. The jury could find that the father breached this duty of care by not noticing when his child unbuckled the seat belt and started climbing into the front seat, and not preventing the child from grabbing the steering wheel. Hence, the case should go to the jury for a determination of whether the father was negligent. (A) is incorrect because the facts do not establish that the statutory standard of care is applicable to these facts. The precise standard of care in a common law negligence case may be established by proving that a statute providing for a criminal penalty applies to the particular case. If that is done, the statute's more specific duty will replace the more general common law duty of care. Violation of the statute establishes negligence per se—a conclusive presumption of duty and breach of duty; the plaintiff must then establish causation and damages to complete the prima facie case of negligence. To prove that the statutory standard applies, the plaintiff must show that (i) she is in the class intended to be protected by the statute, and (ii) the statute was designed to prevent the type of harm that occurred. Here, the statute likely was intended primarily to protect children from injuries caused by not being properly restrained in a vehicle involved in a collision. The motorist has presented no evidence that the statute was intended to protect her from the harm that she suffered. (B) is incorrect because even though the motorist did not establish that the statute applies to her claim, she has presented facts sufficient to allow the jury to find that the father breached the common law duty of care that he owed to other motorists. (C) is incorrect because the father is not vicariously liable for his child's negligent conduct at common law. Any liability of the father in this case would arise from his own potential negligence in failing to control his child while driving.

Answer to Question 12

(D) The cyclist will not prevail because the motorist did not make the cyclist's position any worse. There is no affirmative duty to rescue, except by a professional rescuer. But once any person decides to assist in a rescue, he must act as a reasonable person in an emergency situation. Here, however, the motorist chose not to assist the cyclist, and his actions when he stopped and examined him did nothing to make the cyclist's situation worse (such as causing others not to stop because they believed the cyclist was receiving assistance). Hence, the motorist will not be liable. (A) is wrong because even though it appears that the motorist acted unreasonably, he is not liable because he had no duty to rescue. (B) is similarly wrong; his stopping did not by itself create a duty to rescue. (C) is wrong because it does not address the motorist's conduct in the facts, which raise the issue only of what duty the motorist had once he stopped and got out of his car.

Answer to Question 13

(D) The injured driver will likely not prevail on causation grounds. Even though there is an apparent unexcused violation of the statute, as stated by choice (A), the most that this showing establishes is duty and breach of duty. The plaintiff still must show that the breach of the duty in fact caused the injury to him. The facts indicate that even if the truck driver had been going the legal speed limit, she would not have been able to stop in time. Thus, there is no showing that her breach of this duty in fact caused the harm to the injured driver, and (D) is the best answer. (C) is incorrect. Had the injured driver established a prima facie case, his recovery would have been reduced because of his contributory fault in pulling in front of the truck driver, but under the facts here he cannot establish the prima facie case. (B) is irrelevant; violation of a criminal statute does not establish tort liability in the absence of causation.

Answer to Question 14

(B) The jogger's violation of the ordinance is a concurring actual cause of his injury. When several acts combine to cause an injury, but none of the acts standing alone would have been sufficient, the "but for" test is applied. Here, but for the jogger's violation of the ordinance, he would not have been injured. While it might not be found to be the proximate cause of his injury, the violation of the ordinance was one of several contributing actual causes of his injury. Hence, (A) and (D) are wrong. (C) is wrong because an intervening cause is a force that comes into motion ***after*** the time of the defendant's negligent act and combines with it to cause the injury. The jogger's conduct in jogging on the bike path preceded the motorist's negligence in running the stop sign.

Answer to Question 15

(B) The friend is not liable because proximate cause cannot be established. Although the statute involved appears to be designed to protect persons who contract with construction workers (so the homeowner is within the protected class) and to prevent damage occurring during the performance of construction work (which is the risk protected against), there must be both an actual and a proximate causal connection between the activity of the defendant and the injury to the plaintiff. Here, the friend's decision to park in the homeowner's driveway resulted in injury to the homeowner through intervention of a completely unforeseeable event. Thus, the friend's activities were not the proximate cause of the injury to the homeowner. Therefore, (B) is correct and (C) is wrong. (A) is not the best answer because a member of a protected class may not assume the risk that the statute was intended to prevent. (D) is wrong because the "but for" test establishes actual cause only. Proximate cause is not established because the chain of events was unforeseeable.

Answer to Question 16

(B) The passenger will probably recover from the driver because she was negligent. The driver owes a duty of ordinary care to his passenger regardless of whether that passenger is paying or not paying. The driver also owed a duty to act as a reasonable person would under emergency circumstances after the car was stopped. Her opening of the car door, as well as her failure to maintain her car, constituted negligence under the circumstances. The acts of the criminals were foreseeable, because every day the passenger and the driver commuted through this dangerous neighborhood. (A) is incorrect because this is the standard of care owed to a paying passenger. (C) is incorrect because the criminal activity was foreseeable under the circumstances and therefore does not constitute a superseding cause. (D) is incorrect. The driver owed a duty to her passenger to use reasonable care while in this dangerous area.

Answer to Question 17

(B) The boy's best argument is that his mother's refusal to take him to a physician, if deemed to be negligent, is not imputed to him. A plaintiff has a duty to take reasonable steps to mitigate damages. Thus, in personal injury cases, there is a duty to seek appropriate treatment to effect healing and to prevent aggravation. Failure to do so will preclude recovery for any particular item of injury that occurs or is aggravated ***due to the failure to mitigate*** (this is the avoidable consequences rule). Thus, the boy's not consulting a doctor could limit his recovery to the damages for the original injury only. However, he is a child and his mother decided not to seek medical help for him. In actions against a third party, a parent's negligence is not imputed to the child. Thus, using the argument in choice (B) that any negligence on the part of the boy's mother will not be imputed to him, he should receive a full recovery for ***all*** of his injuries if he prevails in an action against the motorist. On the other hand, if the boy uses the argument in choice (A), he will probably not recover for the aggravated injuries. (A) presents an accurate statement of law, relative to the effect of the avoidable consequences rule. If the boy avails himself of the avoidable consequences rule, he will succeed in salvaging merely his right to recover for the original injury. Thus, (A) does not give him a chance to recover for ***all*** of his injuries, as does (B). (C) is incorrect because it directly contradicts the rule that a plaintiff must take all reasonable measures to mitigate damages after the original injury is inflicted. (D) is incorrect because it misstates the concept of "taking your victim as you find him." This concept refers to the ***physical or mental condition of the victim*** at the time of the injury (*e.g.*, the "eggshell skull plaintiff"); it does not cover the victim's relationship to others and their attitudes or actions. Thus, the attitude of a victim's mother toward medical treatment is not included in "taking your victim as you find him."